THE COLLECTION

STUDIES IN BIBLICAL THEOLOGY · 48

THE COLLECTION

A Study in Paul's Strategy

KEITH F. NICKLE

WIPF & STOCK · Eugene, Oregon

Wipf and Stock Publishers
199 W 8th Ave, Suite 3
Eugene, OR 97401

The Collection
A Study in Paul's Strategy
By Nickle, Keith F.
Copyright©1966 by Nickle, Keith F.
ISBN 13: 978-1-60608-690-2
Publication date 4/17/2009
Previously published by Alec R. Allenson, 1966

Albert Thomas Dyal, Jr.
IN MEMORIAM

CONTENTS

Preface   9

I   The New Testament Account of Paul's Collection: I   13
     1   The Collection in Romans   14
     2   The Collection in I Corinthians   15
     3   The Collection in II Corinthians   16
     4   Events recorded in Acts pertinent to the Collection   22

II   The New Testament Account of Paul's Collection: II   40
     1   The Jerusalem meeting in Galatians   40
     2   The Acts and Galatians versions compared   51
     3   The Collection in Galatians   59
     4   The conflict at Antioch   62
     5   The delivery trip to Jerusalem   67
     6   Summary   72

III   Analogies to Paul's Collection in Contemporary Judaism   74
     1   The half-shekel Temple tax   74
     2   Charitable provisions for the poor   93
     3   The 'apostles' and the Patriarchal tax   96
     4   The evidence from Qumran   97
     5   Summary   99

IV   The Theological Significance of the Collection   100
     1   The Collection as an act of Christian charity   100
     2   The Collection and the unity of the Church   111
     3   The eschatological significance of the Collection   129
     4   Summary   142

V   The Collection after Paul   144
     1   The destruction of Jerusalem and the Temple tax   144
     2   The Collection in the post-Pauline Church   145

Contents

3 The theological impact of the Collection on the later life of the Church 152
4 Summary 155

Bibliography 157
Index of Authors 165
Index of Biblical References 168

PREFACE

THE mystery of the unity of the Church has occupied the minds and efforts of Christians to a greater or lesser extent in every era of the history of the Church. This mystery is best expressed in the enigmatic form of indicative/imperative so typical of the New Testament approach to various aspects of the Christian faith. All Christians are one in Christ; therefore they are to be one in Christ. The paradox becomes reasonable only when the approach of logical definition is abandoned, and it is considered within the context of the dynamic relationship between the Lord and his Church.

With the advent of the ecumenical movement on the modern ecclesiastical scene and the acute awareness of the obvious disunity of the Church which it has animated, theological concern for the unity of the Church has been both greatly increased and intensified. Indispensable to the profitable pursuit of this concern is a careful and sensitive analysis of those events within the history of the Church which contributed to the furtherance or to the deterioration of its fidelity to the Christ-given solidarity of all believers.

The endeavours of the Church to either realize the obligation for unity or protect the unity which was given have, without exception, been intimately bound to its concern for the preservation of the truth of the gospel. Thus the formation of the Canon, the early Christian Councils, the formulation of the creeds, the condemnation of various heresies, and most of the organizational innovations which contributed to the institutional establishment of the Church were motivated by an interest to maintain the unity of the Church 'in the truth'.

This is true also for the first venture which was consciously inaugurated for the purpose of restoring the disrupted unity of the Church—the collection project which Paul organized among his Gentile churches for the indigent Christian community in Jerusalem. With this expression of solidarity Paul was simultaneously insisting on the authenticity of his apostleship to the

Preface

Gentiles and the validity of their election into the fellowship of Christ.

It is proposed in this study to examine Paul's project within the context of the life of the first-century Church in which it occurred, in the hope that it may contribute to the appreciation of the initial Christian attempt to avoid a severance in the Body of Christ. That such an investigation need not be relegated to the category of dry, background material far from the cutting-edge of the vital contemporary interest, but rather can result in a direct, creative contribution to the present concern is evidenced by a recent proposal to use Paul's collection as the analogy for a singular concrete expression of interconfessional fellowship in Christ. Professor Oscar Cullmann has urged on the basis of Paul's endeavour that a reciprocal collection be instituted between Roman Catholics and Protestants (this suggestion has been most completely developed in his book, *Message to Catholics and Protestants*). Dr Cullmann has avoided the naïve assumption that such a project would miraculously restore the unity of the Church. On the contrary, he is so sensitive to the deep and fundamental disagreement existing between the two confessions concerning the nature of the Church that he considers an expression of the *unity* of the Church to be now impossible. Instead, Dr Cullmann would have the collection fulfil a more modest but none the less significant aim as a symbol 'of solidarity, of brotherhood among all who invoke the name of Christ'.

Scholars have consistently recognized the role which Paul's collection played as an expression of the unity of the Church. But other related and equally important factors were also present. Involved in Paul's collection was (1) his awareness that salvation comes to men only as the free gift of the grace of God, (2) his insight that the fellowship of believers has its source and sustenance exclusively in the love of Christ, (3) his conviction of the divinely directed eschatological character of his own apostleship, (4) his understanding of the sequence of events in which the redemptive intent of God was to unfold through the proclamation of the Church. Just as the project extended directly or indirectly over the whole temporal duration of Paul's missionary activity, so did it objectively incorporate the entirety of Paul's ministry in all of its theological depth.

Preface

As a study of the Pauline collection involves not only portions of all four of Paul's major epistles but also a considerable segment of Acts and the problems of chronology thereby raised, the first task in the study is a consideration of all of the external factors which had a bearing on the project. Then, because of an abundance of striking similarities between Paul's collection and certain contributions which were extant in Judaism, an examination of these analagous elements will be made. Next the three levels of significance with which Paul invested his project will be defined. Finally, an attempt will be made to assess the impact which the collection had on the later life of the Church up to AD 150.

In an effort to conserve space and yet sustain some continuity to the references to literature in the footnotes, each work has been completely listed only once in each chapter. Subsequent references to the work are listed by the name of the author followed by an indication in parentheses of the preceding footnote in the chapter where bibliographical data on the work may be found.

All biblical quotations have been taken from the Revised Standard Version unless otherwise indicated. Certain abbreviations have been used in the text which may be easily clarified by referring to the section on sources and reference works in the Bibliography at the back of the work. In addition, because of the frequency with which it was cited, *The Beginnings of Christianity* was shortened to '*Beginnings*', and the commentary of rabbinical references prepared by H. L. Strack and Paul Billerbeck to 'Strack-Billerbeck'.

I would like to take this opportunity to express my deep gratitude to Dr Oscar Cullmann for his invaluable guidance and sustaining interest during the writing of this study, and to Dr Bo Reicke for the innumerable helpful suggestions which he offered. I also want to thank the other members of the Faculty of Theology at the University of Basle who, through a felicitous blending of scholarship with unlimited patience for the peculiar problems confronting a student with a foreign mother-tongue, helped to make my period of study in Basle memorable as well as beneficial. I am indebted to my secretary, Mrs Olga Alford, for her help in preparing the study for publication. Finally my thanks go to my long-suffering wife for her encouragement, confidence and assistance.

K.F.N.

I

THE NEW TESTAMENT ACCOUNT OF PAUL'S COLLECTION: I

IN three of the major epistles of the Apostle Paul[1] (Romans, I and II Corinthians) specific reference is made to a collection which he organized among his missionary churches for the relief of the Jerusalem Christian community. The significance of this collection for Paul was clearly more than that of a simple act of charity. He appears to have devoted a large part of his so-called 'third missionary journey' (Acts 18.23–21.16) to its promotion and collection, and it was while he was in Jerusalem for the purpose of delivering this collection[2] that he was arrested, ultimately to be carried as a prisoner to Rome.

The applicability of a brief reference in the fourth major Pauline epistle, Galatians, to the collection project is contested. Its solution is bound to the complicated question of the relationship of the chronological data in Galatians to the account presented in Acts. Therefore the canonical order will be followed in discussing the collection in Paul's epistles. This sacrifices the advantage of considering them in the chronological sequence in which they were written, but it is offset by the distinct advantage of establishing at the outset of the study that there really was a collection.

Attention will next be turned to those portions of Acts relevant to the instigation of Paul's collection project. These include the report of the sending of famine relief funds to Jerusalem from Antioch and the Acts description of the 'Apostolic Council'.

The second chapter constitutes simply a continuation of the investigation begun in the first. Paul's presentation in Galatians of a meeting he had with the leaders of the Christian community in Jerusalem will be examined. In order to be in a position to come

[1] I assume in this book that the genuine Pauline letters are: Romans, I and II Corinthians, Galatians, Philippians, I Thessalonians, Philemon.
[2] Acts 21.17ff.; cf. Rom. 15.25f.

The Collection

to a conclusion about the possible reference to the collection in the Galatians account of the Jerusalem conference, the contradictions between the Galatians and Acts versions must be analysed. Then an interpretation of the Galatians 'collection passage' will follow.

Because of the light it throws on the nature of the agreement reached in Jerusalem, and the influence which it exerted on the emerging shape of Paul's project, the conflict which occurred between Peter and Paul in Antioch as described in Galatians will next be considered. Finally the sparse information concerning the trip to Jerusalem to deliver the collection will be evaluated.

1. THE COLLECTION IN ROMANS

In the Epistle to the Romans Paul wrote of the collection in connection with the intended extension of his missionary activity into Spain by way of the Christian congregation in Rome[3] (Rom. 15.24ff., cf. Acts 19.21; Rom. 1.10ff.). From this passage we learn that the collection, which was then in the process of being gathered,[4] was intended for the 'poor among the saints'[5] at Jerusalem (vv. 25f.), that the regions of Macedonia and Achaia participated in it (v. 26), that their participation was of their own choosing (vv. 26f.),[6] that nevertheless the act itself was in response to an indebtedness already incurred (v. 27).

Further we see that Paul himself was to deliver the collection (vv. 25, 28), although he was aware of the intense hostility with which the Jews[7] in Judea regarded him (v. 31a). Finally, he was

---

[3] Karl Barth, *The Epistle to the Romans*, trs. of 6th ed., London, 1933, saw a specific reference to the Pauline collection for Jerusalem in Rom. 12.13. However, in a later publication (*A Shorter Commentary on Romans*, London, 1959) he interpreted it in the general sense of referring to the support of those 'devoted to the service of the Lord'. The latter is the position of most commentators.

[4] M. J. Lagrange, *Saint Paul épitre aux Romains*, Paris, 1950, *ad loc.*, rightly emphasizes the normal sense of the pres. part. διακονῶν to indicate that 'Paul is already at the service for the saints'. The variants (aor. infin.—P46, D, G, and the Latin MSS.; fut. part.—ℵ) are secondary, but Alexander Pallis, *To the Romans*, Liverpool, 1920, chooses the infin. reading. Hans Lietzmann, *An die Römer* (Handbuch zum Neuen Testament), 3rd ed., Tübingen, 1928, wrongly interprets the word here and in v. 31 as being used for 'the office of deacon'.

[5] These terms appear to have had a special significance for the Jerusalem church. See below, p. 138.

[6] Cf. *ThWB*: 'εὐδοκέω' on the assertion that the collection was a tax imposed on Paul and the Gentile churches by the Jerusalem community, see below, pp. 90ff., 100ff.

[7] Ἀπειθούντων—lit.: 'The disobedient ones'; the early Church considered the highest form of disobedience to be the refusal to believe in Christ (Rom. 11.30f.);

14

anxious about the reception which the collection he was bringing would receive from the Jerusalem Christians (v. 32b), and he requested from the Roman Christians intercessory prayers for its acceptance by them (v. 30).

2. THE COLLECTION IN I CORINTHIANS

The short passage in I Corinthians (16.1-4) indicates that the collection project had already been introduced[8] to the Corinthians, and that in their letter to Paul[9] they had made inquiries about it.[10] Paul directed them to organize the collection as it had already been organized in Galatia[11] (v. 1). On the first day of the week each of them was to set aside at home as much as he could afford so that the money would be ready when Paul arrived (v. 2). They were to appoint representatives and accredit them with letters[12] to deliver

---

therefore this term came to be placed in opposition to 'those believing', i.e. = 'the unbelieving', cf. *ThWB*; A & G. In the light of this comment by Paul, the conjecture by Ed. Schwartz ('Zur Chronologie des Paulus', *Nachrichten von der königlichen Gesellschaft der Wissenschaften zu Göttingen—Philologisch-historische Klasse*, Berlin, 1907) that the phrase 'of those who have believed' (Acts 21.20) should be stricken, thus having James warn Paul of the Jews who are zealous for the law (p. 290), is certainly attractive; so also Johannes Munck, *Paul and the Salvation of Mankind*, London, 1959, pp. 240f. There is no textual evidence to support it.

[8] A. Robertson and A. Plummer, *First Epistle of St Paul to the Corinthians* (The International Critical Commentary), 2nd ed., Edinburgh, 1914, suggest that this was done through Titus on a trip to Corinth before this letter (p. 382). P. Bachmann, *Der erste Brief des Paulus an die Korinther* (Kommentar zum neuen Testament), Leipzig, 1905, thinks it was initiated during Paul's first long stay; A. Schlatter, *Paulus der Bote Jesu*, Stuttgart, 1956, p. 448, suggests that it was done through Paul's first (lost) letter.

[9] I Cor. 7.1.

[10] Περὶ δέ appears to be the phrase with which Paul introduced those sections of material dealing with specific questions asked him by the Corinthians in their letter (cf. 7.1, 25; 8.1; 12.1). So Johannes Weiss, *Der erste Korintherbrief* (Meyer Kommentar), 9th ed., Göttingen, 1910: Joseph Sickenberger, *Die Briefe des heiligen Paulus an die Korinther und Römer*, Bonn, 1932; Otto Schmitz, *Urchristliche Gemeindenöte*, Berlin, 1939, p. 214; A. Robertson and A. Plummer (n. 8), *ad loc*.

[11] Theodor Zahn, *Der Brief des Paulus an die Galater*, Leipzig, 1905, pp. 105f., suggests that perhaps the instructions in Galatia were not connected with Paul's great collection but to an earlier one limited to the Syrian, Cilician and Galatian churches. Because of the date of this epistle (early AD 55), the implication here that the Galatian churches are still following these instructions and the presence of Galatian representatives with Paul on the trip to Jerusalem (Acts 20.4, see below, p. 68), this does not seem probable.

[12] Ἐπιστολῶν—in Attic Greek the plural form is used for one letter, therefore Schlatter and Bachmann (both n. 8) suggest one letter here. The more natural reading would be the plural, as the great majority of translators and commentators read (cf. A and G, p. 300).

Who writes the letters is of more importance. If 'letters' refers to 'I will send', then Paul is saying that he will send letters of recommendation with the ones chosen.

The Collection

the collection to Jerusalem (v. 3). Paul concluded his instructions by indicating that if it were propitious (ἄξιον) for him to make the trip himself, the representatives would accompany him. It is usual to refer ἄξιον to the amount of the collection, translate it 'worth while', or some similar term, and make Paul's decision to travel to Jerusalem dependent upon the generosity of the collection.[13] This interpretation must be rejected, as it unjustifiably imputes to Paul a pettiness and a shallow appreciation of the significance of the collection, a profound lack of confidence in the Corinthians,[14] and a willingness to manipulate his churches in a rather crude fashion.

Instead ἄξιον should be translated 'advisable' (RSV), 'if it is meet' (ASV), or 'propitious' as has been used above. It is then to be referred to the situation at the destination ('Jerusalem', v. 3) and Paul's awareness of the growing hostility toward him there.[15]

3. THE COLLECTION IN II CORINTHIANS

II Corinthians, in the form in which we know it, is probably a collection of parts of several Pauline letters to the Corinthians.[16]

So Bachmann; Sickenberger (see n. 10); Schmitz (n. 10); Robertson and Plummer (n. 8); Weiss (n. 10); H. Lietzmann, *An die Korinther I–II*, Tübingen, 1949. This overlooks the official character of the representatives and, at the same time, posits an ambiguity in Paul's mind which is both unnecessary and out of keeping with the great concern he felt for this project. Therefore it is better to refer 'letters' to 'approve' and to interpret διά as instrumental rather than of accompanying circumstance. Then these letters formally certified the approval given by the Church to its representatives (so H. Rolston, *Stewardship in the New Testament Church*, Richmond, 1946, p. 66).

J. Héring, *La première épître de saint Paul aux Corinthiens*, Neuchâtel, 1949, and W. Meyer, *Der erste Brief an die Korinther*, Part 2, Zürich, 1945, both suggest that one of the purposes of the delegation was to enable Paul to avoid slander by removing any onus of personal interest in the money.

[13] J. Weiss (n. 10) refers it to the infinitive 'to go', but arrives at the same conclusion.

[14] At the time of the writing of I Corinthians such a lack of confidence is unexplainable. When Paul wrote II Corinthians this element *was* present, as is implied in 9.4.

[15] As was later expressed in Rom. 15.31. W. Schmithals, *Paul and James*, London, 1965, p. 83 n. 12, interprets this phrase to mean Paul is waiting for news from the Jerusalem church as to whether his personal visit is expedient or unwelcome.

Another possible though less satisfactory solution would be to refer ἄξιον to the act of delivering the collection ('to carry your gift', v. 3) and understand it as expressing Paul's interest in avoiding personal criticism in connection with the project (as in II Cor. 8.20f.).

[16] The composite character of the epistle is contested. Those supporting the theory that the epistle contains a combination of originally separate Pauline letters are: H. Windisch, *Der zweite Korintherbrief* (Meyer Kommentar, 9th ed.), Göttingen,

The New Testament Account of Paul's Collection: I

Within this group of epistles are comments about the collection (chs. 8 and 9) which originally belonged to two different letters written within a short time of each other.[17]

Both chapters reveal that the Corinthians had not followed the instructions Paul had given them in I Cor. 16.1-4 and that he was deeply concerned that they rectify the situation. The serious conflict which had arisen between them and Paul had undoubtedly been one of the major factors contributing to this failure. Nevertheless Paul was aware that a tendency to parsimony was also involved (8.13ff.; 9.5ff.) which had encouraged them to use the conflict as a welcome excuse for reneging on their commitment.

A. *The first letter*

In the earlier letter (to which chapter 8 belongs)[18] Paul reminded the Corinthians that they had supposedly been occupied

---

1924, intro.; J. Héring, *La seconde épitre de saint Paul aux Corinthiens*, Neuchâtel, 1958, intro.; G. Bornkamm, 'The History of the Origin of the So-called Second Letter to the Corinthians', *New Testament Studies*, Vol. 8, No. 3, April 1962, pp. 258ff.; *RGG*³ IV, cols. 18ff. For the opposing arguments for the integrity of the epistle as a whole, cf. P. Bachmann, *Der zweite Brief des Paulus an die Korinther* (Kommentar zum neuen Testament), Leipzig, 1909, intro.; Lietzmann (n. 12), intro.

[17] Cf. the literature in the preceding note. The introductory clause of chapter 9 (v. 1) appears to be raising a new subject. Also the emphases of Paul's argument cannot be interpreted as a logical continuation of his comments in chapter 8. It is perhaps possible to account for these discrepancies by assuming a long dictation pause between 8 and 9, but it seems more natural to regard them as two separate portions.

[18] It is difficult to determine the other parts of the letters to which these two excerpts originally belonged. The decision depends to a large extent on the way in which the other parts of letters are arranged with regard to their order of appearance. The most probable order seems to be: 10.1-13.10 (= 'letter of tears', cf. 2.3f., 9; 7.8, 12); 1.1-8.24; 13.11-14.9. Within this general framework, the questions of the place of 2.14-7.4 (independent letter to be placed before 'letter of tears'? part of 'letter of tears'? integral part of 1-8 letter?) and the genuineness of 6.14-7.1 are left open as not germane to this book (cf. Bornkamm and Windisch, pp. 286ff.—'Das Problem des 9. Kapitels'; both in n. 16).

The identification of 10.1-13.10 as the 'letter of tears' is not completely verifiable, but appears to be the most plausible solution. Its significance for our concern lies in the fact that if 10.1-13.10 is seen to correspond chronologically to its present position in II Corinthians, then a failure of the collection in Corinth must be concluded (so Chas. H. Buck, Jr, 'The Collection for the Saints', *Harvard Theological Review*, Vol. XLIII, No. 1, 1950, pp. 3-9); a conclusion which is excluded by Rom. 15.26f. Bornkamm, *ibid.*, p. 161, has made the enlightening suggestion that the 'letter of tears' was placed at the end of this Pauline collection in keeping with a prevailing custom, based on the acknowledged view that the appearance of false prophets is a sign of the 'eschaton'.

The hypothesis which reverses the order of chapters 8 and 9, put forward by J. Héring (n. 16); E. Dinkler, *RGG*³ IV, cols. 18ff. (chapter 9 part of 'letter of tears'!), is improbable.

with the collection for over a year[19] (v. 10; repeated in 9.2). He cited the participation of the Macedonians (v. 1),[20] whose performance, although it did not result in a large sum of money,[21] was nevertheless exemplary. Because of their spontaneously enthusiastic and sacrificial response (vv. 3f.) in the face of persecution[22] and deep poverty (v. 2),[23] the Macedonians' participation illustrated the sort of personal involvement (v. 5) which he hoped to inspire in the Corinthians.[24]

To this end Paul informed them that he was sending Titus,[25] who had helped them to initiate the collection (vv. 6, 16f., 23; cf. 9.5),[26] and two men, appointed by the Jerusalem church to assist Paul with the project (vv. 18f., 22f.; cf. 9.5),[27] to en-

[19] Πέρυσι could = 1–23 months; probably 12–18 months. We do not know how Paul reckoned this time (cf. Windisch [n. 16] on 8.10 for different possibilities); probably according to the Jewish method (New Year in October), so Lietzmann (n. 12), p. 135.
[20] Cf. I Thess. 1.6f.
[21] The circumstances under which the collection was gathered (v. 2) preclude a large sum of money. Not once, either in chapter 8 or in chapter 9, does Paul infer that their gift was therefore inferior.
[22] Cf. I Thess. 2.14; also II Thess. 1.4.
[23] The emphasis that the Macedonians gave so willingly out of their poverty, the reference to Christ's humiliation as 'becoming poor' (v. 9), as well as verses 13ff., indicate that Paul was seeking to counteract one of the excuses used by the Corinthians to avoid contributing, i.e. that their sending a substantial contribution to Jerusalem would leave them economically vulnerable.
[24] Not only is this to be inferred as Paul's reason for citing the Macedonians as an example, but it is in this sense of emphasis on attitude rather than material result that the illogical statement of verse 10 ('not only to do, but to will', ASV) is to be understood.
[25] To set verse 6 ('we have urged Titus') and verse 17a ('he accepted our appeal') over against 17b ('he is going to you of his own accord') by placing an absolute value on the terms, involves Paul in a logical contradiction. He is, of course, simply accentuating Titus's enthusiastic response to his exhortation. It is not necessary to conclude that Paul is correcting himself (Lietzmann, cf. n. 12), or that Titus was so zealous he decided to go before Paul (Bachmann, cf. n. 16), or that Paul wrote verse 17 because he had decided to postpone his own trip (Héring, cf. n. 16). The same logical contradiction is in evidence in verse 3 with reference to the 'free will' of the Macedonians over against the 'grace of God' (verse 1) and the implied activity of Paul.
[26] Verse 6, in the light of verse 10, certainly must refer to the beginning of the collection in Corinth (= 7.15) (against Bachmann, ad loc.). This beginning was made in all probability shortly after the Corinthians had received I Cor., which was perhaps brought to them by Titus. He was evidently in the process of organizing the collection when the conflict espoused by the 'false apostles' (10.13, etc.) broke out into open opposition. These men attacked the integrity both of Paul and of Titus (11.7ff.; 12.13ff., 18; cf. I Cor. 9.3ff.) and, by implication, the collection (cf. 8.20). Titus remained in Corinth through Paul's unhappy second visit (cf. 12.14; 13.1; 2.1ff.) and until the 'letter of tears' had worked its happy effect, after which he returned to Paul with the good news (2.13; 7.6ff., 13ff.).
[27] So W. L. Knox, *Saint Paul and the Church of Jerusalem*, Cambridge, 1925, p. 288 and pp. 294f. n. 27. Χειροτονηθείς (v. 19) expresses the official character of the appoint-

courage them to bring to fulfilment their already expressed intent.
It is not stated in II Corinthians that these two men were appointed by the *Jerusalem* church. Instead the vague designation 'the churches' is used in connection with these men four times (vv. 18, 19, 23, 24), of which two references (vv. 19, 23) are specifically to their having been appointed to work with Paul on the collection project. As the text now stands Paul does not explicitly state which 'churches' he means.

In such a case scholarship has only two alternatives. Either it must be assumed that a more precise identification is impossible or an hypothesis must be proposed which does not violate the circumstances nor the plain intent of the text.

Commentators are practically unanimous in interpreting 'the churches' to mean the Macedonian churches. This interpretation must be abandoned for the following reasons:

1. Paul had already mentioned 'the churches of Macedonia' (v. 1). But in verse 18 the phrase 'all the churches' cannot refer just to the Macedonians. Therefore if Paul meant the Macedonian churches in verse 19 one would expect him to use the same phrase as in verse 1.[28]

2. The two brethren, along with Titus, precede Paul, with whom the Macedonian delegates are to come. Paul's allusion to the possibility of their and his humiliation (9.3f.) is senseless if the two men accompanying Titus are Macedonians.

---

ment. The verb literally means 'elect by raising hands', but a related meaning is 'appoint, install' for a definite office or task (cf. A & G, p. 889). The only other passage in the NT where this word occurs is Acts 14.23, 'when they had appointed elders for them in every church', which clearly has the meaning of 'appoint, install'. Although at the time of Paul's writing this word had not become a technical term for the appointing of church functionaries (Titus 1.5 uses καταστήσῃς for precisely the same function as Acts 14.23), yet the later addition to Titus 1.9 as well as the subscriptions to both Titus and II Timothy indicate that this soon became the case (cf. Didache 15.1; Ignat., *ad Philad.* 10.1; *ad Smyr.* 11.2; *ad Poly.* 7.2). In our passage it is best translated 'appointed', especially in view of the fact that when Paul wanted to specify the means or method of appointment he used a different expression altogether (I Cor. 16.3; cf. n. 12 above). (Against Lietzmann, cf. n. 12; Schlatter, n. 8; Bachmann; and Windisch, cf. for both n. 16.) The official character of the role they filled is reiterated in v. 23 when Paul refers to them as the 'apostles of the churches'.

[28] It should be noted that, other than this passage, whenever Paul used the term 'church' in a plural form or with a plural inference he either meant the whole Church (Rom. 16.16, 23; I Cor. 11.16; 14.33f.; II Cor. 8.18) or he specified the area meant (I Cor. 16.1, 19; II Cor. 8.1; Gal. 1.2, 22; I Thess. 2.14), or the context explains it (Rom. 16.4; I Cor. 4.17; 7.17; II Cor. 11.8, 28; 12.13; Phil 4.15).

The Collection

3. In vv. 20f. Paul gives as the reason for their appointment to assist him that they were to be protection against any threat to his integrity in connection with the project. Why two representatives from the Macedonian churches would be a guarantee against the accusation of embezzlement or some similar charge is obscure. If the Corinthians retained any lingering doubts about Paul, how could the appearance of two unknown Macedonians, recommended to them by Paul himself, assuage their suspicions; especially if these men came in the company of Titus?[29]

All of these considerations do not justify the assertion made above that Paul meant the churches of Judea. They do eliminate as a possibility the usual interpretation of understanding the Macedonian churches to have been meant.

Must this, then, be left as another unknown in the New Testament, or are there other clues which would encourage looking in another direction?

Several scholars[30] have rightly pointed out that since this portion of chapter 8 has all of the characteristics of a letter of recommendation the names of the two 'brothers' certainly were included in the original letter. They further agree that the only possible reason for intentionally leaving the names out of subsequent copies of the letter was that these men were involved in some painful situation in Corinth and were no longer considered worthy to have their names included.

Commentators have nominated a long list of candidates to be identified with these two. They have all failed to take into account the significance of this explanation for the lack of names.

The inquiry must look for two men who were known to have been associated with Paul during his missionary work. In addition it would be helpful if their connection with him was accompanied by some sort of official sanction by a Christian community.

Barnabas and Mark are possibilities, but several considerations make them unlikely. Mark is such a peripheral figure that little is known of him. What little is known hardly lends itself to an identification of Mark with either of the 'brothers' of II Cor. 8.

---

[29] Cf. II Cor. 12.17f.
[30] Windisch (n. 16), Lietzmann (n. 12), and Héring (n. 16) have all made the observations which follow.

The New Testament Account of Paul's Collection: I

If the Antioch conflict (Gal 2.11ff.) occurred soon after the Jerusalem conference (Gal. 2.1ff.), as seems most likely, then both Barnabas and Mark are excluded.

Another pair of names which meet the requirements are 'Judas called Barsabbas, and Silas, leading men among the brethren' (Acts 15.22). Since the information on these men is also very sparse, one must conjecture the circumstances which led them to be with Paul in Greece and later caused their names to be dropped from the II Corinthians account.[31]

These men were first appointed by the Jerusalem church leaders at Paul's request to assist him with the collection project. This appointment took place either soon after what is represented in Acts as the 'Apostolic Council' or, better, at the Acts 18.22 visit. They were appointed for the purpose of protecting Paul from the slander of zealous Jews who would regard his collection as a misappropriation of funds which otherwise would go to the Temple in Jerusalem.[32]

Because of the familiarity with the Pauline churches which they achieved during the gathering of the collection, these same two men were *later* reappointed by the Jerusalem church to distribute the 'Apostolic Decree' (Acts 15.20, 29; 21.25).

On account of the previous bitter conflict in Corinth, and the Corinthians' awareness of Paul's attitude on the subject later handled in the Decree (I Cor. 8, 10), this document was particularly odious to them. They rejected the 'Decree' and the resulting conflict led to the striking of these men's names in Paul's collection passage, as well as the striking of the phrase 'of Judea' in vv. 19, 23, 24.[33]

The author of Acts was acquainted with a vague tradition that Silas and Judas worked with Paul, but he did not know to what extent nor in what capacity (cf. Acts 15.32f., 40). He was also aware that these two men were responsible for the distribution of the 'Apostolic Decree'. He therefore combined these elements in his presentation, producing the impossible result that Paul was

---

[31] Much of what follows is dependent upon the understanding of material discussed later in this study. See particularly pp. 54ff., 60ff. below.

[32] Cf. Knox (n. 27), p. 298 and p. 306 n. 21; also the charge of 'teaching against the Temple' brought against Paul in Acts 21.28. Paul's collection and these Jewish Temple contributions are compared in chapter III below.

[33] Perhaps there was originally the singular 'church of Jerusalem' which was replaced by the general phrase 'the churches' extended from verse 18.

The Collection

associated with the formulation of the 'Apostolic Decree' at the time of the Jerusalem conference.[34]

If the first appointment to assist with the collection (II Cor. 8.19, 23) was made at the Acts 18.22 visit, Silas could have worked with Paul previously (Acts 15.40). Then the identification of each of the two 'brothers' in II Cor. 8 is: verses 18f. = Judas; verse 22 = Silas.[35]

B. *The second letter*

In the second letter (ch. 9) which followed shortly after,[36] Paul changed the direction of his argument. No longer using the Macedonian response as an example for the Corinthians, he instead somewhat frantically informed them that he had used their earlier enthusiasm and expected (but not yet forthcoming) performance as an example for the Macedonians; an example which was instrumental in the success realized there (vv. 2ff.). This intensification of Paul's anxiety was undoubtedly heightened by the rapid approach of his own trip to Corinth,[37] on which he would be accompanied by the representatives[38] of those same Macedonian churches (v. 4).

4. EVENTS RECORDED IN ACTS PERTINENT TO THE COLLECTION

In the Epistle to the Galatians Paul makes a rather cryptic remark about 'remembering the poor' (2.10). The way in which this

---

[34] The validity of such a presentation is absolutely excluded by I Cor. 8, 10; Gal. 2.6, 11ff.; 3–5; Rom. 14.1–4, 14–23.

[35] This would correspond to the 'the brother'-'our brother' differentiation; cf. also the order in which the two are listed in Acts 15.22, 27, 32.
Should this hypothesis be favourably received it would give additional support to the questioning of the 'missionary journeys' structure in Acts. In addition the usual identification of the Silas of Acts with the Silvanus of the Epistles (cf. *RGG*³ VI, col. 34) needs to be re-examined.

[36] Cf. n. 18 above; also the general similarity of the two chapters. It is not known who brought this letter to the Corinthians. We can only conjecture that shortly after Titus and the two 'brothers' of chapter 8 had left, Paul was presented with another opportunity to communicate with the Corinthian Christians (a Christian from Corinth or some other place travelling through Macedonia on his way to Corinth?) which he used to urge and encourage them again to complete the collection and to announce his impending arrival.

[37] This trip probably corresponds to that of Acts 20.2.

[38] Although Paul does not say so, these men are undoubtedly the delegates chosen in Macedonia to accompany him to Jerusalem with the collection. Evidently Paul arranged for such delegates from each of the contributing churches (I Cor. 16.4; Acts 20.4). On the delegates see below pp. 68f.; for their significance, cf. pp. 138ff.

The New Testament Account of Paul's Collection: I

reference is to be understood depends on the interpretation of the immediately preceding account of a meeting in Jerusalem, which in turn involves the complicated question of the relationship of the first two chapters of Galatians to the corresponding material in Acts. Before that can be considered, however, a general summary of the situation of the Jerusalem church as far as it can be discerned from Acts must be sketched out, as this has a decisive bearing on the later events recorded in Acts and stands in the immediate background of Paul's collection.

A. The Antioch famine relief

The poverty of the Jerusalem church

The Christians who lived together in close fellowship in Jerusalem after the dramatic Pentecost experience ordered their common life around a vivid expectation of the imminent consumation of the End. One of the many areas in which this expectation found concrete expression for them was in their attitude toward material possessions,[39] which the author of Acts portrayed in an idealistic pattern.[40] Nevertheless there was an effort at extensive common sharing realized in such a way that, although the practice was undoubtedly based on a definite element in the teaching of

---

[39] Acts 2.42-47; 3.6; 4.32-5.11.
[40] So F. J. Foakes Jackson, *The Acts of the Apostles* (Moffatt NT Commentary), London, 1931; Kirsopp Lake, 'The Communism of Acts', *The Beginnings of Christianity, Part I, The Acts of the Apostles*, ed. F. J. Foakes Jackson and K. Lake (hereafter referred to as *Beginnings*), vol. V, pp. 140-51; Ernst Haenchen, *Die Apostelgeschichte* (Meyer Kommentar), Göttingen, 1959. H. J. Cadbury, in 'The Summaries in Acts', *Beginnings* V, pp. 392-402, asserts that the summaries are much later than the intervening panels and were generalized from the specific adjacent material (pp. 395f.). Thus the summaries dealing with the 'communism' of the Jerusalem Christians were drawn from the specific examples of Barnabas and Ananias and were intended to emphasize the results of the activity of the Holy Spirit among the Jerusalem Christians. These examples, Haenchen points out, 'survived in memory only because they were something unusual; an exception, not the rule' (p. 190 on 4.32ff.). It is probably more accurate to understand the situation as a periodic sale of property to meet the daily needs of the community as intimated in Acts 6.1ff.

The attempt by Knox (n. 27) to maintain the Acts presentation of absolute communal property by analogy to the practice of the Essenes is not convincing (pp. 4 and 19 n. 28). On the basis of the documents found at the Qumran community site, we know that there was an essential difference between the two types of common sharing, in that at Qumran it was an obligatory condition of membership, while the Christian fellowship practised it on a voluntary basis (cf. the 'sin' of Ananias, Acts 5.4).

23

The Collection

Jesus,[41] it was implemented in what proved to be an unrealistic, short-sighted manner.[42]

These financial arrangements were made to meet a pressing need in that the community had to provide relief for its large number of impoverished members (Acts 6.1ff.)[43] and support its leaders.[44] This highly vulnerable financial position was aggravated by the subsequent Jewish hostility and the persecutions under which the Jerusalem Christian community suffered (as reflected in Acts 4.1ff.; 5.17ff.; 6.12ff.; 7.54ff.; 9.1f.; 12.1ff.).[45]

The prophecy of famine

The Christian communities around Jerusalem were certain to have been aware of the state of affairs there. The young church in Antioch would also have learned of this; at first through the Hellenistic fugitives who founded the Christian community there

---

[41] E.g. Mark 4.19 par.; 6.7-11 par.; 10.17-30 par.: 12.41-44 par.; etc. The social and religious significance of poverty is a recurring theme of the Old Testament and found a particularly concrete expression in the Qumran community (cf. *RGG*³ I, cols. 622f., 'Armut' I 1, 2; *RGG*³ III, col. 1735, 'Kommunismus' I 6, II 1).

[42] C. H. Dodd calls attention to this in *The Epistle of Paul to the Romans* (Moffatt NT Commentary), London, 1932: 'They carried (the system of partial and voluntary communism) out in the economically disastrous way of realizing capital and distributing it as income. So far as we can gather, no practical steps were taken to replace the capital thus dissipated; and when hard times came, the community had no reserves of any kind' (p. 230). Cf. also F. J. Foakes Jackson and K. Lake, 'Primitive Christianity', *Beginnings* I, p. 306.

[43] This is implied in the early chapters of Acts and coincides with what the situation in Jerusalem as a great religious centre must have been. Both Robertson and Plummer (n. 8), p. 382, and O. Dibelius, *Die Werdende Kirche*, 4th ed., Berlin, 1941, pp. 45ff., suggest that this already large number of poor was increased by the lack of industry in some members due to an oversensitivity to the nearness of the Second Coming of Christ (as evidenced elsewhere in II Thess. 3.10ff.). Although the Acts 6.1ff. account is opaque, the picture it gives of the charity work in the community corresponds to certain aspects of the usual Jewish charity (cf. below, pp. 93f.) and may have been one of the bases for the popular Jewish assumption that the Jerusalem Christians were a Jewish sect belonging to a 'Synagogue of the Nazarenes' (cf. Acts 9.2; 24.5, 14; also Lake and Jackson, *Beginnings* I, p. 304). Another burden may have been added after a time by the necessity of providing hospitality for Christian pilgrims and visitors (so F. Rendall, 'The Pauline Collection for the Saints', *The Expositor*, 4th Series, Vol. VIII, 1893).

[44] Proportionately there was an extremely large number of Apostles and teachers for the Jerusalem church to support. Whenever Paul spoke either of support for teachers in general or of the question of his own sustenance it was always from the standpoint that Apostles and teachers are unquestionably entitled to such support (cf. especially I Cor. 9.11ff.).

[45] Most commentators recognize this as a significant element contributing to their financial distress. Cf. espec. W. Sanday and A. C. Headlam, *The Epistle to the Romans* (International Critical Commentary), Edinburgh, 1902, p. 412, who rightly see this hostility focused primarily in the Sadducees.

The New Testament Account of Paul's Collection: I

after having fled Jerusalem to escape the persecution[46] precipitated by the death of Stephen (Acts 11.19), then through Barnabas (11.22). Thus when Agabus appeared from Jerusalem in the company of other prophets (11.27ff.) and foretold a famine which would shortly fall upon Jerusalem[47] they were well able to appreciate the gravity of the matter.

This prediction probably came within the context of an eschatological warning that the Second Coming of Christ was at hand, based on the conviction that Caligula's attempt to have his statue placed in the Temple at Jerusalem was 'the desolation sacrilege ... standing in the holy place'.[48] The famine represented one of the tribulations which would strike Jerusalem as the immediate antecedents of the End.[49]

Since the urgent anticipation of the Second Coming was just as decisive for the frame-of-reference of the Antiocheans as it was for the attitudes of the Jerusalem community, they received the prophecy quite literally and prepared to send aid for the relief of

---

[46] W. Schmithals (n. 15), p. 19, has followed Haenchen (n. 40), p. 148, in pointing out the inconsistency in Acts 8.1 which, contrary to the intent of the Acts account, can allow for a persecution of the Hellenist segment only and not of the whole Jerusalem Christian community.

[47] Cf. Acts 21.10f. J. Wellhausen, 'Noten zur Apostelgeschichte', *Nachrichten von der königlichen Gesellschaft der Wissenschaft zu Göttingen—Philologisch-historische Klasse*, Berlin, 1907, asserted that Agabus and the other prophets were not really prophets but some other people who came to Antioch for some other purpose, on the grounds that a prophecy would not be enough to instigate a collection (pp. 7ff.). This same opinion is expressed by J. N. Sanders in 'Peter and Paul in the Acts', *New Testament Studies*, Vol. 2, No. 1, September 1955, p. 136.

[48] Matt. 24.15; Mark 13.14; cf. Dan. 11.31; Rev. 17.1ff. On the Caligula incident, see Philo, *Leg. ad Gaium*; Josephus, *Antiq.* XVIII, vii, 2; *Bel. Jud.* II, x, 1–5; Dio Cass. LIX, xxvi, and xxviii; cf. J. Juster, *Les Juifs dans l'empire Romain*, Paris, 1914, vol. I, pp. 351ff. W. L. Knox (n. 27), pp. 165f., 187 n. 9, held the probability that the prophecy was made in such an eschatological context. The hypothesis has received tentative acceptance by Joachim Jeremias, 'Sabbathjahr und neutestamentliche Chronologie', *Zeitschrift für die Neutestamentliche Wissenschaft*, vol. 27, Giessen, 1928, p. 101. Also by V. Weber, *Die antiochenische Kollekte*, Würzburg, 1917, pp. 28f., who suggested as an alternative that the context was a general talk on love for one's neighbour in which Agabus indicated that a time of need would come and provide an opportunity for the realization of the potentiality of Christian love (p. 68). E. Haenchen (n. 40), p. 322, thinks that the prophecies of Agabus both here and in 21.10f. were originally part of an independent 'personal legend' after the manner in which the popular religious tradition remembered the great men of God, and that Luke arbitrarily incorporated it into his narrative and added the 'under Claudius' notation (11.28) to give it historical authenticity. Cf. also M. Dibelius, *Studies in the Acts of the Apostles*, London, 1956, p. 93; E. Meyer, *Ursprung und Anfänge des Christentums*, vol. III, Stuttgart, 1923, p. 168, n. 2.

[49] In the NT passages at the beginning of the preceding note a famine is one of the eschatological woes accompanying the 'desolation sacrilege' as signs of the approach of the End: Matt. 24.7, Mark 13.14; also Rev. 18.8.

The Collection

their Christian brethren in Jerusalem[50] during the coming trying times (11.29). It would have required a considerable period of sustained effort to bring together a sum which would have been of significant help for the Jerusalem church. The community in Antioch would have also had a large percentage of members who were low on the economic scale. If the above interpretation of the context of the prophecy is correct, then Agabus was in Antioch around the end of AD 40 or the beginning of 41. Therefore a span of time is to be understood between Acts 11.29 and 30, or more precisely, between 11.28a and 11.28b.[51]

When a serious food shortage did occur later which intensified the already critical situation of the Jerusalem Christian community, the Antioch Christians accordingly sent the funds they had been gathering by Barnabas and Paul (Acts 11.30; 12.25).[52]

The analogy to Paul's later project

It should be noted here that the significance of this collection in Antioch as the prototype for Paul's great collection among his Gentile churches for the Jerusalem church cannot be overestimated. The parallels are too striking and too explicit to have been accidental.

The Antioch collection was made for Jerusalem at a time when a serious theological conflict, although still in its embryo stages, had arisen (Acts 11.20ff.). This was the problem of the relationship of the Gentiles to the proclamation of the good news of the Risen Lord. It was probably here for the first time that this problem was

---

[50] Foakes Jackson, *Acts* (Moffatt), *ad loc.*, maintains that the relief was intended not just for Jerusalem but for Judea (possible all of Jewish Palestine). It is possible that the funds were not exclusively used for the Jerusalem church, but it would nevertheless have been sent to Jerusalem as being the most needy, and as being the central 'mother' church around which the other smaller communities were grouped and to whom they looked for leadership.

[51] So W. M. Ramsay, *St Paul the Traveller and the Roman Citizen*, 10th ed., London, 1908, pp. 49–51; and V. Weber (n. 48), p. 28.

In fact, an interval of seven years is indicated by the dating of the delivery maintained below, pp. 29ff. The length of time between the beginning of the collection and its delivery to Jerusalem is the most serious difficulty for the connection of the Agabus prophecy with the Caligula incident.

[52] Both E. Schwartz (n. 7), p. 272 n. 2, and J. N. Sanders (n. 47), p. 136, affirm the probability that Antioch sent some sort of relief, but deny that either Paul or Barnabas were associated with it.

Ferdinand Hahn, *Mission in the New Testament*, London, 1965, pp. 82ff., locates the Jerusalem conference (Gal. 2.1ff.) between Acts 11.25f. and 11.29f., and is led thereby to consider it possible that the Antioch relief collection was a result of the Jerusalem conference agreement.

brought so sharply into focus for the young Jerusalem community.

As far as is known there were no 'Gentiles' in the strict sense of the term in the Jerusalem congregation.

The mission of the Hellenists to the Samaritans (Acts 8.4ff.) was a step in this direction. It apparently caused considerable uneasiness in Jerusalem, for they sent two of their leaders, Peter and John, to see about it (Acts 8.14). Still, the Samaritans were not exactly Gentiles.

The incident of the Ethiopian eunuch (Acts 8.26ff.) is not fixed within any historical framework. It was remembered as one of the earliest of such incidents, but made no claim to be *the* first. Further the man appears to have been associated in some way with Judaism (probably as one of the 'God-fearers'), else why would he be so assiduously studying the prophet Isaiah?

The extended account of Peter and Cornelius (Acts 10.1ff.) is also without a fixed historical setting. The author of Acts obviously introduced it to represent the beginning of the proclamation of the gospel to the Gentiles (11.1, 18), but again this man is described as a 'God-fearer' (10.2, 22).[53]

The first clear reference in the Acts account to a proclamation of the gospel to Gentiles is in 11.20, a result of missionary work of the Hellenist fugitives in Antioch. It was because of this problem that Barnabas had been sent there by the Jerusalem church. Through him the Antioch community knew that the Jerusalem Christians regarded their interest for the Gentiles in a dubious light. Paul was also acutely aware of the radically revolutionary character of this interest, which from the standpoint of Judaism (to which the Jerusalem community was closely affiliated) was inconceivable.

There must have been a certain element of the same conflict within the Antioch church itself, although certainly not so

[53] Also pertinent is the fact that this tradition, as the author knew it, was in a form primarily intended to support the liberal point of view in the controversy over the problem of fellowship at table for the common Christian meal between Jews and Gentiles. This is indicated by Peter's vision (10.10ff.; 11.5ff.; as the account now stands, Peter's interpretation of the vision appears rather forced, 10.28), and by the accusation of the Jerusalem Christians against Peter (11.3; cf. also 15.7ff, 14). In this connection compare Mark 7.14ff., which provided support in the teaching of Jesus for the liberal attitude to this problem.

As we shall see below, pp. 54ff., the controversy over table-fellowship did not reach a critical point demanding formal action until much later.

The Collection

pointedly defined or expressed as by the Jerusalem church, because of the proximity of the Gentile world and its influence to the Antioch community.

The eschatological element also played an important part in this collection. This is represented by the prophecy of Agabus. It is present also in the simple fact that they sent aid to Jerusalem at all. It would be very difficult to maintain the position that they were helping Jerusalem out of gratitude for the missionaries which that church had sent to them. As far as we can gather from Acts the relationship between the Hellenists and the rest of the Jerusalem Christians was strained at the best, and perhaps an overt break was involved. At any rate the Jerusalem church was evidently not informed of their subsequent activities until after they had achieved some success (Acts 8.14; 11.22; cf. 11.1). Then when the Jerusalem Christians did send Barnabas to Antioch[54] it was motivated by a negatively critical attitude (11.22).

The action of the Antioch Christians in sending aid to Jerusalem could have been justified only in view of the role which that place was to fill as the eschatological Zion. Also contributing to their high regard for Jerusalem was the fact that it was the historical point of origin of the Christian faith, and was still the base of operations for the Twelve.

When Barnabas first came to Antioch from Jerusalem he must have shared the misgivings of the Jerusalem Christians which had prompted his being sent there, or they would never have chosen him to go. Therefore, when he had arrived and, after witnessing the vitality of their common life in Christ, had radically reversed his own attitude (11.23), he made himself potentially vulnerable to severe criticism from the Jerusalem church. Paul shared this vulnerability when he became associated with the work in Antioch (11.25f.). Not only their reliability as competent witnesses of the gospel but also the validity of their own concept of their missionary purpose was open to question.

All of these issues were coincidentally involved with the send-

---

[54] The attempt to present Barnabas as one of the Hellenists who left Jerusalem after the persecution of Stephen is not convincing, against E. Haenchen (n. 40), pp. 312ff., and his article, 'Barnabas' in RGG^3 I, col. 879f.

Barnabas was sent to Antioch to check on the work of the Hellenists there precisely in the same way as Peter and John were sent to Samaria to check on the work of the Hellenists in that place (8.14).

The New Testament Account of Paul's Collection: I

ing of famine relief from Antioch to Jerusalem, and played a vital role in the subsequent events which occurred there.

Chronology of the famine and the delivery of aid

There remains to be determined the dates of the famine during which the delivery took place, and then the date of the delivery itself.[55] At first glance it appears as if the author of Acts had fixed the approximate date of the famine for his readers by the insertion of the editorial comment, 'a great famine over all the world ... took place in the days of Claudius' (11.28b). But his assistance becomes less valuable when we realize that there was no 'great world-wide famine'[56] in Claudius' time (AD 41-54).

Suetonius does indicate that the reign of Claudius was marked by recurring food shortages.[57] It is doubtless to this that the author of Acts was referring. Josephus records it as being present in Palestine during the offices of Cuspius Fadus and of Tiberius Alexander (44-48 ?).[58] It is probable that under Tiberius Alexander the dearth was most severe.[59]

The dating of the delivery of the Antioch collection is more problematic in that the author of Acts mentions it twice (11.30; 12.25). The reading 'to Jerusalem' (εἰς Ἰερουσαλήμ) in 12.25 has such weighty manuscript confirmation that it must be regarded as the original reading.[60] The secondary emendations 'out of'

---

[55] The attempt to place the delivery of the collection before the outbreak of the famine must be regarded as highly improbable. So most commentators; but cf. A. Schlatter, *Die Apostelgeschichte*, Stuttgart, 1958, pp. 143f.; H. Braun, 'Christentum' I 6, *RGG*³ I, cols. 1693f.

[56] The Greek expression for this phrase would naturally have this meaning (cf. A & G, pp. 563f.). Thus K. Lake and H. J. Cadbury, *Beginnings* IV, *ad loc.*, consider it more probable to view the phrase as a natural exaggeration. Another possibility is to assume an Aramaic expression behind it (kōl 'arʿā = all the land = Palestine), which has the pleasing advantage of eliminating the difficulty altogether (so F. F. Bruce, *The Acts of the Apostles*, London, 1959, p. 239; cf. also O. Michel, *ThWB* V, p. 160).

[57] 'Assiduae sterilitates', Claud. XVIII, 2; cf. also XIX; Tacitus, *Ann.* XII, 43.

[58] *Antiq.* III, 15, 3; XX, 2, 5; 5, 2. Both periods of office fell within the time span 44-48. It is not possible to determine precisely when Tiberius Alexander replaced Cuspius Fadus; scholars fluctuate between 46 and 47.

[59] W. L. Knox (n. 27), p. 186, n. 8, conjectures that Tiberius Alexander was sent to Palestine to replace Fadus for the purpose of handling the increasingly serious emergency. He was an able man, but was undoubtedly repugnant to the Jews, as he was himself a renegade Jew. For a lucid summary of the intricate chronological problems relating to the famine, cf. K. Lake, 'The Chronology of Acts', *Beginnings* V, pp. 452-5.

[60] Foakes Jackson, *Acts* (Moffatt), *ad loc.*, and Lake and Cadbury, *Beginnings* IV, p. 141, recognize the probable authenticity of the reading, but insist it is impossible to explain.

The Collection

(ἐξ Ἰερ.) or 'from' (ἀπὸ Ἰερ.) were substituted to eliminate the apparent contradiction in the Acts account.[61] Therefore the author of Acts must be understood as having recorded a trip by Paul and Barnabas *to* Jerusalem in both passages.

The only alternative to the exceedingly problematical conclusion that the author of Acts was actually describing two different trips to Jerusalem is the resolution of the difficulty by understanding both passages as referring to the same visit. The 11.30

---

[61] Westcott and Hort conjectured an alternative reading, substantially followed by Haenchen (n. 40), p. 330, *ad loc.*, which related the return of Barnabas and Paul 'after they had completed the collection service in Jerusalem'. The only external support for this conjecture is found in the Commentary of Ephraem on Acts (4th century): 'Shavul autem et Barnabas qui tulerant cibaria sanctorum in Ierusalem, reversi sunt cum Iohanne qui vocatus est Marcus, et Lucas Cyrenaicus.' (The text of this commentary, prepared from three thirteenth-century MSS by F. C. Conybeare, and presented with parallel passages from a twelfth-century Armenian Catena which amalgamated Ephraem, Chrysostom, and several others, is available in *Beginnings* III, pp. 373ff.) This conjecture places full value on the aorist participle 'having completed'. But the aorist participle was often used in Greek, especially in relation to a main verb in the aorist, to express 'time coincident with that of the verb when the action of the verb and of the participle is practically one' (W. W. Goodwin and C. B. Gulick, *Greek Grammar*, Boston, 1930, p. 274, sect. 1291; cf. the examples listed there). Thus it is perfectly acceptable to interpret the participle as a participle of attendant circumstance and translate the phrase, 'Barnabas and Saul returned to Jerusalem fulfilling the collection service'.

It might be suggested that the author would not have used the term 'return' in referring to this trip by Paul and Barnabas *to* Jerusalem. But it should be remembered that Barnabas, the one sent from Jerusalem to Antioch, occupied the leading role in the Antioch account. Also the author had earlier described an extensive and active visit by Paul to Jerusalem (Acts 9.26ff.). Although his version of this visit is certainly incorrect (cf. Gal. 1.18f.), yet nevertheless from his viewpoint it would not have been inconsistent to speak of Paul's 'return' to Jerusalem.

A further difficulty could be seen in the reference to John Mark, who, according to 12.12, lived in Jerusalem. As the author is introducing him into his narrative here for the first time, and had just mentioned his home in Jerusalem, one could suppose that he naturally imagined Mark to be in Jerusalem, where he joined Barnabas and Paul. However, the paucity and vagueness of the references in Acts to the figure of Mark indicates a certain lack of definiteness to the tradition at the author's disposal. (Acts 15.37ff. is in all probability a construction by the author to explain why Barnabas was replaced with Silas. Otherwise he is mentioned twice during the so-called 'first missionary journey', 13.5b, 13b, which references are not only vague, but also the whole account of the journey is questionable.) Evidently Mark was associated with Paul's missionary work at a later time (Philemon 29).

It is quite possible that the author conjectured that Mark had previously travelled to Antioch, although he did not know when. Because of the relative insignificance of John Mark for his narrative he did not take the trouble to correct this inconsistency with an insertion into the Antioch account to indicate Mark's arrival there. The occasion can only be imagined (he was associated with the Hellenists and had to leave Jerusalem at the time of the persecution?—he came with Agabus and the other prophets?—more probably, if the Col. 4.10 reference to a family relationship is correct, he came with Barnabas?—or came to help Barnabas after the latter had been there for a while?). Note the same type of difficulty with Silas in 15.33, 40 and the variant readings which were inserted (v. 34) to correct it!

reference is a natural conclusion to the preceding material, but the 12.25 reference appears to be placed more correct chronologically.[62] There was certainly no food shortage during Herod's reign (cf. Acts 12.30).

This judgement which interprets a duplicate presentation by the author of the same event must not be arbitrary. Some reason must be offered which would reasonably explain why he had so constructed his account. As a matter of fact, such an explanation does suggest itself which provides the best sense for the passage, and indicates that the author was doing his best with the scanty material and hazy traditions at his disposal to maintain a dependable chronological sequence.

Evidently the author had completed the account of the Antioch collection and had followed it with the account of the Herod persecution from another source. But he was aware that the Antioch collection was not brought to Jerusalem until after Herod's death, although the prophecy preceded it. Therefore in order not to disrupt the Antioch anecdote by splitting the beginning from the ending with the insertion of the Herod persecution, he included it intact. Then, to maintain the chronological validity of his narrative, he again recounted its delivery after recording Herod's death.[63]

Joachim Jeremias, in his article 'Sabbathjahr und neutestamentliche Chronologie',[64] has given a very helpful and conclusive suggestion to facilitate the dating of the delivery in Jerusalem. He has established that the Jewish year of 47–48 (from Fall to Fall) was a Sabbath year in which the fields lay fallow.[65] For this to occur at a time marked by shortages and privation undoubtedly caused a drastic intensification of an already critical situation which was not relieved until the harvest of the next year (i.e.

[62] Cf. V. Weber, *Der Heilige Paulus vom Apostelübereinkommen bis zum Apostelkonzil* (Biblischen Studien, vol. VI, Heft 1(2), Freiburg, 1901, p. 5; J. Jeremias (n. 48), p. 101; W. M. Ramsay (n. 51), pp. 50f.; G. Ricciotti, *Der Apostel Paulus*, Basle, 1950, p. 140. It is not necessary to read into 'διακονία' a stay by Paul and Barnabas for some time in Jerusalem during which interval they distributed the relief (so Ramsay, p. 51).

[63] To attempt to interpret Acts without taking into consideration the short, disconnected, often legendary nature of the sources available to the author not only depreciates his veracity but also fails to appreciate his extraordinary literary capabilities. See the informative discussion by E. Haenchen, 'Apostelgeschichte', 4b, *RGG*³ I, cols. 405f.; also the literature listed at the end of the article.

[64] *Zeitschrift für die neutestamentliche Wissenschaft*, vol. 27, Giessen, 1928.

[65] See espec. Lev. 25.1–7; cf. also *RGG*³ II, 'Erlassjahr', cols. 568f.

The Collection

AD 49). It would appear then that AD 48 would have been the most logical time for the Antioch Christians to have forwarded their previously prepared aid to Jerusalem.[66]

B. *The 'Apostolic Council'*

The next portion of Acts relevant to this study is the section of verses (15.1ff.) preparatory to the account of the 'Apostolic Council'. The entire fifteenth chapter is of the utmost importance for the study of primitive Christianity in that if the 'Apostolic Council' of Acts and the meeting described by Paul in Gal. 2.1–10 are found to be concerned with the same event, then the most important point of correspondence between Acts and the Pauline literature is established. At the first examination the similarities between the two accounts seem to make this identity self-evident. On closer investigation the apparent analogy of the two is so severely impaired by the large number of serious contradictions that critical research has been led to offer several alternative solutions, none of which is completely satisfactory.

The provocation

The Acts account is introduced with the appearance in Antioch of men, designated rather generally as 'from Judea' (15.1). This term is the same somewhat vague expression as is found in 11.29. Most probably they came from Jerusalem itself.[67]

Of more significance is the question of in what capacity they were acting. The position of high honour and authority which Barnabas occupied in the Christian community in Jerusalem (Acts 4.36ff.; 11.22, etc.) indicates that these men would not have ventured to openly contradict him if they were officially representing the entire Jerusalem church.[68]

If Barnabas' previous actions in Antioch (11.23ff.) had resulted in criticism and suspicion in Jerusalem, these men could very well have been the exponents of an extremist faction there, sent to Antioch to correct what was in their view an intolerable situa-

[66] So also W. L. Knox (n. 27), p. 184 n. 2; H. W. Beyer, *Apostelgeschichte* (Das Neue Testament Deutsch), 2nd ed., Göttingen, 1935, *ad loc.*; F. Hahn (n. 52), p. 92.
[67] The variant reading of D in verse 2 explicitly stated that these men were from Jerusalem, which assertion is supported by verse 24.
[68] The author of Acts obviously did not consider these men to be officially representing the Jerusalem church, as he portrays James in his speech before the council (15.24) as completely repudiating them.

tion.⁶⁹ Yet to seriously entertain this possibility is erroneous. The demand which they made rules it out.

The men insisted that it was essential for Gentiles to become members of the Jewish nation as a prerequisite for being accepted into the Christian fellowship. This was the intent behind their demand for circumcision 'according to the custom of Moses' (15.1).

The later textual addition, 'and walk according to the custom of Moses' (in D), was again an attempt to identify these men with the Christian Pharisaic faction by altering their demands to coincide with the requirements demanded by that faction in verse 5. This change probably seemed relatively insignificant to the later correctors, but actually it was doing great violence to the author's intent.

It is inconceivable that the author of Acts, who was writing at a time when the question of the relationship of Christians to Judaism was still a very live issue, was unaware of the significance of the difference in the demands made by the two groups in verses 1 and 5. Rather it must be assumed that he was purposely making a determinative distinction.

Only in Acts is there found specific mention of a Pharisaic party in the Jerusalem church. In presenting them as a separate group the author of Acts clearly intended for them to be understood as a group who, although they believed in the messiahship of the risen Christ, still held themselves bound to the regulations of their Pharisaic background. Such a group would never have suggested nor supported a demand for adherence of Gentiles to Judaism which required *only* circumcision. The demands described in verse 5 as presented by the Pharisaic faction are characteristic if the 'Law of Moses' is understood in its full rabbinical sense.

Therefore the author of Acts could not have conceived of the men in verse 1 as belonging to the party of the Pharisees. In all probability they belonged to or were associated with the nationalistic 'Zealot' movement which was rapidly becoming more

⁶⁹ It was this understanding of the function these men were to fulfil in Antioch which resulted in the later addition in ψ, 614, and a few other MSS of the phrase 'of those having believed from the faction of the Pharisees' (cf. 6.7). This interpretation naturally enough, but wrongly, identified these extremists with that 'party' mentioned in verse 5.

The Collection

vigorous at that time. The requirement of circumcision alone coincided admirably with their programme.[70]

The demand which these men made resulted in a sharp conflict between them and Paul and Barnabas (v. 2a). They must have found support for their position from within the Antioch church itself. This is implied in the subsequent remark that the matter was referred to Jerusalem. If the men from Judea had evoked no response in Antioch, the controversy would have aborted.[71]

In response to the dissension within their own fellowship resulting from this disturbance, the Antioch Christians decided to refer the problem to the Jerusalem community,[72] where it could be resolved under the counsel and judgement of the Apostles and elders there (v. 2b).

The proceedings at the 'Council'

Accordingly Paul and Barnabas and 'some of the others'[73] travelled to Jerusalem. When they arrived they rehearsed before the church leaders[74] the progress made in their missionary work

[70] See below, pp. 46ff., 64ff.

[71] That the Antioch community had a certain element within it that was susceptible to their strain of argumentation is confirmed in Paul's account of his later conflict with Peter there (cf. Gal. 2.13).

[72] The Greek has no specific antecedent for 'they appointed'. Grammatically it would most naturally refer back to the men from Judea. The variant reading in D made this explicit, and at the same time implied a strong dependence of Paul and Barnabas on the Jerusalem church (cf. Schwartz [n. 7 above], p. 269 n. 2). K. Lake and H. J. Cadbury, *Beginnings* IV, p. 170, point out that it is very unlikely that the author regarded these men as official representatives of the Jerusalem leaders in that he describes James in verse 24 as thoroughly repudiating them. As it is very difficult to see how they would possess enough authority to 'appoint' the two main leaders in Antioch opposing them for a trip to Jerusalem, it seems better to refer the act of 'appointing' to the Antioch community itself which took such an action out of concern for its own disrupted missionary programme. This again indicates with what high regard the Antioch Christians valued the Jerusalem church, although they hardly regarded it as the direct source of their foundation and growth. As the Twelve were directly associated with the Jerusalem congregation, it was the logical place to appeal for clarification on any question of the faith.

[73] Commentators who hold the identity of Acts 15 and Gal. 2 include Titus as one of these. One would expect representatives of both sides of the issue to have been sent by the Antioch church. There is no way of determining if the 'men from Judea' returned to Jerusalem (cf. the variant reading to verse 5). The activity during the trip described in verse 3 implies that only those favourable to Paul and Barnabas were sent. Verses 4ff. give the impression that the Jerusalem church had no prior knowledge of the problem.

[74] The phrase 'apostles and elders' was apparently the stylized formula used in the source employed by the author to designate the leadership in Jerusalem. It appears in 15.2, 4, 6, 22, 23, and in 16.4 with reference back to the events recorded in chapter 15. Other than these passages the phrase does not occur in the NT.

Perhaps the expressions used in Acts 21.17b, 18 were the result of an attempt by the author of Acts to paraphrase this fixed designation in his tradition, in order that

(v. 4). While they were there, however, adherents to the strict Pharisaic party within the Jerusalem Christian community insisted upon the necessity of the circumcision of Gentile believers[75] and their acceptance of the cultic restrictions of the Mosaic Law (v. 5).

Leaving aside for the moment the question of the correspondence of this account with that of Paul, serious questions concerning the inner integrity of the Acts account are nevertheless raised. The problem in Antioch was whether or not to require Gentiles who believed to be circumcised; in Jerusalem the problem was circumcision and observance of the Mosaic Law. Although Barnabas had been described earlier as an official deputy of the Jerusalem church (11.22) his position does not come into play here either in Antioch or at Jerusalem. The retinue accompanying Paul and Barnabas is apparently composed exclusively of those favourable to their position. In addition verse 3 gives the impression that their journey was made in a more leisurely manner than the serious situation in Antioch would have allowed.

When they arrive in Jerusalem neither Paul nor Barnabas expressly bring up the crucial problem which was the alleged cause for their trip. When the problem is raised it is raised in a different form by another interest group than that to which the men who

---

it would be consistent with his conception of the leadership of the Jerusalem community of that time. Evidently he thought the Twelve were no longer located in, nor directly associated with, the Jerusalem church; a conception which could very well be wrong (see below, pp. 54ff.).

[75] The text reads, 'It is necessary to circumcise *them* and to charge *them* to keep the law of Moses.' These requirements are usually understood to have been directed toward Gentile believers in general by assuming that the report of verse 4 was similar to that of verse 2 and 14.27, and that these members of the Pharisaic party were present when the report was made. The Antiochene text represented by H and L adds 'and that (God) had opened a door of faith to the Gentiles' from 14.27 to make this reference plain (the reading is presented in *Beginnings* III, p. 140, ed. by J. H. Ropes).

In their commentary, Lake and Cadbury (*Beginnings* IV) cite the article 'Composition und Entstehung der Apostelgeschichte' by Lekebusch which suggests that 'them' here refers to 'some of the others' of verse 2. According to this suggestion the Pharisaic party was making the demands of someone who accompanied Paul, which would then provide a convenient point of contact with the Galatians account (cf. Gal. 2.3).

W. L. Knox (n. 27) sees the raising of this demand as turning the attitude of the Jerusalem community decisively in favour of Paul's views, since the demand for observance of the whole Mosaic Law implied a censure by the Pharisaic faction on all except James and Paul himself. 'The demand was not put forward with any serious expectation that it would be accepted, but rather with the characteristic contempt of the extremist for those less logical than himself' (pp. 224f.). Cf. Paul's argument concerning the whole law in Gal. 5.3.

The Collection

initiated the controversy in Antioch belonged. The manner in which they are described as raising the issue gives the impression that they were originating a demand about which the Jerusalem church had not previously been concerned (but see 11.1ff., 20ff.!).

It is perhaps possible to resolve most of these inconsistencies by assuming the necessary details were left by the author in the background as being unessential for his concise report, but to do so requires a great amount of reading between the lines. It is more probable that the author was here writing of an event, the actual details of which were almost completely unknown to him, or that he was without any personal knowledge of the event and had to rely on an unfortunately sketchy and inaccurate source.

The author of Acts continued his account with the description of a somewhat formal church meeting[76] avowedly held to deal with the problem in the form in which it was raised by the Pharisaic faction (vv. 6–29).[77] In the course of this meeting Peter and James both made speeches in support of a mission to the Gentiles essentially freed from the requirements of the Mosaic Law (vv. 7–11, 13–21).[78] Paul and Barnabas again told of their work with

---

[76] It is not pertinent to this study to examine the ensuing material in detail. Some of the major problems involved in the narrative are indicated in the footnotes, as well as the literature which may be consulted for a closer analysis. Apparently the author of Acts erroneously combined traditions of what were originally two separate events into his one account of the 'Apostolic Council' (see below, pp. 53ff.).

[77] Verses 9f., 20f. and 28f. are all understandable only over against the demand that fulfilment of the entire Mosaic Law be imposed upon Gentile believers.

[78] These speeches, as all the speeches throughout Acts, are to be understood as the products of literary imagination rather than factually grounded reproductions of what was actually said (cf. H. J. Cadbury, 'The Speeches in Acts', *Beginnings* V, pp. 402ff., and the literature listed there: pp. 402f. n. 2).

There are certain uncharacteristic elements in both addresses. Peter could conceivably have uttered verse 10 if he was referring directly to the strict demand of the Pharisaic faction that the Mosaic Law in its fullest sense must be fulfilled. But verse 11 indicates that the author envisaged Peter as referring to the salvation of Christians placed over against the Mosaic Law in general, which attitude is contradicted by his position in Gal. 2.11ff.

James is described as using quotations from the LXX, and inaccurately at that (vv. 16ff.); cf. W. L. Knox, *The Acts of the Apostles*, Cambridge, 1948: '(Luke) would have felt quite justified in putting into James's mouth a favourite testimony from the LXX to prove God's intention of converting the Gentiles: he probably would not have known that there was any difference between the Greek and the Hebrew at this point; he would certainly have held that the Greek was right as against the Hebrew, since it foretold that purpose of converting the Gentiles which was already being fulfilled' (pp. 45f.).

His statement in verse 21 that 'from early generations Moses has had in every city those who preach him, for he is read every sabbath in the synagogues' has proved exceedingly difficult for scholars to interpret. Usually it is explained as the author's attempt to have James justify the proposal that only the 'Apostolic Decrees' were

the Gentiles (v. 12), and the subsequent decision of the assembly validated their missionary approach (v. 25). However, to facilitate the common fellowship of Jews and Gentiles within the same Christian community, the assembly recommended the so-called 'Apostolic Decrees' (vv. 20, 29).[79]

The 'Decrees' were clearly intended to make possible close fellowship within the same Christian community between Gentiles who were free from the Mosaic Law and Jews who were

---

necessary. Lake and Cadbury, *Beginnings* IV, pp. 177-8, cite an article by J. H. Ropes (in *Journal of Biblical Literature*, No. XV, 1896, pp. 75-81), in which he suggests that this verse is intended to clarify James's quote from Amos 9.11 (v. 17): 'To prove that the prophecy means more (than just Israel), James puts in the argument that the Jews have synagogues all over the world, and thus "the nations which are called by my name" covers not only the old Kingdom of David, but the whole civilized world.'

The most glaring inconsistency in the two speeches is the cryptic references to the Cornelius episode (vv. 7ff., 14), which might have been discernible to a reader, but which would not have been clear to an audience listening to a speech. These references lend the weightiest support to the hypothesis that the Cornelius episode was closely associated with the Jerusalem meeting represented in this second part of the author's account of the 'Apostolic Council'. They either belonged together in the source used or the Cornelius source was a parallel tradition, in which case the 11.1ff. Jerusalem meeting is a duplicate to the 15.6ff. meeting. Note the phrase 'apostles and brethren' (11.1), which closely corresponds to the phrase 'apostles and elders' in chapter 15 (see n. 74 above; also the awkward construction resulting from an amalgamation of the two phrases in 15.23).

If the parallelism is the author's own construction, this could well have been instigated by his schematic parallelism between the figures of Peter and Paul throughout Acts. On the Cornelius episode, see *Beginnings* II, pp. 156ff.; IV, pp. 112ff.; M. Dibelius (n. 48), pp. 94f., 109ff.; O. Cullmann, *Peter: Disciple, Apostle, Martyr*, 2nd ed., London, 1962, pp. 37f., and the literature listed there in n. 12; also his contention on p. 43: '(Peter), just like Paul and Barnabas, interrupted his missionary travels to go to Jerusalem for the so-called Apostolic Council.'

Nevertheless it is quite probable that the general tone of the speeches, which are both strongly in support of a liberal attitude to Gentile converts, were constructed by the author to reflect the actual attitudes of Peter and James toward the Gentile element in the Church. (See *Beginnings* V, pp. 426f.; O. Cullmann, *op. cit.*, pp. 52f.)

[79] See Acts 21.25; also Rev. 2.14, 20; Eusebius, *Hist. Eccles.* V, i, 20: 'How could such people eat children, when they are not even permitted to eat the blood of irrational animals?' (in connection with the persecution of AD 177). Cf. also Mark 7.14ff.; Col. 2.16, 20ff.; I Tim. 4.3f.; Titus 1.14f.; Heb. 13.9.

The reading which presents the 'Decrees' as Jewish cultic restrictions is to be preferred (so J. Munck, n. 7 above, p. 235; W. M. Ramsay, n. 51 above, p. 43; H. Lietzmann, 'Der Sinn des Aposteldekretes und seine Textwandlung', *Amicitiae Corolla*, London, 1933, pp. 203ff.; F. F. Bruce, n. 56 above, p. 300; E. Haenchen, n. 40 above, p. 401; W. L. Knox, *The Acts of the Apostles*, Cambridge, 1948, pp. 46f.; K. Lake, *Beginnings* IV, p. 177; V, pp. 204f.) over the secondary reading in the Western text which gives them an ethical character (chosen by Rudolf Steinmetz, 'Das Apostoldekret', *Biblische Zeit und Streitfragen*, Heft 5, Berlin, 1911, pp. 29ff., 43ff.). See also A. von Harnack, 'Das Apostoldekret und die Blass'sche Hypothese', *Studien zur Geschichte des Neuen Testament und der alten Kirche*, vol. I, 1931, pp. 1-32; J. H. Ropes, *Beginnings* III, pp. 265-9; J. Wellhausen (n. 47), pp. 19ff.; Walter Lüthi, *Die Apostelgeschichte*, Basle, 1958, p. 239; Foakes Jackson, *Acts* (Moffatt), pp. 140f.

The Collection

committed to keep that Law. It is of the utmost importance for a correct chronological reconstruction of the events recorded in Acts to grasp that this problem of fellowship could not have reached the critical point requiring formal action until after the prior question of the eligibility of the Gentiles to join the new faith without being circumcised had *already been decisively resolved*.

They recorded their decision in a letter (vv. 23ff.)[80] and appointed Judas and Silas[81] to travel with Paul and Barnabas to Antioch to convey their judgement to the troubled Christians there (v. 22).

A further inconsistency is to be seen in the destination of the letter. Supposedly the whole controversy originated and was centred in Antioch. But the letter is addressed 'to the brethren who are of the Gentiles in Antioch and Syria and Cilicia' (v. 23, cf. v. 41). Then in 16.4 Paul and Silas and Timothy unexplainedly are described as delivering the Jerusalem decision in Galatia. In the meantime at least one of the two men appointed to travel with the letter returned to Jerusalem after having visited only Antioch (15.33; cf. the variant reading, and v. 40).

Chronology of the 'Council'

As the account stands in Acts, it is not possible to say with certainty when the author of Acts considered the 'Apostolic Council' to have occurred. If the 'Gallio inscription' is understood to place the proconsulship of Gallio in Achaia during AD 51/52,[82] and if Paul's encounter with him there (Acts 18.12ff.) took place early in his term of office and toward the end of Paul's stay (Acts 18.11),[83] then it may be concluded that the author

---

[80] In all probability the contents of the letter, as were the speeches, is a product of the author's own creativity (see K. Lake, 'The Apostolic Council of Jerusalem', *Beginnings* V, p. 211).

[81] When the question of social intercourse was considered the Jerusalem church evidently did send a letter to the Gentile churches bearing their decision (K. Lake, *ibid*., p. 212). It has been suggested above (pp. 21f.) that the letter was carried by these two men because they already had previous knowledge of the Gentile churches from their travels with Paul while working on the collection project. By combining two functions which they carried out into one, the author of Acts unwittingly produced a construction irreconcilable with the testimony of Paul. See below, pp. 54ff.

[82] Another possibility is AD 52-53. In *Beginnings* V, pp. 460ff., the text and a translation of the inscription are presented along with a discussion of the problems involved in interpreting it and the various results possible. Cf. also RGG^3 II, col. 1196.

[83] Both assertions are not explicitly stated in the Acts account, but seem to be implied by the context.

understood the Council to have taken place around AD 48.[84]

However, considering the author's proclivity for inserting historical reference points (whether correct or not) into his narrative, the absence of such a specification in Acts 15 may mean that he was not sure precisely when it was held.

[84] So E. Haenchen (n. 40), p. 58; J. Jeremias (n. 48), p. 100; E. D. Burton, *The Epistle to the Galatians* (International Critical Commentary), Edinburgh, 1921, intro., p. xliv; cf. also H. Conzelmann, *RGG*³ III, 'Heidenchristentum', sect. 6. E. Schwartz's theory, which places the 'Council' at AD 43-44, before the persecution by Herod, appears unlikely (n. 7 above; pp. 267f.). At the other extreme of improbability is the assumption by Anders Nygren (*Commentary on Romans*, trans. C. C. Rasmussen, Philadelphia, 1949, p. 455) that the meeting with the Apostles took place in AD 52.

II

THE NEW TESTAMENT ACCOUNT OF PAUL'S COLLECTION: II

THIS chapter continues the investigation begun in the first chapter. Following the analysis of the 'Apostolic Council' account in Acts 15, the next step is to examine Paul's account in Gal. 2.1ff. of the Jerusalem conference. In order to reach some judgement concerning the alleged identity of the meeting described in the two accounts the Acts 15 and Gal. 2 versions will next be compared.

Attention is then turned to the conflict which occurred between Paul and Peter in Antioch. This account immediately follows Paul's Jerusalem conference presentation (Gal. 2.11ff.). As will be seen below, the events and attitudes involved in the Antioch conflict provide important corroborative evidence to the issues and decisions of the Apostolic Council.

Lastly, the meagre information available on the delivery trip to Jerusalem and the reception accorded it there will be considered.

1. THE JERUSALEM MEETING IN GALATIANS

Paul composed his version of a meeting which took place in Jerusalem as an integral part of the evidence he was offering to the Galatians[1] to prove that his apostleship was legitimate and that

[1] The question as to whether Paul wrote Galatians to the churches in ethnic Galatia (North-Galatian theory) or in the Roman province of Galatia (South-Galatian theory) has never been resolved. Either theory is possible; neither has been conclusively established; cf. H. Schlier, *Der Brief an die Galater* (Meyer Kommentar, 10th ed.), Göttingen, 1949, on 1.2. The strong points of one theory are the weak points of the other. The South-Galatian theory is assumed to be correct in this study.
For a discussion of the North-Galatian theory, see J. B. Lightfoot, *Saint Paul's Epistle to the Galatians*, London, 1892, intro., pp. 18ff.; H. Lietzmann, *An die Galater* (Handbuch zum neuen Testament), Tübingen, 1932, pp. 3f.; A. Oepke, *Der Brief des Paulus an die Galater* (Theologischer Handkommentar zum neuen Testament), 2nd ed., Berlin, 1957, intro., pp. 5-8, pp. 168f.; Pierre Bonnard, *L'épitre de saint Paul aux Galates*, Neuchâtel, 1953, intro., pp. 10f.; M.-J. Lagrange, *Saint Paul épitre aux Galates*, Paris, 1950, pp. iii, xiiiff. For the South-Galatian theory, see W. M. Ramsay, *The Church in the Roman Empire before AD 170*, 9th ed., London, 1907, pp.

The New Testament Account of Paul's Collection: II

the gospel he preached was neither dependent upon nor received through human agency. This was called forth by the presence of men among the Galatian communities who were seeking to discredit Paul and his previous work there by charging that he was subservient to the congregation in Jerusalem and had disobediently distorted the gospel which he had been authorized by them to preach (Gal. 1.1, 6–12, 15–17a, 18–19, 22).

An understanding of the situation which lay in the background of the defence Paul here made of his apostleship and the gospel he preached is essential for a full appreciation of the dependability of the account which he presented. As a source his writings would in any case be considered the more trustworthy in that they were written by a man who was directly involved in the events they describe, and who recorded his impressions of them relatively soon after they had occurred. In this particular passage the reliability of the information given is considerably heightened by the circumstances under which it was written. Paul was under attack. He wrote this passage to refute the charges which were levied against him. If he had purposely or accidentally omitted or distorted any of the events which had a bearing on the situation he would have provided his opposition with the perfect opportunity to claim vindication for their assertions on the basis of his own defence. The oath which he wrote in 1.20 dramatically underscored that he was very well aware of this danger and was being particularly cautious in this defence.[2]

To answer the allegations brought against him, Paul rehearsed the significant facts in his life pertaining to the accusations from the period before his conversion up until the recent past (Gal. 1 and 2).[3] Within this enumeration is the account of the Jerusalem meeting (Gal. 2.1–10).

8ff., 97ff.; *St Paul the Traveller and the Roman Citizen*, 10th ed., London, 1908, pp. 89ff.; E. D. Burton, *The Epistle to the Galatians* (International Critical Commentary), Edinburgh, 1921, intro., pp. xxvi, xlivff.; Theodor Zahn, *Der Brief des Paulus an die Galater*, Leipzig, 1905, intro., pp. 9ff.; W. L. Knox, *Saint Paul and the Church of Jerusalem*, Cambridge, 1925, pp. 236ff.; also the related word study on pp. 216ff.; Wilhelm Oehler, *Ein Missionar kämpft um seine Gemeinden*, Neukirchen, 1960, pp. 8f.

The significance of choosing the South-Galatian over against the North-Galatian theory for this study is that it thereby is possible to substantiate the participation of Galatia in Paul's collection and to identify its representatives (see below, p. 68).

[2] Cf. John Knox, *Chapters in a Life of Paul*, Nashville, 1950, pp. 52f. On Paul's use of such an oath compare Rom. 9.1; also I Tim. 2.7.

[3] There does not seem to be any sufficient reason for understanding an extended

The Collection

A. *The discussions with the 'Pillars'*

Paul began his account by mentioning that Barnabas and Titus went with him to Jerusalem (v. 1).[4] The motivation for this trip was an ecstatic mystical experience.[5] The fact that the impetus for this trip was the result of such a 'revelation' is important for an understanding of the meeting in Jerusalem. Paul was neither commanded to appear by the Jerusalem leadership nor was he ordered to go there by anyone representing them. His being delegated by another group of Christians to make the trip (i.e. Antioch, Acts 15.2) is also to be excluded. Rather his trip was instigated by a direct command of God and was immediately concerned with the clarification of an essential element in the primitive Church's understanding of the manner of execution of its missionary enterprise within the '*Heilsgeschichte*'.

The purpose of the trip was to come to a mutual understanding with the Jerusalem leadership over the form, scope and direction of future missionary activity, as well as to obtain their approbation of the work already accomplished. This is expressed in the phrase 'lest somehow I should be running or had run in vain' (v. 2). Certainly if the Jerusalem church, to which the majority of the eyewitnesses of Jesus' earthly ministry belonged, should judge Paul's gospel unChristian it would have been disastrous.[6] But the central thrust of the apprehension expressed here involved more than just that.

---

period of time between the 'Antioch conflict' of 2.11ff. and the writing of this epistle. If the allusive reference in Acts 18.22 indicates a Jerusalem trip, the writing of this epistle certainly occurred before then or Paul would have had to mention it here.

[4] The chronological specification, 'after fourteen years', is discussed below, p. 58.
The manner in which Paul listed his companions, 'I went up again to Jerusalem with Barnabas, taking Titus along with me', indicates that Paul held Barnabas in high regard as his fellow labourer. He probably mentioned Barnabas so predominantly because the prestige of that person as a witness to what Paul was to relate would lend weight to his argument (H. Schlier, *Der Brief an die Galater*, Meyer Kommentar, 10th ed., *ad loc.*). Titus, an *aide* of Paul's or simply one chosen by Paul to travel with him on this trip, was mentioned because of the role he played in the incident described in verses 3ff. Perhaps there were others who came with them, but as they were unessential to Paul's narrative he omitted mention of them.

[5] Paul nowhere employs the term 'revelation' for a communication mediated by another human (against F. Hahn, *Mission in the New Testament*, London, 1965, p. 79, who erroneously maintains the revelation was made known to Paul through the mouth of a prophet). It is always eschatologically oriented, so P. Bonnard (n. 1), on 1.16; cf. also *ThWB* III, pp. 586ff. The form of the experience is not known; H. Schlier (n. 1), *ad loc.*, discusses the different possibilities.

[6] So H. Lietzmann; E. D. Burton; both n. 1 above, *ad loc.*

There would not have been a serious conflict of opinion over whether the Gentiles were to be allowed to share in the salvation of the gospel. The main point of concern was the question of at what point within the *'Heilsgeschichte'* the gospel would go to them. Was the main attention to be focused first on the conversion of Israel, and only after that was completed would there be a concentrated effort made to spread the gospel among the nations? If so, then any individual Gentile who sought to become a Christian before the latter stage was reached could reasonably be required to accept circumcision and become a member of the Jewish nation.[7] Or was it conceivable that it was the will of the risen Christ that a simultaneous mission to the Gentiles be established? In terms of this question Paul was certainly justified in being apprehensive as to whether he had prematurely begun the mission to the Gentiles for which he was convinced he had been specifically called by God (cf. 1.15f.).[8]

It was to settle this question that he met together privately with James, Peter and John (v. 2, cf. v. 9).[9] After hearing of the effective working of the Spirit in and through him, the 'Pillars' unconditionally[10] acknowledged the validity of the form, method

---

[7] Certainly the problem of the circumcision of Gentiles would have been at some time brought up by the Jerusalem 'Pillars' as a related question to the discussion of Paul's gospel within this context. The events of verses 3ff. lent a note of real urgency to that particular phrase of their talks. But the question of receiving circumcision as a *requisite for salvation* was never the dominating issue in the private discussions (against Floyd Filson, *Three Crucial Decades*, Richmond, 1963, p. 107). Note that in 5.2ff. Paul categorically condemns those who hold such a view of circumcision in relation to the gospel of Christ as being 'severed from Christ . . . fallen away from grace'! His relations with Jerusalem would have been seriously disrupted, rather than an agreement reached, had they sought to maintain that extreme position.

[8] It is this understanding of the relationship between Paul and the leaders of the Jerusalem church which is one of the main themes in *Paul and the Salvation of Mankind*, by Johannes Munck, London, 1959.

[9] Verse 2 reads: '. . . I laid before them the gospel . . . but privately before them who were of repute' (ASV). Grammatically the first 'them' refers to the whole Christian community in Jerusalem implied in verse 1; the second 'them' to James, Peter and John, specified later in verse 9. Many commentators have therefore erroneously understood two different meetings to have been listed by Paul here (for example: Lightfoot, Bonnard, Zahn, Oepke, Burton: for all, see above, n. 1). Yet the text as it stands could only mean one meeting; the latter phrase being a limitation to the former (so H. Schlier, n. 1 above). The suggestion of two meetings here would never have arisen were it not for the obviously contradictory description of a general assembly in Acts 15 which could in no way be construed to have been judged as 'privately before them who were of repute' by Paul.

[10] 'Added nothing to me' excludes any restriction, correction, or additional requirement imposed upon Paul by the Jerusalem leadership. Verse 10 ('only they would have us . . .') is grammatically but not intrinsically a condition to verses 6f., 9 (against Karl Holl, 'Der Kirchenbegriff des Paulus in seinem Verhältnis zu dem

43

The Collection

and objective of the gospel Paul and Barnabas had been preaching (vv. 6f., 9).

James, Peter and John were brought to this recognition which contradicted their concept of the order of the spreading of the gospel when they 'saw that (Paul) had been entrusted with the gospel to the uncircumcised, just as Peter had been entrusted with the gospel to the circumcised' (v. 7) and 'had perceived the grace that was given to (Paul)' (v. 9). The second phrase is clarified by the first. 'Grace' is to be understood here in a very concrete sense. Paul related the progress of his work among the Gentiles and told of the great success it had realized, abundantly accompanied by indubitable evidences of the presence and activity of the Spirit (cf. 3.5; compare I Cor. 9.1f.).

In the face of the obvious approbation of the resurrected Christ the 'Pillars' were compelled to accept the validity of the work Paul was doing. It was evident that God had led him to enter upon a new phase of missionary work which they had not envisioned as being begun so soon.

The parenthetical remark in verse 8[11] expresses not only Paul's personal conviction, but is also a further clarification of the preceding passive, 'when they saw that *I had been entrusted*'. Verse 8 affirms that the 'Pillars' clearly recognized that the missionary work done by Paul had been instigated and maintained by God (cf. 1.15f.). On the other hand, they remained just as convinced of the validity and urgent necessity of their mission to Judaism which was under the leadership of Peter.

They proceeded to formulate general areas of responsibility for the future missionary endeavour of the Church (v. 9; cf. vv. 7f.).[12]

---

der Urgemeinde', *Gesammelte Aufsätze zur Kirchengeschichte*, vol. II, Tüginben, 1928, pp. 44–67; cf. also H. Lietzmann, n. 1 above, pp. 12f.). H. Schlier, *ad loc.* and pp. 76f.; and A. Oepke, *ad loc.* and pp. 51–55 (both n. 1 above), by overemphasizing 'to me', erroneously assert that only to Paul personally was there nothing added.

[11] 'For he who worked through Peter for the mission to the circumcised worked through me also for the Gentiles.'

[12] Walter Schmithals, in *Paul and James*, London, 1965, sees the central question at the Jerusalem conference to have centred around Paul's custom of proclaiming an antinomian gospel to the Jews. Consequently the agreement reached was a strict ethnographic one in which Paul relinquished his practice of preaching to the Jews (pp. 25, 44ff.).

This view would demand the arbitrary and forced conclusion that from this time on Paul ceased to have any interest in actively converting Jews to the Christian faith. The conclusion is contradicted by Rom. 9–11 (among numerous passages) as well as by one of the main purposes of the collection, as will be seen below.

The New Testament Account of Paul's Collection: II

Rather than subjugate Paul's work to direct Jerusalem supervision and revise it to conform to their understanding of the order of the spreading of the gospel, they agreed upon the simultaneous coexistence of two missionary enterprises relatively independent of each other: Peter, working from the Jerusalem church, would be responsible for the efforts to convert Judaism; Paul, working from Antioch, would devote himself to the Gentile mission. Implied in this compromise was the corollary understanding that Peter's mission was of necessity to operate within the restrictive borders of cultic Judaism under the Mosaic Law; Paul's mission was to be free of these restrictions in so far as the Gentiles were concerned.[13]

It is of the utmost importance for the understanding of this entire passage to see that the agreement reached between the Jerusalem 'Pillars' and Paul was not the result of a reserved 'partial surrender' by either or both sides. The agreement was reached in a positive, perhaps even enthusiastic, attitude. They recognized Paul's apostleship and his special commission (vv. 7f.). They imposed no restrictions on him (v. 6). They gave to Paul and Barnabas the 'right hand of fellowship' (v. 9), expressing thereby their sharing equally in a common task toward a common goal in obedience to the same Lord.[14]

To support his argument Schmithals holds that for the agreement to have been other than strictly ethnographic would have made it 'so vague and therefore useless from the outset' (p. 46, n. 22). But is this not precisely what the subsequent incident of conflict at Antioch indicates?

[13] Not once does Paul assert in his epistles, nor is he pictured as asserting in Acts, that Jewish-Christians should abandon their observance of the Law. Neither does he maintain that it is of any use for a Gentile-Christian to place himself under the Law; cf. I Cor. 7.17ff.; Gal. 5.6; 6.15. The circumcision of Timothy, which is probably historical, occurred under very different circumstances and does not contradict this, see p. 50 below. I Cor. 9.19ff. is an excellent summary from Paul's own experience of the attitude which produced and which was expressed in this agreement by the leaders in Jerusalem, Paul, and Barnabas toward the continuing missionary enterprise of the Church.

[14] Against Albert Schweitzer, *The Mysticism of Paul the Apostle*, London, 1931, who questioned that the 'attempt at agreement' was ever seriously made, p. 155. Schmithals (n. 12), p. 50, misses the importance of the precedent set by this agreement when he implies that it was simply a clarification and confirmation of a *modus operandi* already in effect as a result of Paul's first Jerusalem visit.

Practically all commentators see in the giving of the right hand of fellowship a completely sincere expression of harmonious understanding. So, for example, H.-J. Schoeps, *Paulus*, Tübingen, 1959: 'I come to the conclusion that the handclasp with which the στῦλοι dismissed Paul from the apostolic convention meant their sincere recognition of the Pauline apostleship to the Gentiles, that Paul was to be entrusted with the gospel to the uncircumcised just as Peter with the gospel to the circumcision, that both men laboured together and not against each other, and James, as the

The Collection

In addition they requested Paul to 'remember the poor' (v. 10).[15]

B. *The demand to circumcise Titus*

During this visit to Jerusalem by Paul and his fellow workers certain men demanded the circumcision of Titus (vv. 3-5).[16] These men had affiliated themselves with the Jerusalem Christians[17] not as the result of their faith in the gospel but to infiltrate the community in the hope of being able to use it for their own purposes. It was these motives which led them to insist upon Titus' circumcision.

Neither the identity of these men nor their motives are made explicit in the Galatians account. But they are clearly implied.

The 'false brethren' had apparently insinuated themselves by devious means into being accepted as members of the Christian group. If the passive phrase, 'secretly brought in' (v. 4), is to be interpreted with its full literal force, then it must be assumed that there were certain Jewish Christians already belonging to the

---

head of the Jerusalem community, gave his blessing to this arrangement, to the intense displeasure of the intransigent "zealous for the Law" in the Jerusalem community' (pp. 62f.). Cf. also the study in Burton's commentary, pp. 95f.; Filson (n. 7), p. 108.

[15] See below, pp. 59ff.

[16] If the main question which brought Paul to Jerusalem to confer with the Apostles there was that described in pp. 42f. above, then it is misleading to credit him with bringing Titus along as a practical test-case for the question of circumcision (so A. Schlatter, *Die Briefe an die Galater und Epheser*, Stuttgart, 1920, *ad loc.*; E. D. Burton, on vv. 1 and 3). Filson (n. 7), p. 108, more accurately interprets Titus's role as being 'Exhibit A' of what God had been doing for and through the Gentiles.

H. Schlier and P. Bonnard (both n. 1 above) interpret verse 3 in the passive sense that, although Titus, an uncircumcised Gentile, was present, there was no demand made that he be circumcised. This interpretation eliminates any direct connection between the Titus incident and the 'false brethren'. It seems more probable, however, that verses 3-5 are to be seen as belonging together (so the majority of commentators).

[17] There is no evidence in this account that the 'false brethren' were active in Antioch (against A. Schlatter, n. 16) or in the Gentile communities in general against A. Oepke; H. Lietzmann; P. Bonnard; all n. 1 above; H. Schlier, p. 40, assumed on the basis of the definite article before 'false brethren' that they were known to the Galatians). Neither are verses 4 f. to be seen as an accusation formulated by Paul, but having no direct relation to the Jerusalem meeting (so J. Munck, n. 8 above, pp. 95ff.).

Rather the account which Paul wrote gives the impression that the opposition by these men was an unexpected factor which arose in the course of his stay there and which had to be rebuked at all costs. E. D. Burton (n. 1 above) most thoroughly developed the position that Paul was here speaking of an incident which occurred in Jerusalem. W. L. Knox (n. 1 above) affirmed its occurrence in Jerusalem, but erroneously concluded that Titus *was* circumcised as a result (pp. 182, 189f., n. 19).

Jerusalem church who sponsored them.[18] However, the following phrase, 'who slipped in to spy out', expressed their own activity in the matter. So it is possible that they joined the Christians on their own initiative.

In the only other passage in which Paul used the designation 'false brethren' (II Cor. 11.26) he explicitly differentiated the 'false brethren' from both genuine Jews and Gentiles. This confirms what one would naturally suspect, that the phrase is descriptive of their relationship to the Christian faith.

A correct understanding of this negative epithet as Paul used it in referring to these men is crucial for an accurate identification. By 'false brethren' Paul meant 'men who claimed to be Christian but are not' rather than 'men who genuinely believed in Christ but expounded a distorted theology' (i.e. heretical Christians).

Throughout the New Testament, whenever the prefix ψευδο- is applied to a personal title or category, it is always in the sense of 'falsely claiming to belong to that category'. The most obvious example is the designation, 'false christs' (Mark 13.22, par.), who are quite clearly those who claim to be the Christ, the Messiah, but are not.

In the same manner Paul uses the term 'false apostle'[19] for those who claimed apostolic authority for themselves although they had not received an apostolic commission from Christ. 'False witnesses' are those who claim to have experienced or observed something for which, in reality, they have no reliable supporting information.[20] A ψευδολόγος is someone who by his word maintains the veracity of something which he knows actually is not so (= liar).[21] 'False prophets' are not genuine prophets who have distorted the word of God to their own ends (something as Ezek. 13.2 ff.), but are those who, without authorization, claim for themselves the role of prophet.[22]

---

[18] It is maintained in the subsequent material that these 'false brethren' were activists in a growing Jewish nationalistic movement. If this is correct then it must be concluded that there were already those belonging to the Christian fellowship who were inclined in this nationalistic direction. That such an element was indeed part of the Jerusalem church is borne out in Paul's account of the Antioch episode (Gal. 2.12), see below, pp. 64ff.
[19] II Cor. 11.13; cf. Rev. 2.2.
[20] I Cor. 15.15; cf. var. Matt. 26.60.
[21] I Tim. 4.2; cf. ψευδής: Acts 6.13; Rev. 2.2; 21.8.
[22] Matt. 7.15; 24.11, 24; Mark 13.22; Luke 6.26; Acts 13.6; II Peter 2.1; I John 4.1; Rev. 16.13; 19.20; 20.10.

The Collection

The analogous comparison implied in II Peter 2.1 between 'false prophets' and 'false teachers' makes it most probable that, although 'false teachers' are directly associated with 'destructive heresies', the designation expresses: 'those who wrongly claim they have been called to the charismatic office of teaching', which false claim is evident, then, in the 'destructive heresies' they teach.

Therefore it seems probable that the *expression*, 'false brethren', which Paul used in Gal. 2.4 (and, by analogy, in II Cor. 11.26) as well as the *context*, indicates that he was speaking not of the Christian brethren whose theology was wrong, but of men who unjustifiably claimed to be Christian brethren when, in reality, they were not 'brethren' at all. They were *counterfeit* Christians, not simply erroneous ones.[23]

The motive of the 'false brethren' for affiliating with the Jerusalem church was the same as their motive for demanding the circumcision of Titus. They had become part of the Christian community for the purpose of enlisting the support of this new and vigorous 'Jewish sect' for the emerging nationalistic movement dedicated to the goal of restoring the political independence and prestige of the Jewish nation.

They learned that Titus, who professed to belong to this sect, was an uncircumcised Gentile. In keeping with their intent of enrolling the Christians as supporters of a rigid Jewish nationalism they demanded the circumcision of Titus in order that he might be regarded as a member of the Jewish nation.

Several factors in Paul's account lend support to this interpretation.

The only demand they made of Titus was that he be circumcised. There is no suggestion that any other aspect of the Mosaic Law was specified. If the motivation for the demand had been primarily the establishment of a relationship acceptable to cultic Judaism, an obvious and well-known compromise solution as a 'God-fearer' was already in existence.[24]

Paul protested that these men were attacking the 'freedom

---

[23] It is probably in this sense that the term is used in Polycarp, *ad Phil.* 6.3, where the Philippian Christians are warned to avoid 'those who tempt others to sin, and the false brethren, and those who hypocritically bear the name of the Lord, who lead foolish men astray' (against A & G, p. 899, who interpret it as 'Christians with wrong beliefs').

[24] Cf. K. Lake, 'Proselytes and God-fearers', *Beginnings* V, pp. 74-95, for a discussion of this and other possible relationships of varying strictness to Judaism.

The New Testament Account of Paul's Collection: II

which we have in Christ Jesus' to 'bring us into bondage'. The sign of this 'bondage' for Paul was undoubtedly the requirements of the Mosaic Law (Gal. 4.8ff.; 5.1–6). But by freedom he meant more than just exemption from the law. He was maintaining the position that in Christ Jesus the redemptive purpose of God is no longer bound exclusively with an ethnic-politic-cultic group (cf. espec. 3.6ff.; 6.13–16) the distinctive sign of which had been circumcision.[25]

Instead of making their demands directly to Titus or Paul, the 'false brethren' indirectly brought pressure to bear on them by appealing to the 'Pillars'. The latter in turn raised the question of Titus' circumcision for discussion in their private deliberations with Paul.[26]

That these men should have such free access to the attention of the Jerusalem leaders is not surprising. Paul's use of the designation 'false brethren' in referring to them indicates that they were generally regarded as 'brethren'. That is, they were accepted by the Jerusalem Christians as genuine Christians; as 'brothers in Christ'.

This recognition in turn implies that the 'Pillars' either were unaware of their real intent or they did not comprehend the seriousness of the menace which these men represented, and therefore tolerated them. If the 'false brethren' could have induced the Jerusalem leaders to support their demands in this concrete case involving Titus they would have attained the precedent and authoritative recognition necessary to their purpose.

When the 'Pillars' at the instigation of the 'false brethren' brought the matter up with Paul he categorically refused to yield to the demand (v. 5). The tone of v. 3 gives the impression that although the demand was made known to Paul by the 'Pillars' it

---

[25] Cf. the strong emphasis on circumcision in Gal. 5.1–15. The force of Paul's argument here and in chapter 3 is that if a man accepts circumcision as a necessary requirement for participation in God's salvation he obligates himself, *even if it was not his intention to do so*, to observe the whole law. This argument was useful, however, only against those who demanded fulfilment of only certain aspects of the law; in this case circumcision.

[26] Διὰ δὲ τοὺς παρεισάκτους ψευδαδέλφους (v. 4) states that the circumcision of Titus was raised 'because of' and not 'by' the 'false brethren'. Therefore it seems best along with E. D. Burton and H. Lietzmann (n. 1 above), *ad loc.*, to assume that the demand was not made directly to Paul, Barnabas, or Titus, but indirectly through the 'Pillars'. This view is opposed by H. W. Beyer, *Der Brief an die Galater* (Das Neue Testament Deutsch), 2nd ed., Göttingen, 1935.

was not accompanied by any strong pressure or insistence on their part. Verses 5f. testify that in the face of Paul's firm rejection of the proposal they agreed with him that it was not necessary or even useful.[27]

c. *Titus and Timothy*

Superficially the circumcision of Timothy appears to contradict the position Paul took in Jerusalem concerning the circumcision of Titus. But the contradiction is only superficial, for the circumstances under which Timothy was circumcised were very different. Titus was a Greek, that is, a full Gentile; Timothy was half Jewish. Walter Lüthi[28] has pointed out that, according to the Jewish Talmud, Timothy was a Jew in the eye of other Jews because his mother had been Jewish. With Timothy the question was not the necessity of receiving circumcision to become a legitimate member of the Christian community, as it was with Titus. Rather, the motivation for his circumcision lay in the practical necessity of his being acceptable to the Jewish communities in the Diaspora as he journeyed with Paul assisting him in his missionary labours.[29]

It is significant that Paul, in Gal. 5.11, sought to counteract one of the charges brought against him; a charge of inconsistency in his attitude toward circumcision. He had preached the gospel divorced from the requirement of circumcision to them, yet there was some tangible event known to the Galatian Christians that his opponents could point to as evidence that Paul had advocated circumcision. On the basis of the assumption that the South-Galatian theory is correct, this tangible event was very probably

---

[27] Julius Richter (*Die Briefe des Apostels Paulus als missionarische Sendschreiben*, Gütersloh, 1929, p. 103), W. L. Knox (n. 1 above; p. 182) and K. Lake (*Beginnings* V, pp. 196f.), all interpreted the Galatians passage as meaning that Titus was actually circumcised. This interpretation led Lake in his commentary on Acts (*Beginnings* IV), to suggest that the account of the circumcision of Timothy (Acts 16.1-3) 'is a confused and perhaps erroneous memory of the story of Titus' (p. 184). There is so little similarity between the accounts that such a proposed identity between them seems impossible. The Timothy incident has the appearance of being historical. It is difficult to conceive of a reason for the author of Acts including it in his account unless he had a well-developed tradition concerning the incident, or was acquainted with Timothy.

[28] *Die Apostelgeschichte*, Basle, 1958, p. 249.

[29] W. Schmithals (n. 12), pp. 94f., considers the explanation of Timothy's circumcision as being expedient for Paul's mission work to be a construction of the author of Acts. He describes as Paul's real reason his desire to keep the agreement reached in Jerusalem (which is understood in a strict ethnographic sense) by giving no grounds for the charge of preaching the gospel freed of the Law to Jews.

the circumcision of Timothy. Therefore Paul explicitly recorded with his own hand his actual attitude, and the attitude of the Jerusalem 'Pillars', toward circumcision: 'For neither circumcision counts for anything, nor uncircumcision, but a new creation'.[30]

2. THE ACTS AND GALATIANS VERSIONS COMPARED

The contradictions between Paul's account in Galatians and the narrative presented in Acts are of such a serious nature that the New Testament research has not been able to arrive at a solution in regard to their interrelationship satisfactory enough to receive general acceptance. It is not directly significant for this study to give a detailed analysis of every attempt to reconcile the two versions. Among the various authors four major solutions can be discerned.[31] These four explanations will be briefly summarized in the text accompanied by the indications of the main problems raised by each. Representative discussions of each solution are listed in the footnotes. It should be observed that within these four general directions there are many minor variations among the different exponents.

A. *The first solution: Acts 15 = Gal. 2*

The most general solution offered by those seeking to maintain the factual integrity of both Acts and the Pauline epistle is the identification of Acts 15. 1–29 with Gal. 2. 1–10.[32]

The major problems involved in this identity are: (1) Acts 15 is presented as Paul's third trip to Jerusalem; Paul described it as

[30] Gal. 6.15; cf. 5.6; I Cor. 7.17ff.
[31] An interesting but unconvincing solution which does not fit into any of the four discussed here is that suggested by John Knox, *Chapters in a Life of Paul*, Nashville, 1950, pp. 68f. Knox proposes that Acts 15 and Acts 18.22–23 are a duplicate account of the Gal. 2.1ff. meeting which is to be chronologically located in the Acts account at the chapter 18 position.
[32] J. B. Lightfoot (n. 1), p. 123; cf. also his article, 'St Paul and the Three', pp. 292ff., in the back of his commentary; R. Steinmetz, 'Das Aposteldekret', *Biblische Zeit und Streitfragen*, Heft 5, Berlin, 1911, pp. 29ff., 43ff.; M. Dibelius, *Studies in the Acts of the Apostles*, London, 1956, pp. 93ff.; A. Schlatter, *Die Apostelgeschichte*, Stuttgart, 1958, pp. 179f.; also (n. 16), on Gal. 2.1; M.-J. Lagrange (n. 1), intro., p. iv, and on Gal. 2.1; E. D. Burton (n. 1), pp. 115ff.; F. Filson (n. 7), p. 107. F. J. Foakes Jackson, *The Acts of the Apostles* (Moffatt NT Commentary), London, 1931 pp. 132f., and T. Zahn (n. 1), pp. 107ff., both make this identification but admit that the two accounts are irreconcilable. H. Schlier (n. 1), pp. 66ff., rejects the Acts 9 visit, identifies Acts 11.27–30; 12.25 with Gal. 1.18–24; thus Gal. 2.1–10/Acts 15 are both Paul's second visit.

his second, (2) Acts maintained he was sent by the Antioch church; Paul claimed that he went by revelation, (3) in Acts the 'Apostolic Decrees' were imposed upon the Gentile Christians; Paul insisted that nothing was added to his gospel, (4) Acts pictured the council as a public meeting; Paul, as a private consultation, (5) Titus was not mentioned in Acts, but played a significant role in Paul's account, (6) The Pharisaic faction provided the opposition in Acts; they can hardly be equated with the 'false brethren' in Galatians.

B. *The second solution: Acts 11 = Gal. 2*

A second solution, again intended to preserve the integrity of both the Acts and the Galatians accounts, is the identification of Gal. 2.1–10 with the trip to Jerusalem described in Acts 11.27–30; 12.25.[33]

The problems raised here are: (1) the author of Acts knew nothing of what occurred after Paul arrived in Jerusalem, (2) it was necessary for the Jerusalem church to ratify later in public session (Acts 15) what had already been decided upon by its leaders privately with Paul, (3) a chronological inconsistency arises in the span of time from Paul's conversion to this trip,[34] (4) the conflict in Antioch over the social relations between Jewish-Christians and Gentile-Christians occurred before the question of the admittance of Gentiles to the Christian fellowship had been decisively solved, (5) Paul had to have written Galatians before Acts 15, or some explanation must be found to account for his lack of mentioning that subsequent meeting.

[33] V. Weber, 'Der Heilige Paulus vom Apostelübereinkommen bis zum Apostelkonzil,' *Biblischen Studien*, Vol. VI, Heft 1/2, Freiburg, 1901, p. 5; also by V. Weber, *Die antiochenische Kollekte*, Würzburg, 1917, pp. 28f.; W. M. Ramsay, *St Paul the Traveller and the Roman Citizen*, 10th ed., London, 1908, pp. 54ff.; F. F. Bruce, *The Acts of the Apostles*, London, 1959, pp. 241f.; W. L. Knox (n. 1), pp. 181ff.; also by W. L. Knox, *The Acts of the Apostles*, Cambridge, 1948, pp. 49f.; C. H. Buck, 'The Collection for the Saints', *Harvard Theological Review*, Vol. XLIII, No. 1, 1950, p. 17 (he identifies Gal. 2.1 with Acts 11.30; Acts 12.25 with Acts 15.2); C. W. Emmet, 'The Case for the Tradition' (*Beginnings* II, pp. 265–97), pp. 277ff.
Characteristic to this solution are the placing of the 'Antioch Conflict' of Gal. 2.11–14 at Acts 15.1ff. and the assigning of an early date for the writing of Galatians (often between Acts 15.2 and 4).
[34] Even if the chronological data provided by Paul in Gal. 1.18; 2.1 is understood to total thirteen years (cf. p. 58 below) this would place Paul's conversion at AD 31. The longer period of fifteen years would push it back to AD 29. Both dates are too early. Apart from this it is extremely difficult to read either thirteen or fifteen years into the Acts account between chapters 9 and 11.

The New Testament Account of Paul's Collection: II

C. *The third solution: Acts 11 (15) = Gal. 2*

Another approach has been offered by scholars who regard Paul's account as the primary source, and therefore seek to correct the narrative in Acts to make it correspond to the Galatians presentation. One direction taken by this approach is to consider Acts 11.27–30; 12.25 and Acts 15.1–29 as duplicate accounts, taken from two different sources, of the one event described in Gal. 2.1–10, which coincided chronologically with the Acts 11 material.[35] This solution poses the following questions: (1) as in the preceding solution, a chronological difficulty must be solved concerning the span of time between Paul's conversion and the 'Council', (2) a delivery of financial aid from Antioch to Jerusalem before the famine occurred is involved, (3–7) the same difficulties as were listed in problems 2–6 for the first solution described above[36] must be dealt with, (8) a major rearranging of the narrative sequence of Acts is necessary, particularly in regard to the 'first missionary journey' (Acts 13–14).

D. *The fourth solution: Acts 15 (11) = Gal. 2*

The fourth major solution is similar to the third in that it also maintains that Acts 11 and Acts 15 are double accounts of the same trip described by Paul in Galatians 2. This solution, however, regards the Acts 15 version as being in the correct chronological position.[37]

---

[35] H. Lietzmann (n. 1), p. 9; J. Wellhausen, 'Noten zur Apostelgeschichte', *Nachrichten von der königlichen Gesellschaft der Wissenschaften zu Göttingen—Philologisch-historische Klasse*, Berlin, 1907, pp. 7ff.; E. Schwartz, 'Zur Chronologie des Paulus', *Nachrichten von der königlichen Gesellschaft der Wissenschaften zu Göttingen—Philologisch-historische Klasse*, Berlin, 1907, pp. 267ff.; E. Meyer, *Ursprung und Anfänge des Christentums*, Stuttgart, 1923, vol. III, pp. 170f.; H. Windisch, 'The Case against the Tradition', (*Beginnings* II, pp. 298–348), pp. 322ff.; H. Braun, *RGG*³ I, 'Christentum' I, 6, col. 1693.

Proponents of this position often maintain the martyrdom of John together with James, his brother, during the Herodian persecution of AD 44 (Acts 12) to justify an early dating of the 'Apostolic Council'; so especially Schwartz, pp. 267f.; Meyer, vol. III, pp. 174ff.

[36] See the preceding page.

[37] O. Dibelius, *Die Werdende Kirche*, 4th ed., Berlin, 1941, pp. 158f.; A. Oepke (n. 1), pp. 51–55 (attempts to retain the 'Decrees' as an integral part of the meeting); H. W. Beyer, *Apostelgeschichte* (Das Neue Testament Deutsch), 2nd ed., Göttingen, 1935, *ad loc.*, on Acts 11.27–30; 15.6; J. Jeremias, 'Sabbathjahr und neutestamentliche Chronologie', *Zeitschrift für die neutestamentliche Wissenschaft*, Vol. 27, p. 101; Bo Reicke, 'Der geschichtliche Hintergrund des Apostelkonzils und der Antiochia-Episode, Gal. 2.1–14', (*Studia Paulina*, Haarlem, 1953, pp. 172–87), pp. 173f.; P. Bonnard (n. 1), pp. 44–48; K. Lake, 'The Apostolic Council of Jerusalem', *Beginnings* V, pp. 195–212.

The Collection

The difficulties raised by this solution are, again, those listed as 2-6 in the first solution. For the sake of clarity they are listed here again: (1) Acts maintained Paul was sent by the Antioch church; Paul claimed that he went by revelation, (2) in Acts the 'Apostolic Decrees' were imposed upon the Gentile Christians; Paul insisted that nothing was added to his gospel, (3) Acts pictured the council as a public meeting; Paul, as a private consultation, (4) Titus was not mentioned in Acts, but played a significant role in Paul's account, (5) the Pharisaic faction provided the opposition in Acts; they cannot be equated with the 'false brethren' in Galatians. In addition, (6), this solution, as does the preceding one, radically questions the reliability of the sequence of events as recorded in Acts.

The problems discussed

This fourth solution provides the most satisfactory explanation for the discrepancies which exist between Acts and Galatians. The problems which it raises are serious and demand radical alteration of one of the two versions if their resolution is to be achieved.

(1) The motivation which brought Paul to Jerusalem must be understood as the eschatologically oriented 'revelation' which he mentioned in Gal. 2.2.[38] The Antioch community participated in sending this delegation also, but only in a secondary way; i.e., only in connection with the famine relief which they had collected for the Jerusalem church. The conflict over circumcision in Antioch and its result as described in Acts 15.1-3 are to be understood as mainly the construction of the author of Acts to introduce his presentation of the 'Apostolic Council'. This is not to say that he simply invented the incident. His representation probably reflects an indefinite trace of the 'Antioch conflict' described in Gal. 2.11-14, and is to be placed together with Acts 15.36ff., which also contains a distorted echo of that conflict.

(2) The section in Acts 15 dealing with the formulation of the 'Apostolic Decrees', the discussion preceding it, and the letter communicating these Decrees to the Gentile churches (vv. 6-29) is to be understood as occurring not at this meeting but at a later time.[39] The author of Acts erroneously placed it in the Acts 15

---

[38] See p. 42 above.
[39] Because of Paul's very clear assertion in Gal. 2.6 that nothing was added to him, the suggestion has often been made, and correctly so, that the 'Apostolic

The New Testament Account of Paul's Collection: II

location because of his confusion concerning the roles filled by Judas and Silas.[40]

The 'Decrees' were formulated not as the fundamental requirements which a Gentile had to fulfil in order to become a Christian but as those basic regulations necessary to make full fellowship between Gentile and Jewish Christians within the same Christian community possible.[41] As such they were not at all foreign or contradictory to Paul's conception of the relationship of the Christian to the Mosaic Law. It is therefore even more extraordinary, if they had already been formulated and distributed, that he failed to mention them, not only in Galatians, but even more in I Corinthians and Romans.

In searching for some later occasion that suggests itself as a possible context for a meeting during which the 'Decrees' were formulated, Acts 21.25 is a strong and interesting alternative. It is the only other passage in Acts which mentions the Decrees. In its present form it certainly stands in contradiction to Acts 15, for it gives the impression that Paul received his first information of the 'Decrees' then.[42]

This passage could well represent a clue unwittingly provided by the author of Acts for the correct location of the actual formulation of the Decrees. That is, he knew that the Decrees were involved in this later meeting, but either was unsure of the way

---

Decrees' were not formulated during this meeting: so O. Cullmann, *Peter: Disciple, Apostle, Martyr*, 2nd ed., London, 1962, p. 51; H. Lietzmann (n. 1), on Gal. 2.6; also Lietzmann, 'Der Sinn des Aposteldekretes und seine Textwandlung', *Amicitiae Corolla*, London, 1933, pp. 207f.; H. W. Beyer, *Apostelgeschichte* (Das Neue Testament Deutsch), 2nd ed., Göttingen, 1935, *ad loc.*, on Acts 15.6; E. Haenchen, *Die Apostelgeschichte* (Meyer Kommentar), Göttingen, 1959, pp. 404f.; J. N. Sanders, 'Peter and Paul in the Acts', *New Testament Studies*, Vol. 2, No. 1, 1955, p. 141; K. Lake, *Beginnings* V, p. 211; H. Conzelmann, *RGG*³ III, cols. 136f.; G. Bornkamm, *RGG*³ V, 'Paulus', 2c, col. 176. If the 'Decrees' had been decided upon, and Paul had failed to mention them in Galatians, he would have provided those opposing him in Galatia with a weighty argument to substantiate their accusations.

[40] See pp. 21ff. above.
[41] F. Filson (n. 7), pp. 110ff., correctly recognizes that the thrust of the 'Decrees' was in the direction of the problem of table-fellowship in mixed Christian communities. On the practical impossibility of table-fellowship between Jews and Gentiles, see H. L. Strack and Paul Billerbeck, 'Die Stellung der alten Synagogue zur nichtjüdischen Welt', *Kommentar zum Neuen Testament aus Talmud und Midrasch*, Munich, 1926, vol. IV, Part I, pp. 374ff. But cf. Mark 7.14ff.
[42] It has been suggested by O. Cullmann (*op. cit.*, p. 50), and H. Beyer (*op. cit.*, on Acts 15.6), that Acts 21.25 represents the first time that Paul was introduced to the 'Decrees' which were decided at some earlier meeting from which he was absent. This is a possibility; especially if the speech is regarded as being part of or directly dependent upon the 'we-source'. F. Filson (n. 7), p. 110 opposes it.

The Collection

in which they were involved or he altered his source so that Acts 21 did not conflict with the Acts 15 account.

The following factors lend credence and support to this possibility. (*a*) The Decrees were not inconsistent with Paul's theology. (*b*) The author of Acts could hardly have fabricated the association of Paul with the formulation of the Decrees; he must have had a tradition which already contained this association. (*c*) If the agreement reached between Paul and the 'Pillars' described in Gal. 2.1–10 is to be taken seriously, it is inconceivable that the Jerusalem church would later compromise itself so severely as to impose regulations on that portion of the missionary enterprise of the Church which they had ceremoniously recognized as being under the leadership of Paul, *without first consulting him*. (*d*) Paul was one of the principal figures involved in the 'Antioch conflict' (Gal. 2.11–14), one of the earliest episodes which made the ultimate necessity of some such formulation as the 'Decrees' evident.[43] (*e*) According to the hypothesis stated above,[44] the two men appointed by the Jerusalem church to distribute the letter containing the 'Decrees' began that trip only after returning to Jerusalem with Paul after he had completed his collection project; i.e., after 21.15. (*f*) The antagonism generated against the Christian community in Jerusalem by the rapidly coagulating Jewish Zealot movement made it imperative that some gesture be made to exemplify correctly the true Christian attitude toward the Law.[45]

It should be noted that if this hypothesis is correct it indicates an extremely early tradition testifying to the presence of Peter in Jerusalem, still acting as the head of the Christian mission to the Circumcision, around A.D. 56.

After the portions specified in (1) and (2) above have been subtracted, the Acts account of the Jerusalem meeting is reduced to only vv. 4–5. Yet even within this abbreviated version essential corrections must be made.

(3) The meeting in Jerusalem is to be understood as a private consultation between Paul and the 'Pillars', James, Peter and John, with Barnabas also participating, as described in the Galatians account. The author of Acts used the phrase 'apostles and

---

[43] See below, pp. 62ff.
[44] See pp. 21ff. above.
[45] This concern is reflected also in verses 20–24, 26 of the Acts 21 account.

The New Testament Account of Paul's Collection: II

elders' in 15.14 to refer to the Jerusalem leaders to make it conform with the set phrase employed in his source for the rest of the meeting.

(4) One may see a vague trace of the controversy over the circumcision of Titus in Acts 15.5.

(5) As has been already indicated, it is not possible to identify the Pharisaic faction in Acts 15.5 with the 'false brethren' of Gal. 2.4.[46] That the author of Acts conceived of the opponents of Paul in such a manner indicates that he was not aware either of the central question under discussion or of the nature of the adversaries whom Paul had to resist. He probably mentioned the faction as an extension of Acts 6.7 into the later life of the Jerusalem community to provide a logical transition in his narrative from the demand for circumcision (15.1) to the general consideration of the implications of the Mosaic Law for social intercourse between Gentile and Jewish Christians. Not only the extent of influence but even the existence of such a clearly defined faction within the Jerusalem church must be regarded as questionable.[47]

(6) With the acceptance of the identification of the Acts 11 (12) and Acts 15 Jerusalem trips as being two versions of the same trip described by Paul in Gal. 2, a discontinuity in the narrative sequence of Acts is automatically involved. Even if the Acts 11 trip was understood by the author to have taken place after the persecution by Herod,[48] yet chapters 13 and 14 are still left stranded from the flow of events. It is practically impossible to identify this material with the missionary activity in Syria and Cilicia mentioned by Paul in Gal. 1.21.[49] The only other alternative is to locate these chapters, to the extent that they represent

---

[46] See above, pp. 46ff.
[47] Against W. L. Knox (n. 1), pp. 1ff., also 12 n. 3; 13 n. 8, who maintained that, although the Pharisaic faction was numerically small, it nevertheless exercised considerable influence within the Jerusalem community. Perhaps some Pharisees did become Christians. Undoubtedly there was an element within the Jerusalem community which did favour a close relationship of all Christians to the Law (= the predecessors of the Ebionite Christians); cf. K. Lake, 'Paul's Controversies', iii, *Beginnings* V, pp. 220ff. That this group exercised a decisive influence in the Jerusalem church is indirectly excluded both by the results of the Gal. 2.1ff. meeting and by the later formulation of the 'Apostolic Decrees'. That they were given consideration at all was prompted by the urgent necessity for the Jewish mission of the Jerusalem church to maintain unobstructed lines of communication with cultic Judaism.
[48] See pp. 29ff. above.
[49] If there is any parallel to the activity in Syria and Cilicia in Acts, it is probably in the vague presentation of 11.25f.

The Collection

an actual period of Paul's missionary activity,[50] after the second Jerusalem trip, that is, after the Jerusalem meeting of chapter 15.[51]

Chronology of the meeting

After the adjustments suggested above have been made it appears that the only detail of the meeting left in the Acts presentation to the credit of the author of Acts is the approximate chronological location. On the basis of the date determined for the delivery of the Antioch collection[52] and the tentative date suggested for the Acts 15 account[53] the meeting is in all probability to be dated in AD 48.

Only when this has been established is it possible to make use of the chronological particulars mentioned by Paul in Galatians (three years, 1.18; fourteen years, 2.1). As the customary method for reckoning periods of time in Paul's day was to include both the beginning and the concluding units whether they were entirely involved or not, these numbers are best understood as 'two years' and 'thirteen years'.

Even with the date of the meeting established these details can provide only approximate results for the Pauline chronology. In 1.18 Paul was quite clearly designating his first trip to Jerusalem as having occurred 'two years' after his conversion. The second trip to Jerusalem occurred 'after thirteen years', but scholars are about evenly divided as to whether Paul was again counting from his conversion or from his first Jerusalem trip. Grammatically both are possible; the choice depends on the inflection and emphatic weight given to 'then' and 'again' in 2.1. On the basis of the date established for the second Jerusalem trip, the first inter-

---

[50] Both the first and the second missionary journeys appear to be, to a large extent, a construction either by the author of Acts or by the author of his source, compiled to conform with the material and form of the 'we' source for the purpose of providing a connective narrative vehicle for the disconnected Pauline anecdotes he desired to include in his account. Nevertheless his formulation of the trips must have been based on a general awareness that Paul was involved in missionary activity beyond the immediate vicinity of Antioch and Tarsus.

John Knox (n. 31), pp. 40ff., makes an accurate assessment of the questionable reliability of the 'three great missionary journeys' structure in Acts.

[51] This positioning has been proposed, with some minor variations, by E. Schwartz (n. 35), pp. 271ff.; J. Wellhausen (n. 35), pp. 7ff.; K. Lake, 'The Chronology of Acts', *Beginnings* V, pp. 468ff.; cf. also G. Bornkamm, *RGG*³ V, col. 176; H. Conzelmann, *RGG*³ III, col. 133f.; H. Braun, *RGG*³ I, col. 1481.

[52] See pp. 29ff. above.
[53] See pp. 38f. above.

pretation would locate Paul's conversion at AD 35; the second at 33.[54]

3. THE COLLECTION IN GALATIANS

As a result of the foregoing study, it seems probable that in Paul's remark concerning one aspect of the agreement reached in Jerusalem, 'only they would have us remember the poor, which very thing I was eager to do' (Gal. 2.10), a double allusion must be understood: (1) an allusion to the famine relief brought by Paul to Jerusalem from Antioch and which stood immediately in the background of this meeting; (2) an allusion to Paul's subsequent efforts to collect money from all of his Gentile churches for the assistance of Jerusalem.[55]

The aid from Antioch brought by Paul and Barnabas to Jerusalem and presented to the church there at the same time as Paul was having his discussions with the 'Pillars' provided a very concrete expression of the reality of the Holy Spirit working in their midst, calling them to faith in Christ and to Christian concern for their brothers in the faith. The tangible result of this concern was the timely provided and urgently needed relief funds for the poor in the Jerusalem church suffering under increased deprivation as a result of the severe food shortage.

This relief contribution provided undeniable corroborating evidence to Paul's claim that his call to apostleship for the purpose of proclaiming the gospel to the Gentiles was genuine. He supported this claim by relating the success of his endeavours and by telling of the plain evidence of the accompanying presence of the Holy Spirit in his activity as manifested through the wonders and miracles which occurred. Paul's claim was recognized as valid by

---

[54] I am more inclined to the latter, but the former is also possible.
[55] The force of the verb in the phrase, 'only they would have us remember the poor', is that of continued action. E. D. Burton (n. 1), *ad loc.*, has correctly interpreted it to refer to an action already begun which is to be continued, rather than to an action conceived as a repetitive practice in the future, which is grammatically also a possibility.

J. B. Lightfoot, intro., p. 55, and H. Lietzmann, *ad loc.* (both n. 1 above), saw an additional reference to Paul's great collection in Gal. 6.7-10. It seems more probable that here Paul was exhorting them to provide, too, for the physical needs of: (1) the teachers in the community (v. 6), (2) those in want (v. 10a), (3) especially Christian brothers in want (v. 10b). The resemblance arising from the similarity of expression and argument (cf. II Cor. 9.6–10) reflects the extent to which Paul's involvement in his collection project moulded the vocabulary he used to refer to sharing of sustenance for any purpose (cf. Rom. 12.13; I Cor. 16.15; Phil. 1.5; 2.30; 4.14ff.).

The Collection

the 'Pillars' after they had 'perceived the grace that was given to (him)', the most immediate sign of which was the relief he had brought with him.

Finally, the famine relief expressed not only the gratitude of the Antioch church for the role which the Jerusalem community had played as the source from which their knowledge of the gospel had come (however indirectly), but even more a deep veneration for the Jerusalem church. This veneration can be understood only as coinciding with that eschatological self-understanding of the Jerusalem church concerning its role in the '*Heilsgeschichte*' and the impending consummation of the End.[56]

Each of these aspects was to bear an essential significance in the motivation and purpose of Paul's later collection. Although the Gal. 2.10 statement clearly indicates that this project was decided upon then, it is not possible to determine to what extent the details for the collection were discussed. If Acts 18.22 is correct in its implication of a later Jerusalem visit by Paul, and if the later visit was devoted to the further planning of the collection,[57] and if Galatians was written before that later visit,[58] then perhaps it would be more accurate to understand this verse to be referring to a preliminary stage in the development of what later became his great collection.[59]

This interpretation of the Gal. 2.10 reference to the collection opens the possibility for a largely conjectural reconstruction of the sequence of events which occurred between the Jerusalem Conference and the stage of development reached with the collection

---

[56] Most commentators have agreed that this collection denoted a form of recognition of the special position occupied by the Jerusalem church, but have not been united concerning either the type of recognition or the nature of the special position being recognized.

[57] Both of these assumptions are possible; neither is verifiable.

[58] The same necessity would have required Paul to at least have mentioned this later trip, as the necessity which has given those commentators who maintain a one-to-one identification of Acts 15 with Gal. 2 so much trouble in trying to explain why Paul did not mention his second (Antioch relief trip) in his Galatians narrative. If the Acts 18.22 trip had occurred before the composition of Galatians and Paul had not mentioned it, his opponents among the Galatian churches could have maintained that the early accord was the result of the implications of Paul's position not having been fully realized by the Jerusalem leaders at first, but that they placed heavy restrictions on him at the subsequent Jerusalem meeting which he refused to mention in his letter.

[59] The advantage provided by these assumptions is that they allow time for Silas to have assisted Paul in his missionary activity during the intervening period between the Acts 15 and the Acts 18 trips, thereby lending some credibility to the presentation of their common labour by the author of Acts (15.40, etc.).

The New Testament Account of Paul's Collection: II

project as represented by the references in I and II Corinthians and Romans.

At the time of the Jerusalem agreement neither Paul nor the Jerusalem leaders conceived of his missionary endeavours as covering so large a geographical area in so short a time as actually was to occur. Probably they were all thinking in terms of his working from the base of the Antioch church in the surrounding vicinity just as Peter was working from the Jerusalem church. Accordingly the collection work which Paul agreed to assume as part of his labours was envisaged as a sort of extension of the Antioch relief already sent, by which the double goal of providing urgently needed assistance for the Jerusalem poor and the establishment of stable bonds of solidarity between the Jewish-Christian and Gentile-Christian wings of the Church could be realized.

But when Paul and Silas, who had by this time replaced Barnabas as Paul's co-worker as a result of the Antioch conflict, entered into the new work they were confronted by two major factors which had not been foreseen. One was the extraordinary enthusiasm with which the Gentiles received their proclamation; an enthusiasm which opened doors of opportunity far beyond the borders of their originally contemplated activity. The second was the bitter hostility with which the Jewish communities regarded their work; a hostility which became most intense in reaction to the collection activity which the Jews regarded as an open infringement on the rights of the Temple, since, in their eyes, Paul was competing with the traditional Temple tax.

It is not possible to determine either from Paul's letters or from the undependable presentation in Acts the actual scope of this initial missionary endeavour. It is at least certain that it extended to Galatia, for Paul's mention of the collection in 2.10 implied that they were already acquainted with the project.[60]

When Paul and Silas were confronted by these two major factors they returned to Jerusalem (Acts 18.22),[61] where it was

---

[60] To this extent it is possible to agree with T. Zahn (n. 1), pp. 105f., that the Gal. 2.10 reference was to a collection limited to a small area of Gentile churches (he suggested Syria, Cilicia, Galatia). However, the sharp distinction which he made between this and Paul's later large collection must be rejected in favour of the understanding that it represented a preliminary stage of the same project.

[61] John Knox (n. 31), pp. 53ff., in keeping with his identification of the Jerusalem conference with the Acts 18 Jerusalem visit, denies the possibility of any interim visit to Jerusalem between the Council visit and the delivery of the collection.

The Collection

agreed that in order for them to take advantage of the opportunities opened to them, they would no longer work from Antioch but would be relatively independent. Because it was vitally necessary for the Jerusalem Christians to maintain good relations with Judaism for the sake of their mission, it was decided that, rather than drop the urgently needed and theologically significant collection project, Silas and one other well-known Jerusalem Christian, Judas called Barsabbas, were to be specifically assigned to assist with the collection work. This provided the Jerusalem leaders with a concrete means of assuring the orthodox Jews that no poaching of potential Temple funds would occur.

In Paul's letters traces of the further development of the mechanics of the collection project are discernible. When he wrote I Corinthians he had already worked enough on the project to have devised and implemented in Galatia an operative means of organizing the collection within a community. At that time he intended to involve only those communities capable of giving without too great a sacrifice. But the subsequent unsolicited response of the Macedonian Christians opened the possibility of a complete representation by all of the large areas of Pauline activity in the collection. Thus by the time of the writing of II Corinthians the project had reached such immense theological proportions that it became imperative to reactivate the previously expressed but not yet realized enthusiasm of the Corinthian Christians. Paul evidently also anticipated the eventual involvement of the non-Pauline Gentile-Christian communities.[62]

4. THE CONFLICT AT ANTIOCH

Also of relevance to this study are certain aspects of the disagreement between Paul and Peter at Antioch (Gal. 2.11–14), soon after the Jerusalem meeting, which reflect something of the nature, and something of the inadequacy, of the agreement reached there.

A. *As a critique of the Jerusalem agreement*

The conflict in Antioch could not have occurred if the previous Jerusalem discussions had also been concerned with the difficulties arising within a Christian community composed of both

---

[62] See below, pp. 69f.

The New Testament Account of Paul's Collection: II

Jewish and Gentile believers.[63] But the Jerusalem meeting was instead devoted to the mutual recognition of two general directions in the missionary enterprise of the Church founded on basically contradictory conceptions of the order to be followed in the spreading of the gospel. The agreement reached at that time did not resolve the contradiction, but expressed an understanding of partnership in the call and the goal of the two missionary endeavours. It ignored the practical situation already apparent in Antioch and soon to become crucial in the other Gentile churches founded by Paul: the situation of mixed congregations including Jewish as well as Gentile Christians.

The acute question arising from this situation was whether the Jewish element should abandon those aspects of their observance of the Law which hindered their fellowship with the Gentile Christians, or whether the Gentile Christians should take upon themselves as an accommodation to the Jewish Christian members those minimum regulations necessary to remove any obstacle to their full participation in the common fellowship. The report of the incident in Antioch is the closest Paul ever came in his known letters to advocating that Jewish Christians should, under certain circumstances, abandon observance of certain requirements of the Mosaic Law. He explicitly stated this position only in terms of his own personal conduct (Gal. 2.19; I Cor. 9.20ff.).

B. *Peter's initial attitude*

Before Peter came to Antioch the community had regularly practised an unrestricted fellowship together (v. 13), and therefore the problem had not yet arisen. As subsequent events were to prove, it lay just beneath the surface. Likewise during the first part of Peter's visit this potential difficulty was suppressed in that he, who was the recognized leader of the Christian mission to the Jews, did not hesitate to freely join in fellowship with the Gentile Christians there (v. 12). This attitude reflected his personal point of view concerning the relationship of Christian freedom to the Law; a position analogous to that maintained by Paul.[64]

---

[63] The fact that it did occur provides additional support for the position maintained above, pp. 54ff., that the 'Apostolic Decrees' were not formulated at that meeting.

[64] Paul testified in this passage to the real nature of Peter's attitude on this question when, in reference to Peter's subsequent behaviour, he termed the reversal of

The Collection

C. *The motivation for Peter's hypocrisy*

However, in response to the activity of men who had arrived in Antioch on a commission from James,[65] Peter inconsistently reversed his position concerning the free association of Gentile and Jewish Christians.

It is not possible to conclude from the text whether the strife these men caused was a direct result of their commission from James, or whether they made this attempt to sunder the Antioch church on their own initiative. Other considerations commend the latter view.[66] If these men were a part of that element within the Jerusalem community which, because of its involvement in the emerging Jewish nationalism, had been instrumental in introducing the 'false brethren' of Gal. 2.4 into the Christian fellowship there, such an attempt would have been the next logical move to make to try and salvage at least the Jewish-Christian element for their cause after the defeat which the 'false brethren' had suffered in connection with the Titus incident. The role played by James as one of the 'Pillars' participating in the Jerusalem agreement excludes him from active involvement with this element.[67]

The motivation which caused Peter to commit this 'hypocrisy' was 'because he feared those of the circumcision' (v. 12). The basis for his fear cannot be interpreted as apprehension over against

---

that attitude 'hypocrisy' (v. 13) and considered Peter as standing 'condemned' because of it (v. 11). There are also traces indicating that Peter represented such an attitude in Acts: cf. O. Cullmann (n. 39), pp. 48, 66ff.

[65] The description of these men as 'from James' most likely refers not to the geographical point of origin (against H. Lietzmann, *ad loc.*; H. Schlier, *ad loc.*; both n. 1 above), but to the purpose of their travelling to Antioch; i.e., on business commissioned by James as the head of the Jerusalem church (so E. D. Burton, n. 1 above, p. 101).

Burton, *ibid.*, pp. 100f., pointed out that the conflict in Antioch was the result of both sides attempting to implement in this concrete situation the viewpoint each represented in the Jerusalem agreement, thereby bringing to light the 'essentially contradictory character' implied in that agreement.

[66] Against Schmithals (n. 12), p. 65, who held that these men had been commissioned 'to check the development which had been set going (in Antioch)'.

The position taken above also opposes the suggestion of Hans Lietzmann, *A History of the Early Church*, London, 1961, vol. I, pp. 108f., that these representatives from James were really Judas and Silas using the 'Apostolic Decrees' as a weapon against Paul.

[67] Perhaps their leader within the Christian community was Simon the Zealot of Luke 6.15; Acts 1.3; cf. Matt. 10.4; Mark 3.18.

The New Testament Account of Paul's Collection: II

the position which James held as leader of the Jerusalem church,[68] nor as anxiety over an extremist faction within the Jerusalem community.

Although Paul used the noun 'circumcision' fifteen times in Romans, once in I Corinthians, six times other than this passage in Galatians, and twice in Philippians, not once did he use it as a designation for a faction of Jewish-Christians. On the contrary, he employed the term fourteen times to refer to the cultic practice: Rom. 2.25-29 (six times); 4.10f. (three times); I Cor. 7.19; Gal. 5.6, 11; 6.15; Phil. 3.5; seven times *as a designation for the Jews*: Rom. 3.30; 4.12 (twice); 15.8; Gal. 2.7-9 (three times!); and twice in an ambiguous manner which contains both of the preceding nuances: Rom. 3.1; 4.9.[69]

It seems incontestable that Paul blamed Peter's dissimulation on his fear of the Jews and not of Jewish Christians.[70]

Bo Reicke, in his article, 'Der Geschichtliche Hintergrund des Apostelkonzils und der Antiochia-Episode', has connected this fear which caused Peter to disemble with the emerging Jewish nationalist movement which was becoming very militant in its zeal for the Law.[71]

There could very well have been an element of personal anxiety for his own physical safety involved. That such an element was

---

[68] It is not possible to discern a limited use of the term φοβέω by Paul that refers only to fear before a higher authority, and thereby maintain that Peter's action was caused from fear of James's reaction. Paul does use the term in that sense (Rom. 11.20), but also employs it in a more rhetorical manner to express his apprehensive concern for the errors of the Christians in Corinth (II Cor. 11.3; 12.20). Here Paul was simply stating that Peter's hypocrisy was caused by fear of 'them that were of the circumcision' (ASV).

[69] This corresponds with the use of the word in the LXX and by Philo and Josephus (cf. *ThWB* VI, pp. 73f.). The last two texts mentioned above, (Rom. 3.1; 4.9), illustrate the process by which the term for the cultic act was abstracted to designate collectively those who had submitted to the act. In one passage (Phil. 3.3) Paul asserted that all Christians were the 'true circumcision', but this referred to the life 'in the Spirit' as placed in sharp contrast to corporeal circumcision (Phil. 3.5).

This use of the term as referring either to the cultic act or to Jews collectively dominated beyond Paul's time (so Col. 2.11 = cultic act; 3.11; 4.11; Eph. 2.11 = the Jewish people). Only in Titus 1.10 and Acts 11.2 do we find the use of the term for a group of Jewish Christians especially oriented to the Mosaic Law. The development of this use was possible only after a complete break between such a group and the rest of the Christian Church had been made (= the Ebionites?). Only within the Christian society would this use of the term have been understandable. Acts 10.45 testifies that even at the comparatively late date of its composition the term was so ambiguous that the explanatory phrase 'they of the circumcision *that believed*' (ASV) had to be added to make the reference to Jewish Christians clear.

[70] Against Lightfoot, Burton, Lietzmann, Schlier (all n. 1 above).
[71] *Studia Paulina*, Haarlem, 1953, pp. 177ff.

The Collection

present in Peter's character is evidenced by the famous denial incident (Mark 14.70–72 and par.; John 18.25–27). Acts 4.1ff.; 5.17ff.; 12.3ff. indicate that he had already had first-hand experience of Jewish hostility. In addition, the persecution wreaked on the Hellenists following the martyrdom of Stephen must have impressed upon him and the whole Jerusalem community the viciousness with which this hostility could react against any challenge to the established Jewish order.

Even more influential from his standpoint, however, were two related factors. If reports of his indiscriminate ignoring of Jewish cultic regulations should filter back to Jerusalem, which was almost certain after the 'men from James' arrived, the Jerusalem community would thereby have been made even more vulnerable to persecution by the already suspicious Jews.[72] In addition, the mission to Judaism which was his direct responsibility would have been seriously compromised.[73]

D. *The consequences of the conflict*

Because of these considerations, and because Paul did not specifically mention that Peter acceded in the face of his condemnation of the latter's shift of attitude (a result the mention of which would have materially strengthened this passage as evidence for the validity of Paul's independent apostleship), it must be concluded that Peter resisted Paul's reprimand and did not resume

---

[72] Cf. Acts 11.2, 22 (see above, pp. 26ff.); 20.22; 21.11, 20, 28; 23.12ff.; 24.5ff.; 25.2f.

[73] The negative role played by the surging nationalistic inclination to independence, which simmered beneath the surface in Palestine under Roman domination since the Maccabean Wars and was again swiftly gaining impetus, in materially affecting the course followed by the Jerusalem Christian community and subsequently the whole Christian Church, has been largely underestimated by the New Testament research; cf. V. Weber (n. 33), p. 14.

For information on the Zealots and the Sicarii, cf. Emil Schürer, *Geschichte des Jüdischen Volkes im Zeitalter Jesu Christi*, 3rd ed., Leipzig, 1898, vol. I, pp. 486f., 573ff.; R. Travers Herford, *The Pharisees*, London, 1924, pp. 187ff.; Wilhelm Bousset, *Die Religion des Judentums im späthellenistischen Zeitalter*, 3rd ed., Tübingen, 1926 (= Handbuch zum neuen Testament, Vol. 21), pp. 86ff.; F. J. Foakes Jackson and K. Lake, *Beginnings* I, pp. 421ff.; R. H. Pfeiffer, *History of New Testament Times*, New York, 1949, pp. 35ff.; Martin Hengel, *Die Zeloten*, Leiden, 1961.

The willingness of the people to recognize Jesus as a politically oriented Messiah is a theme which recurs often in the Gospels, and illustrates their receptivity to a radical nationalism. One of the Twelve was a Zealot (Luke 6.15; Acts 1.3, cf. Matt. 10.4; Mark 3.18). It is possible to etymologically identify two others with this movement (Peter and Judas Iscariot; cf. O. Cullmann [n. 39 above], pp. 23f.). However, it should be noted that a specific 'Zealot party' did not come into being until post-Pauline times.

his former attitude of unrestricted social intercourse with the Gentile Christians in Antioch. This resulted in a rupture in the cordial relationships hitherto existing between the two missionary leaders which was not healed until they met again in Jerusalem much later. At this subsequent meeting a specific compromise solution, the 'Apostolic Decrees', was decided upon to alleviate this very difficult and sensitive problem.

This conclusion receives additional support from the following considerations. If the Antioch conflict is to be located with the material in Acts following that version of the 'Apostolic Council', that is, with Acts 15.30–40, then the split between Barnabas and Paul resulted from Barnabas' behaviour in this conflict (Gal. 2.13) and not from a disagreement over John Mark. It seems highly improbable that Barnabas would have continued to contradict Paul's position had Peter again reversed his attitude in response to Paul's criticism. It is more likely that Barnabas abandoned his earlier interest in the mission to the Gentiles and joined Peter in his work with the Circumcision. Finally, if Peter and Paul, both the leaders of their respective missionary enterprises, had come to a workable mutual understanding concerning the relationship of Jewish to Gentile Christians in mixed communities as a result of this conflict, it requires a great deal of imagination to explain how the problem subsequently became so acute that a compromise solution had to be found and formally ratified: the 'Apostolic Decrees'.

In Rom. 15.31b Paul expressed real anxiety about the possibility of his collection being refused by the Christians in Jerusalem. There must have been a specific situation which prompted him to this apprehension. This situation could only have been the conflict in Antioch. He feared that if the collection sent by the Gentile churches to Jerusalem were rejected the rupture begun in Antioch would be irreparably confirmed.[74]

5. THE DELIVERY TRIP TO JERUSALEM

Finally, there remains to be considered the trip made by Paul and the representatives of his churches to Jerusalem bearing the

---

[74] Against H.-J. Schoeps (n. 14 above), who discounted the Antioch conflict as 'only an episode' and saw in Paul's collection activity confirmation that 'nothing seemed to have altered the positive relationship', pp. 62f.

The Collection

collection. Although the author of Acts did not say so (Acts 19.21; 20.1–21.16), Rom. 15.24f. leaves little doubt that this was the purpose of the last trip to Jerusalem.[75]

A. *The contributing churches and their delegates*

By comparing Acts with the Pauline epistles, a fairly complete list of the participating churches may be constructed. I Corinthians indicates that Galatia had already begun collecting (16.1). II Corinthians adds the completed participation of Macedonia (8.1ff.; 9.2, 4). In Romans the involvement of both Macedonia and Achaia (including Corinth) is confirmed (15.26).[76]

Fortunately the Acts account of the trip is composed to a large extent from the 'we' source, which lends more weight to the reliability of its presentation.[77] The list of representatives named there (Acts 20.4) includes Sopater of Beroea,[78] Aristarchus and Secundus of Thessalonica (all from Macedonia), Gaius of Derbe[79] and Timothy of Lystra[80] (Galatia), Tychicus and Trophimus of Ephesus[81] (Asia). In addition the author of the 'we' source is to be included.[82]

Apparently the list is not complete.[83] The Corinthian delegates

---

[75] The addition in some MSS of the comment that the delegates accompanied him only as far as Asia was evidently the result of a mistaken assumption that the 'them' of Acts 21.1 included these men as well as the Ephesian elders.

[76] C. H. Buck (n. 33) maintained that neither Corinth nor Galatia participated in the collection. He felt that II Cor. 10–13 was written after 1–9, causing a final break between the Corinthians and Paul which thereby eliminated any possibility of their contributing (pp. 9f.). Rom. 15.26, however, establishes their participation. Because Paul did not mention Galatia in this verse, Buck concluded that they also were not involved (p. 12), which is contradicted by the presence of Galatian representatives in Paul's travelling retinue.

[77] Cf. F. J. Foakes Jackson and K. Lake, 'The Internal Evidence of Acts', *Beginnings* II, pp. 158ff., on the significance of the 'we' source.

[78] Probably this man and the Sosipater of Rom. 16.21 are the same person (cf. H. Lietzmann, *An die Römer* [Handbuch zum Neuen Testament], 3rd ed., Tübingen, 1928; T. Zahn, *Der Brief des Paulus and die Römer*, Leipzig, 1910; E. Haenchen, n. 39 above; F. F. Bruce, n. 33 above; against Lake and Cadbury, *Beginnings* IV, *ad loc.*). Besides the linguistic similarity, the remark in 16.23 probably refers to the aggregate group of representatives in Corinth.

[79] The variant reading in D assigning him to a town in Macedonia is to be understood as a secondary correction to make the text conform with 19.29. The name was frequent. There was also a Gaius in Corinth (Rom. 16.23; I Cor. 1.14).

[80] Cf. Acts 16.1ff.

[81] D specifically designated them as being from Ephesus (cf. Acts 21.29; Eph. 6.21; II Tim. 4.12, 20).

[82] Perhaps he represented Philippi (compare 16.16 and 20.6—the 'we' source ceases in the first and is resumed in the second).

[83] O. Dibelius (n. 37), *ad loc.*, suggested that the author may have listed only seven representatives for the symbolic effect.

were not mentioned, although Paul was there for three months (20.3) and had informed the Romans that Achaia was one of the main contributors (Rom. 15.26). It is not sufficient to explain this silence by assuming that Paul himself represented the Greek churches. Paul's own instructions (I Cor. 16.3), the practice he evidently established in all of the other contributing churches, and the significance which the representatives held for him[84] indicate that delegates from Corinth probably also went on the trip to Jerusalem.

One can surmise that additional representatives were picked up along the trip. Perhaps delegates were included also from Troas (Acts 20.5, 6bff.),[85] Philippi (Acts 20.6),[86] Tyre (Acts 21.4),[87] Ptolemais (Acts 21.7)—certainly Caesarea, possibly Cyprus (Acts 21.16).

Particularly intriguing is the section in Acts 20.17-38 relating Paul's encounter with the Ephesian elders. Verses 33-35 contain paraphrased echoes of Paul's collection project, including an otherwise unknown quotation from Jesus. One is tempted to speculate that a group of representatives came from Ephesus to join Paul in Miletus, bringing with them the bulk of the collected funds which had been previously forwarded to Ephesus. Perhaps Paul's long stay in Ephesus represented his attempt to use that city as a collection point for the contributions of the various churches before sending them on to Jerusalem; an attempt frustrated by the outbreak of Jewish hostility there.

It seems possible that Paul contemplated the later voluntary participation of the Roman Christians in the collection.[88] Perhaps it was this project in the back of his mind which led him, in speaking of their care for fellow Christians, to use language strikingly reminiscent of the collection (Rom. 12.13; cf. Rom. 15.26; II Cor.

---

[84] See below, pp. 129ff.
[85] Cf. Acts 16.8, 11; II Cor. 2.12.
[86] Cf. Acts 16.12; Phil. 2.2. Paul's emphasis on their generosity in sending him personal support (Phil. 1.5; 4.15ff.) indicates the probability of their participation in his collection project. The author of the 'we' source may have represented them; see n. 82 above).
[87] Cf. Acts 15.23, 41; Gal. 1.21. The remark in Acts 21.6 makes their participation questionable.
[88] J. Sickenberger, *Die Briefe des heiligen Paulus an die Korinther und Römer*, Bonn, 1932, p. 297, and Franz-J. Leenhardt, *L'épître de saint Paul aux Romains*, Neuchâtel, 1957, p. 211, suggest this as a possibility. If Paul did intend to do so, it probably was as the result of the unexpected participation of all of his own communities which added a deeper dimension to the significance of the collection.

The Collection

8.4; 9.13). Supporting this conjecture is the statement by Paul in Rom. 1.13 that he desired to 'reap some harvest among you as well as among the rest of the Gentiles'. The harvest image recalls Paul's collection argument (cf. II Cor. 9.6–10) and could hardly refer to making converts (cf. Rom. 15.20, 24).

B. *The reception of the collection*

Acts does not inform us whether the collection Paul brought to Jerusalem was well received by the church there or not. It does not even mention if it was delivered. As a matter of fact, the only mention made of the collection at all in Acts is an obscure reference in Paul's speech before Felix (Acts 24.17; cf. 24.26). For the structure of this study, a discussion of possible reasons why the collection was, to all practical purposes, ignored in the Acts narrative belongs in a later chapter.[89] Let it suffice to note here that in this one minor allusion the author of Acts either intentionally or ignorantly pictured it as a delivery by Paul of traditional Jewish contributions from the Diaspora to Jerusalem.[90]

Nevertheless, on the basis of the study completed in these two chapters it may be confidently conjectured that the collection was well received. Two factors which have already been developed at some length point to this conclusion.

The first is the interpretation that the trouble-makers with whom Paul had to contend were not Jewish Christians but Jews who had associated themselves with the Christian community for political reasons. They wanted to enlist the Jewish Christians in the cause for Jewish nationalism.[91] Neither the leaders nor a large majority of the Jerusalem Christians were in any way opposed to the work that Paul was doing among the Gentiles.

Paul had to counteract demands propagated by this nationalistic movement both at the Jerusalem meeting (the Titus incident) and during the subsequent disagreement with Peter in Antioch (the men 'from James'). Only in terms of this nationalism can the description by the author of Acts of the opponents of Paul in Antioch preceding the 'Apostolic Council' (Acts 15.1) be understood.

---

[89] See below, pp. 148ff.
[90] See next chapter.
[91] This point was made above, pp. 46ff.

Further, at the time he was writing Galatians, Paul clearly stated that his opponents in Galatia were motivated in making their erroneous demands from a fear of being persecuted by *Jews* (6.12f.; cf. 4.29; 4.11). In 6.12f. Paul emphasized twice that, in addition to the fear of being persecuted if the Gentile Christians were not circumcised, his opponents were seeking their circumcision to 'glory in your flesh'. This could only mean that they wanted to impose circumcision as a physical verification that they had enlisted the active support of the Gentile Christians for the Jewish cause.

Paul testified elsewhere that the Jewish Christian communities in Judea suffered bitterly under Jewish persecution by the *same men* who had attacked Paul and were continually impeding his efforts.[92]

Finally Paul expressed his concern to the Romans (15.31a) that when he delivered his collection to Jerusalem he would be placing himself in serious danger from the *Jews*. The 'disobedient ones' is a circumscription for 'Jews'[93] as distinguished from Jewish Christians (= the 'saints', v. 31b). The polemic nature of the term could have developed and been comprehensible only within the context of a bitter conflict between Christianity as a whole and Judaism, not in a struggle between two factions within Christianity.

This understanding of Paul's opponents as Jewish nationalist radicals contradicts the presentation in Acts 21.20. There James, in his *welcoming* speech (!), remarked to Paul of 'how many thousands there are among the Jews of those who have believed; they are all zealous for the law'.

At this point the hypothesis offered by E. Schwartz is highly attractive.[94] He suggested that, although there is no textual justification, the phrase 'of those who have believed' should be struck as a construction of the author of Acts, in order to make the passage credible. The result of this textual emendation expresses both the source and the object of Paul's polemic: 'how many thousands there are among the Jews zealous for the law'. This

---

[92] I Thess. 2.14ff.; cf. II Cor. 11.22ff.; Phil. 3.2ff., 18f. (in contrast to 'our commonwealth', v. 20).
[93] Rom. 1.5; 2.8; 10.21; 11.30f.; also John 3.36; Acts 14.2; Eph. 5.6.
[94] E. Schwartz (n. 35), p. 290. Both J. Munck (n. 8), pp. 240ff., and W. Schmithals (n. 12), p. 90, endorse his solution.

The Collection

would correspond to the preliminary stages of what within a decade was to solidify into the Zealot Party.

The second factor which indicates that the Jerusalem church accorded Paul's collection a favourable reception was the subsequent formulation of the 'Apostolic Decrees'.[95] After the rupture in relations between Peter and Paul resulting from the conflict in Antioch, there was a strain between the two missionary wings of the Church. This tension was most sharply focused on the problem of table-fellowship in mixed Jewish and Gentile Christian communities.

The effect of the collection and of the witness to the power of Christ working among the Gentiles as symbolized by the representatives who brought the collection made a deep impression on the Jerusalem Christians. It provided the impetus for the Jerusalem church, in the face of a very real and rapidly increasing danger from fanatic Jews, to meet finally the problem of common fellowship in mixed Christian communities. Together with Paul they formulated in the 'Apostolic Decrees' a solution which did not distort or violate the gospel message.

6. SUMMARY

In these two chapters it has been seen that the collection project, which Paul discussed to a greater or lesser extent in each of his four major epistles, was a direct outgrowth of the emerging delicate situation created by the simultaneous diffusion of the gospel in two different yet intermingled directions under the auspices of two conflictingly oriented missionary enterprises. The prototype of the Pauline collection was the famine relief sent from Antioch to Jerusalem, which had effectively proven itself as an instrument of reconciliation.

Paul's collection was instigated, ostensibly as a simple act of Christian charity, at the Jerusalem meeting during which Paul and the 'Pillars' had discovered their basic accord in acknowledging that the salvation of God was made available to men solely as the gift of his grace, and that no other works except faith in Christ were necessary to participate in it. Nevertheless, because of

---

[95] It has been maintained above, pp. 54ff., that the 'Decrees' listed in Acts 15 were first decided upon by Paul and the Jerusalem church only at the later meeting in Acts 21 when Paul delivered his collection.

their differing views concerning the order in the 'Heilsgeschichte' in which the gospel was to be made known to the Gentiles by a concentrated effort, they agreed to embark on two contemporaneous missionary endeavours, Paul leading the one to the Gentiles while Peter was to head the one to the Jews.

The unresolved conflict which subsequently arose in Antioch seriously ruptured the previously established harmony and impelled Paul out of revulsion at the prospect of a permanent division within the Christian fellowship to invest his collection with an additional theological purpose. He successfully organized the project among his Gentile churches in the succeeding years and delivered it to the Jerusalem Christian community in the company of representatives from the contributing Gentile areas. It had the desired effect of promoting a reconciliation which resulted in the formulation of the 'Apostolic Decrees' as a guide for the maintenance of mixed fellowship at the liturgical meals of the community.

III

ANALOGIES TO PAUL'S COLLECTION IN CONTEMPORARY JUDAISM

WITHIN the sphere of Judaism contemporary with the early Church, several contributory practices were prevalent which were directly in the background of Paul's collection. Paul appropriated certain aspects from these practices which are discernible in the external elements of the collection. There is also revealed a striking correlation in the underlying symbolic significance.

In this section the relevant Jewish monetary institutions will be discussed in the order of the importance of their analogical relationship to the Christian collection project: the half-shekel Temple tax; the Jewish contributions for charity; the Patriarch tax. This will be followed by a brief examination of the place these contributions held in the fellowship of the Qumran community.

1. THE HALF-SHEKEL TEMPLE TAX

The Jewish tax from which Paul borrowed most heavily[1] was the half-shekel tax collected primarily for the maintenance of the cultic sacrifices offered in the Temple at Jerusalem on behalf of aggregate Judaism.[2] The correspondence between this tax and

---

[1] It is indicative of the careful consideration with which Paul conceived and implemented his collection that he made such extensive use of this Jewish contribution. In that the collection of famine relief in Antioch (see pp. 23ff. above) had established the precedent and provided the impulse for Paul's collection (see pp. 26ff.; 59ff. above), there were other contributions within Judaism which would have suggested themselves, at least to superficial reflection, as corresponding more immediately to his project than the Temple tax (for instance, the Jewish contributions for the poor, see below, pp. 93ff.).

[2] In the following discussion of the Temple tax I am indebted to the studies presented by: Emil Schürer, *Geschichte des Jüdischen Volkes im Zeitalter Jesu Christi*, 3rd ed., Leipzig, 1898, vol. II, pp. 258ff.; H. L. Strack and Paul Billerbeck, *Kommentar zum Neuen Testament aus Talmud und Midrasch*, Munich, 1926, vol. I, pp. 760ff. (on Matt. 17.24); Jean Juster, *Les Juifs dans l'empire Romain*, Paris, 1914, vol. I, pp. 377ff.; all of which the reader may profitably consult for further details on the tax which have been omitted in this study as not being directly relevant to the task at hand.

Analogies to Paul's Collection in Contemporary Judaism

Paul's collection is so distinct that it has been noted by many scholars.[3]

A. In the New Testament

The Temple tax is specifically mentioned in the New Testament only in one passage; in the account peculiar to the Gospel of Matthew concerning Jesus' attitude to the tax (Matt. 17.24–27). A less direct reference is to be seen in the money-changers who were one of the objects of Jesus' attack at the cleansing of the Temple.[4]

B. In the Old Testament

The Temple tax for the provision of sacrifices was first paid by the people during the post-exilic rebuilding of Jerusalem in Nehemiah's time.[5] Apparently before the Exile the Temple sacrifices offered for the whole nation were provided by the Kings.[6] According to the Nehemiah passage, one provision of the covenant assented to by both the leaders and all the people was to 'lay upon ourselves the obligation to charge ourselves yearly with the third part of a shekel for the service of the house of our God' (Neh. 10.32). Here it is seen that the tax was annual, applicable to the entire nation, and designated for the support of the cultic worship (the uses are itemized in the following verse).[7]

---

[3] So, for example: O. Cullmann, *Peter: Disciple, Apostle, Martyr*, 2nd ed., London, 1962, p. 45; also, *Message to Catholics and Protestants*, Grand Rapids, Michigan, 1959, p. 34; H.-J. Schoeps, *Paulus*, Tübingen, 1959, p. 63; C. Tresmontant, *Paulus in Selbstzeugnissen und Bilddokumenten*, Hamburg, 1959, pp. 9f.; W. L. Knox, *Saint Paul and the Church of Jerusalem*, Cambridge, 1925, pp. 284ff.; Karl Holl, 'Der Kirchenbegriff des Paulus in seinem Verhältnis zu dem der Urgemeinde', *Gesammelte Aufsätze zur Kirchengeschichte*, vol. II, Tübingen, 1928, pp. 59ff.; A. Schweitzer, *The Mysticism of Paul the Apostle*, London, 1931, p. 156; V. Weber, *Die antiochenische Kollekte*, Würzburg, 1917, p. 69; M. Meinertz, *Theologie des Neuen Testaments*, vol. II, Bonn, 1950, pp. 182f.

[4] Matt. 21.12; Mark 11.15; John 2.14f.; cf. Shekalim 1.3; also J. Jeremias, *Jesus' Promise to the Nations*, London, 1958, p. 65. It is curious that the author of Luke-Acts, who did not mention Paul's collection in Acts, is the only one who did not mention the money-changers in his version of the cleansing of the Temple (Luke 19.45f.; cf. the addition in D to correct this deficiency). Perhaps he omitted referring to them because he understood the incident to have occurred at a time well before the Passover (first mentioned in 22.1) whereas the money-changers set up their tables in the Temple only a few days before that festival (on the 25th of Adar; cf. Shek. 1.3).

[5] Neh. 10.32f.

[6] Ezek. 45.13, 17, 21ff.; cf. also Ezek. 46.4ff.; I Kings 8.62ff.; I Chron. 16.2; II Chron. 30.24; 31.3; 35.7.

[7] 'The showbread, the continual cereal offering, the continual burnt offering, the sabbaths, the new moons, the appointed feasts, the holy things, the sin offerings to make atonement for Israel, and for all the work of the house of our God.'

The Collection

Although the tax as described in the Nehemiah covenant amounted to only one-third of a shekel, it was increased at a later time to one-half of a shekel.[8] Ex. 30.11–16 provided the scriptural basis for this increased tax.[9] In that account Moses was instructed by God to take a half-shekel from each person counted in the census as 'a ransom[10] for himself to the Lord' (v. 12) to be used 'for the service of the tent of meeting' (v. 16). To be sure, the contribution was described there as having been collected only once, and not yearly. But by the time of the writing of II Chronicles, at the latest, the Exodus collection was understood to constitute a basis for raising funds for the support of the Temple. Joash is described there as having revived the Mosaic 'tax' for the purpose of raising money to restore the Temple.[11]

c. *Amount paid in Paul's time*

Evidence in the LXX, Philo, Josephus

The Greek term which corresponded to the 'half-shekel' of Ex. 30.13 is obscure. The Septuagint translated the Exodus phrase as 'one-half of two drachmas'.[12] Thus one shekel was equal to two drachmas. This was the way in which Philo understood it. So he spoke of the Temple tax: 'We are meant to consecrate one

---

[8] The increase may have been necessitated by a reduction in the purchase power of the coin. Cf. M. H. Segal (*The Babylonian Talmud, Seder Moʻed*, ed. by I. Epstein, vol. IV, London, 1938), in the introd. to his translation of 'Shekalim', p. v, who maintained that the half-shekel preceded the third-shekel tax and the reduction in the amount was caused either by the changing value of the shekel or by the poverty of the people under Ezra.

[9] That the tax was first one-third of a shekel and then raised to half a shekel is contested (cf. preceding note: Strack-Billerbeck, I, p. 760; A. R. S. Kennedy, 'Money', Hastings' *Dictionary of the Bible*, vol. III, Edinburgh, 1902, p. 422). The position taken in the text has followed E. Shürer, (p. 74 n. 2), vol. II, p. 259; J. Juster, (p. 74 n. 2), vol. I, p. 377 n. 5; Wilhelm Bousset, *Die Religion des Judentums im neutestamentlichen Zeitalter*, 2nd ed., Berlin, 1902, p. 117; R. H. Pfeiffer, *History of New Testament Times*, New York, 1949, p. 178; and numerous others. Note also that in Shek. 2.4, knowledge of the payment of a regular tax extended only back to 'when the Israelites came up out of the captivity'.

Strack-Billerbeck, p. 761, noted that the rabbinical scholars considered the tax in Nehemiah's time to have been a half-shekel. They came to this conclusion by interpreting Neh. 10.32f. to refer not to the amount of the tax but to the number of times in the year that the tax was delivered to the Temple (i.e. three times, which corresponded to the three appropriations for the sacrifices made in the Temple; cf. Shek. 3.1. By extension this was the basis for the three baskets, Shek. 3.2).

[10] Λύτρα (LXX). Cf. Philo, *De spec. leg.* I, xiv, 77: 'These contributions are called "ransom money" (λύτρα); *Quis rer. div. her.* XXXVIII, 186.

[11] II Chron. 24.4–14; but cf. II Kings 11.21–12.14.

[12] Τὸ ἥμισυ τοῦ διδράχμου; so also verse 15.

Analogies to Paul's Collection in Contemporary Judaism

half of (the consecrated didrachmon), the drachma, and pay it as ransom for our own soul.'[13]

But when discussing the amounts specified in Lev. 27.1ff. to be paid for the satisfaction of a vow, Philo interpreted 'fifty shekels' (LXX: 'fifty didrachmon'), to be equal to two hundred drachmas;[14] i.e. one shekel equalled four drachmas. This corresponds to Josephus' understanding of the tax. He stated that '(Moses) imposed on (the people) a contribution of half a shekel for each man, the shekel being a Hebrew coin equivalent to four Attic drachmas'.[15] In another passage he termed it 'two drachmas',[16] and in yet another he used the same term as was used in Matt. 17.24: 'the didrachmon'.[17]

The half-shekel tax was paid according to the 'shekel of the sanctuary'.[18] According to rabbinical tradition, 'All money, of which the Law speaks, is Tyrenian money'.[19] Thus a half-shekel would equal two drachmas.[20] However, an alternative rabbinical tradition held that the 'holy shekel' was worth twice as much as the ordinary shekel.[21] As a result, in the Talmudic tractate 'Shekalim' the tax was always referred to as a 'shekel'. It is undoubtedly this usage which was behind the term used in Matt. 17.24.

One could conjecture that the translator of the Septuagint passage was familiar with both the Greek and the Hebrew term for the tax (didrachmon = shekel) and therefore erroneously made a literal translation of the term in Exodus (one-half of a shekel = one-half of a didrachmon). Philo, however, who must have had to pay the tax himself, certainly was aware that the tax was more than one drachma. Apparently in the passage quoted above[22] Philo simply appropriated the Septuagint term as a convenient illustration for his argument on the unity of God and the division into opposites within the human sphere.

[13] *Quis rer. div. her.* XXXVIII, 186; cf. also 187; XXXIX, 189.
[14] *De spec. leg.* II, viii, 33; the same shekel evaluation is maintained for the other sums mentioned there.
[15] *Antiq.* III, viii, 2.   [16] *Antiq.* VII, vi, 6.
[17] *Antiq.* XVIII, xx, 1. 'The "stater" of Matt. 17.27 was a tetradrachmon, equal to a whole shekel, and therefore payment for two': Hastings' *Dictionary of the Bible* vol. IV, 'Tribute', p. 813.
[18] Ex. 30.13. On the 'shekel of the sanctuary', cf. Ex. 30.34; 38.24-26; Lev. 5.15; 27.3, 25; Num. 3.47, 50; 7.13-86; 18.6.
[19] Tosephta Kethuboth, XII, quoted in Schürer (n. 2), vol. II, p. 259.
[20] So Schürer, *ibid.*; Kennedy (n. 9), p. 422.
[21] Mentioned by M. H. Segal (n. 8), intro. p. v.
[22] Pp. 76f.

The Collection

Evidence in 'Shekalim'

Although the tractate 'Shekalim' spoke of the tax as a 'shekel' tax, it was understood by the scholars to amount to one-half of a shekel. This is confirmed by the rabbinical attempts to explain *why* the tax was half of a shekel. One such attempt understood the half-shekel as the result of the sin of the golden calf (Ex. 32.1ff.), because it occurred in the middle of the day. Another explanation held that it was because the money was to atone for their breaking of the ten commandments (one shekel = twenty gerahs in Ex. 30.13; thus one-half of a shekel = ten gerahs).[23]

The actual value of the half-shekel for the tax appears to have fluctuated according to the economic conditions of the times and the worth of the coins in use.[24]

D. Regulations for collection of the tax
Preparation for collection

The tax was collected in time for the funds, at least from the immediate surrounding area, to be available for the provision of sacrifices during Passover.[25] At the beginning of the month preceding this festival, Adar,[26] the collection of the Temple tax was proclaimed.[27] On the fifteenth of Adar the money-changers set up their tables in the provinces of Palestine outside of Jerusalem, and on the twenty-fifth of the month the tables of the money-changers were set up in the Temple.[28] The function of the money-

---

[23] Both explanations are quoted in Strack-Billerbeck, I, p. 761.

[24] Shek. 2.4: 'R. Judah says: Shekels also have no fixed value. For when the Israelites came up out of the captivity they used to pay the shekel in darics, then they paid the shekel in sela'ʻs, then again they paid it in Tibʻin, and finally they sought to pay it in denars.'

[25] This festival was celebrated on the 15th of Nisan. Contributions received from areas beyond Palestine were received at later intervals and were used to provide the two succeeding appropriations: Shek. 3.1; cf. Strack-Billerbeck, I, pp. 765f.

[26] The Jewish civil year began with the month of Tishri (in October), but the liturgical year began with the 1st of Nisan. The tax became due according to the liturgical year. Thus the preceding month, Adar, was devoted to the collection of the tax. Because both the 1st of Nisan and the 1st of Tishri were holidays (Festivals of the New Year), appropriations for the Temple sacrifices could not be made on those days (Shek. 3.1), and were therefore transposed to the preceding days.

[27] Shek. 1.1: 'On the first of Adar public announcement is made concerning the payment of the shekels.'

[28] Shek. 1.3; cf. Matt. 21.12; Mark 11.15; John 2.14f. Although the Temple tax ceased to exist as a religious contribution after the destruction of the Temple in AD 70 (see below, p. 86), the edict issued by Hadrian commanding the rebuilding of the Temple in Jerusalem as a Roman shrine resulted in the erection of money-changers' tables by two men named Pappos and Julianus, evidently in an attempt to revive the Temple tax (Strack-Billerbeck, I, p. 770).

Analogies to Paul's Collection in Contemporary Judaism

changers was, of course, to change the coins then in use in the economy into coins ritually acceptable for paying the Temple tax; the 'holy' shekel.[29] A slight surcharge[30] was added to the payment of the tax of those who did not themselves go to the money-changers in order that the Temple would not have to pay for changing the ritually unacceptable coins.[31]

Those obligated to pay the tax

Every male Jew who was twenty years of age or older was obligated to pay the half-shekel tax to the Temple.[32] The Talmud listed them as 'Levites and Israelites, proselytes and freed slaves, but not women or slaves or minors'.[33]

The latter groups could, however, voluntarily pay the Temple tax,[34] in which case they were not liable to the surcharge for changing it into the 'holy' shekel. Priests also were not required to pay the tax,[35] although the rabbinical authorities contested the justness of their exemption.[36] In addition, some Rabbis maintained that they were themselves free from paying the tax.[37] A contribution from a Samaritan or a Gentile for the Temple tax was to be rejected.[38]

Delinquent contributions distrained

When the money-changers set up their tables in the Temple on the twenty-fifth of Adar this was a sign that the period of grace (from 1-25 Adar) was over and the tax *had* to be paid. Collectors

---

[29] See above, p. 77; also Strack-Billerbeck, p. 761.
[30] The Rabbis were not agreed as to whether the surcharge should amount to one ma'ah (= 1/12 of a shekel) or half a ma'ah (= 1/24 of a shekel): Shek. 1.7.
[31] Shek. 1.6, 7; cf. Strack-Billerbeck, pp. 764f. Those who were not legally obligated but paid the Temple tax voluntarily were not subject to the surcharge: Shek. 1.6.
[32] Ex. 30.14; cf. Philo, *De spec. leg.* I, xiv, 77; Josephus, *Antiq.* III, viii, 2, where the age of obligation is described as from twenty to fifty years.
[33] Shek. 1.3.
[34] Shek. 1.3, 5, 6. A special case arose when a father paid the shekel for his son. He was not obligated to do so, but if he paid it once, then he was obligated to continue paying it each year; Shek. 1.3.
[35] Shek. 1.3: 'No distraint was levied on the priests, in order to promote peacefulness.' Accordingly a priest was not liable to a surcharge if he voluntarily paid the tax: Shek. 1.6.
[36] Shek. 1.4.
[37] Cf. the rabbinical sayings on this point quoted in Strack-Billerbeck, pp. 771f.
[38] Shek. 1.5: 'If a heathen or a Cuthean (a resident of Cuthea = a Samaritan; cf. II Kings 17.24) paid the shekel it is not accepted of them.'

The Collection

were sent out to compel payment of the tax from all of those subject to a mandatory contribution.[39]

This was done not just to ensure the reception of a large sum but for the theological reason that thereby the entire people were represented in the sacrifices bought with the tax money.[40] Nevertheless, the system was not completely efficient, for one of the thirteen horn-shaped chests maintained in the Temple was marked 'Old Shekels' and was intended to receive delinquent shekels for the tax of the preceding year.[41]

It was evidently not only a prudent but also a common practice that an individual set aside money during the year to be used for the payment of the half-shekel tax. This custom was not limited exclusively to the tax, but was frequently followed for a large number of financial obligations to the cult.

Because of the fluctuations in the price of sacrificial articles[42] and the relative instability of the value of money,[43] it often occurred that more money had been set aside for these purposes than was actually needed. The general rule in such cases was that the surplus of money set aside for a particular cultic purpose must be donated to the Temple as a freewill offering (in the case of sin- or guilt-offerings) or devoted to the specific purpose for which it had been set aside.[44]

However, the money set aside for the payment of the half-shekel tax formed a special case. The surplus remaining after this tax was paid was considered free to be used at the discretion of the owner unless he had verbally committed all of the coins to holy purposes (in which case it was contested whether the money was at his disposal or limited to be spent for consecrated purposes as a freewill offering).[45]

---

[39] Shek. 1.3; this was the function of 'the collectors of the half-shekel tax' in Matt. 17.24, who demanded of Peter whether his 'teacher' paid the tax. Their inquiry may reflect the prevalent uncertainty of the position of rabbis in relation to the tax.

[40] The rabbis justified the distraint by emphasizing Ex. 30.16: 'You shall *take* the atonement money from the people of Israel.' One rabbi compared the distraint applied to a doctor who amputated a wounded foot in order to restore health (quoted in Strack-Billerbeck, pp. 761f.).

[41] Shek. 6.5: 'Whosoever has not paid his shekel in the past year may pay it in the coming year.'

[42] The Temple revised its evaluation of prices once every thirty days (Shek. 4.9).

[43] Cf. above, p. 78.

[44] Shek. 2.5 presents a long list of the regulations governing restricted use of such surplus funds.

[45] Shek. 2.3: 'If a man saved coins and said: Lo, these are for my shekel, Beth

Set dates for delivery

The tax was delivered to the Temple three times during the year, which deliveries corresponded to the three appropriations made from the shekel funds in the Temple treasury preceding by half a month the major cultic pilgrimage festivals.[46] Thus the appropriation preceding Passover was made on the 29th of Adar (or the 1st of Nisan)[47] from the tax money received from Palestine; the second appropriation preceding Pentecost was made on the 1st of Sivan from the money received from the lands close to Palestine, the third appropriation was made on the 29th of Elul preceding the Feast of the Tabernacles from the tax paid by Jews in the distant Diaspora.[48]

Elaborate precautions were taken to insure that each succeeding appropriation was taken from tax-money just delivered so that the sacrifices were purchased from funds drawn equally from all three deliveries.[49] Nevertheless, with the first appropriation all shekel funds contributed for that year were considered to have become the property of the Temple, whether they had already been delivered in Jerusalem or not.[50]

E. Payment of tax

The normal procedure for making the half-shekel contribution, at least within Jerusalem proper, was to cast the special coin obtained from the money-changers into the chest marked 'new

---

Shammai say: The surplus (of the coins goes to the chests of) freewill offerings. But Beth Hillel say: The surplus thereof is common property. (If he said: From these coins) I shall offer my shekel, (both schools) agree that the surplus thereof is common property.' Cf. also Shek 2.5.

[46] Cf. Strack-Billerbeck, I, pp. 765f.; RGG³ II, 'Fests und Feiern' II, 4, a, cols. 912f.
[47] See the uncertainty over this date expressed in Shek. 3.1.
[48] Comp. Shek. 3.1 and 3.4. The phrases used in the latter passage for the three areas are: 'the land of Israel; the cities near thereunto; Babylon and Media and other distant countries'.
[49] Shek. 3.4. A leather covering was spread over the coins remaining from the previous appropriation in order that the new deliveries could be kept separate and not be mixed with them. Stack-Billerbeck recorded a rabbinical provision which required that the remainders of appropriations for the current year could not be mixed with shekels left over from the previous year in case it proved necessary to make a supplementary appropriation should the money already ceremonially taken out not be sufficient (I, p. 767).
[50] Cf. Strack-Billerbeck, I, p. 767, who comment: 'Every Israelite could now say to himself that the sacrifices which were daily offered in the Temple for all Israel, and thereby for him, were offered from his own means'; also Shek. 2.1.

The Collection

shekels' which stood in the Temple.[51] An exception, probably remembered as a sign of singular piety, was the practice of the household of R. Gamaliel, who made their contribution directly to the Temple official responsible for taking the appropriation from the Temple treasury.[52]

The tax in the outlying areas of Palestine and from the Diaspora was paid to central collection points in the various population centres[53] which employed chests in each locality similar to the ones used in the Temple.[54]

Delivery from the Diaspora

The payment of the half-shekel tax from the Diaspora was especially important, both for the Temple and for the Jews who lived so far away from Palestine.[55] Because the Jews in the Diaspora were so numerous,[56] the amount of contributions flowing annually to the Temple was significantly rich. There is evidence of such contributions having been sent from Egypt[57] and Cyrenaica[58] in Africa, Asia (Minor),[59] 'Europe',[60] Italy (Rome),[61] Mesopotamia and Babylon.[62] According to Josephus, not only

[51] Shek. 6.5.
[52] Shek. 3.3: '(Members) of Rabban Gamaliel's household used to enter (the chamber) with their shekel between their fingers, and throw it in front of him who made the appropriation while he who made the appropriation purposely pressed it into the basket.' The basket referred to was the one used to measure the appropriation taken from among the contributed shekels, cf. Shek. 3.2. His action of placing their contribution directly into the basket instead of placing it with the other coins in the treasury was to ensure that their payment was definitely used for the purchase of sacrifices and did not fall into the residue of the contributions which were subsequently employed for other purposes, cf. Shek. 4.2, 3.

Strack-Billerbeck have concluded on the basis of this passage that the inhabitants of Jerusalem were not subjected to the same sort of force to pay the tax in advance as were those Jews living in outlying districts.

[53] Philo, *De spec. leg.* I, xiv, 78: 'In practically every city there are banking places (ταμεῖα = local treasury; cf. *Quod omn. prob. lib. sit* 86) for the holy money where people regularly come and give their offerings.'

[54] Shek. 2.1: 'Just as there were chests in the Temple so were there chests in the province.'

[55] Cf. W. Bousset (n. 9), pp. 81f.; 127.

[56] Josephus, *Antiq.* XIV, vii, 2f.; Philo, *De spec. leg.* I, xiv, 76, 78; cf. Schürer (n. 2), vol. III, pp. 3ff.

[57] Josephus, *Antiq.* IV, vii, 2. Cf. also J. Juster (n. 2), vol. I, p. 378 n. 6; cf. A. Deissmann, *Light from the Ancient East*, new ed., London, 1927, pp. 105, 355.

[58] Josephus, *Antiq.* XIV, vi, 5.

[59] Cicero, *Pro Flacco* 28.66, 68; Josephus, *Antiq.* XIV, vii, 2; XVI, vi, 2, 3, 4, 6, 7; Philo, *De leg. ad Gaium* XL, 315.

[60] Josephus, *Antiq.* XIV, vii, 2.

[61] Cicero, *Pro Flacco* 28.67; Philo, *De leg. ad Gaium* XXIII, 156.

[62] Josephus, *Antiq.* XVIII, ix, 1; cf. the rabbinical witnesses listed by J. Juster (n. 2), vol. I, p. 381 n. 3. See Juster, pp. 180–209, for a list of the localities for which there is evidence of Jewish settlement in the Diaspora.

the Jews (which would include full proselytes), but also those who were only partially affiliated to Judaism contributed.[63]

After the Temple tax contributions had been collected in the local communities, the custom followed in the Diaspora was to send the funds to central receiving points[64] from which the large aggregate sums were forwarded to Jerusalem. They were accompanied for protection from banditry by a large retinue consisting of paid mercenary guards,[65] pilgrims, and deputies[66] from the communities which had contributed; of which the last named were charged with representing the local Jewish fellowship in person at the sacrifices in Jerusalem.[67]

Roman protection of delivery

The delivery of the tax and other religious contributions was facilitated by the special privileges which the Roman authorities granted to the Jews.[68] Perhaps as early as the beginning of the

[63] *Antiq.* XIV, vii, 2: 'God-fearers.' On the relationship of these 'half-proselytes' to Judaism, cf. J. Juster, vol. I, pp. 274ff.; R. Pfeiffer (n. 9), pp. 194f.; K. Lake, 'Proselytes and God-fearers', *Beginnings* I, pp. 74ff.

[64] Josephus specifically mentioned Nisibis and Neardea, *Antiq.* XVIII, ix, 1. W. L. Knox (n. 3), pp. 296ff., maintained, on the basis of Josephus, *Antiq.* XVI, vi, 4, 7, that Ephesus was another such centre for this gathering together of the collection. His position is further supported by the quotation from Strabo in *Antiq.* XIV, vii, 2, concerning '800 talents of the Jews' confiscated by Mithridates in Cos. Josephus understood it to have been transferred there from Asia Minor for the purposes of safety. The logical point of origin would have been Ephesus. Cf. the letter to the Ephesian magistrates from the proconsul Gaius Norbanus Flaccus concerning the protection of the Jewish funds, quoted in Philo, *De leg. ad Gaium* XL, 315; also the letter of Dolabella to the officials in Ephesus, quoted by Josephus, *Antiq.* XIV, x, 12.

Rome is also to be included as a centre of collection on the basis of the witnesses in n. 61 above. There were certainly others.

[65] Cf. Shek. 2.1, and the rabbinical comment to this section which is quoted in Strack-Billerbeck I, p. 767, to the effect that should banditry occur, if the appropriation had already been made at the Temple (see above, p. 81), the Temple suffered the loss; if the appropriation had not been made, the tax had to be paid by the community again. However, if the contributions were sent to Jerusalem unescorted by paid guards, the community was held liable for loss through banditry, even if the appropriation had already been made at the Temple, because of their irresponsibility.

[66] 'Ἱεροπομποί' (Philo, *De spec. leg.* I, xiv, 78; *De leg. ad Gaium* XXXI, 216; XL, 312) was evidently the official title given to them. The foremost men of the community were selected to fulfil this important and honourable function: 'At stated times there are appointed to carry the sacred tribute envoys selected on their merits, from every city those of the highest repute, under whose conduct the hopes of each and all will travel safely. For it is on these first-fruits, as prescribed by the law, that the hopes of the pious rest' (*De spec. leg.* I, xiv, 78). Cf. also Josephus, *Antiq.* XVIII, ix, 1.

[67] Philo, *De leg. ad Gaium*, XXIII, 156; cf. XL, 312.

[68] Cf. J. Juster (n. 2), vol. I, pp. 338ff., where the various special concessions enjoyed by the Jews under Roman rule are conveniently grouped and discussed, together with extensive source references.

first century BC, certainly by mid-century, the Jews had been permitted to collect and dispatch their contributions to Jerusalem.[69]

Julius Caesar reiterated and extended these concessions[70] as an expression of his gratitude for the military assistance provided him during his Egyptian campaign by the Jewish general, Antipater, with support of the High Priest, Hyrcanus.[71] They were enforced by Caesar's successors,[72] apparently still being in effect at the time of the destruction of Jerusalem by Titus (AD 70).[73]

F. *Appropriation and uses of the Temple tax*

When the funds had been delivered into the Temple treasury in Jerusalem and the time for the corresponding appropriation had arrived,[74] the money was measured by the treasury officer into three baskets.[75] This taking of the appropriation was very ceremoniously[76] and exactly[77] done.

Exaggerated care was taken to ensure that the one making the appropriation was not suspected of pilfering for his own private gain: 'He who made the appropriation did not enter the chamber wearing either a bordered cloak or shoes or sandals or "tefillin" or an amulet, lest if he became poor people might say that he became poor because of an iniquity committed in the chamber, or if he became rich people might say that he became rich from the

---

[69] Juster, vol. I, p. 379; Bousset (n. 9), p. 82. The possibility for dating the Roman protection of Jewish fund-shipments so early depends upon whether Josephus was correct in considering the funds confiscated by Mithridates at Cos (88 BC) to have originally been raised in Asia Minor (*Antiq.* XIV, vii, 2). The confiscation of Jewish money in Asia Minor for which crime Flaccus had to be defended (Cicero, *Pro Flacco*) confirms that such protective decrees were in force c. 62 BC.
[70] Cf. Josephus, *Antiq.* XIV, x, 2–8.
[71] *Ibid.* XIV, viii, 1–3; *Bel. Jud.* I, ix, 3–5.
[72] Josephus, *Antiq.* XIV, x, 9–26; xii, 3–6; XVI, ii, 3; vi, 2–7; Philo, *De leg. ad Gaium* XL. Because of the Jewish persecutions resulting from Caligula's sharp anti-Semitic attitudes, Claudius (AD 41) reconfirmed the previously granted concessions; Josephus, *Antiq.* XIX, v, 2–3; vi, 3; XX, i, 2.
[73] During the siege of Jerusalem the Roman protection of Jewish contributions was mentioned by Titus in a speech to the Jews: 'We permitted you to exact tribute for God and to collect offerings, without either admonishing or hindering those who brought them—only that you might grow richer at our expense and make preparations with our money to attack us!', Josephus, *Bel. Jud.* VI, vi, 2.
[74] Shek. 3.1, 4.
[75] They were marked so that the money could be used from each basket in the order in which they were filled: Shek. 3.2.
[76] Shek. 3.3. Cf. Strack-Billerbeck, I, pp. 768f. (5g), for the formulas spoken at the appropriations.
[77] Shek. 3.4.

Analogies to Paul's Collection in Contemporary Judaism

appropriation in the chamber. For it is a man's duty to be free of blame before men as before God, as it is said:[78] "And be guiltless towards the Lord and towards Israel". And again it says:[79] "So shalt thou find favour and good understanding in the sight of God and man." '[80]

The funds obtained through the appropriations were devoted primarily to the provision of daily and special sacrifices.[81] In addition, the guards who protected the grain to be used to prepare offerings in the seventh (Sabbath) year were paid from the appropriation money.[82] Any money remaining in the appropriation after the above necessities had been provided was used either to purchase gold leaf for the interior of the Holy of Holies, or to buy the 'Dessert' for the altar,[83] or for the vessels of ministration in the Temple.[84]

The surplus of funds from the half-shekel tax which remained in the Temple treasury after the appropriations had been made were put to a variety of uses.[85] As well as being expended for secondary cultic purposes[86] it was also employed for civic purposes.[87] Apparently, therefore, the riot which Pilate provoked

---

[78] Num. 32.22.   [79] Prov. 3.4.
[80] Shek. 3.2. Strack-Billerbeck, I, p. 766, list the additional rabbinical precautions taken; of searching the official both before he went into the chamber and when he came back out, and of talking with him continually while he was in the chamber so that no coins could be hidden in his mouth. Another suggestion was that to avoid suspicion the appropriation should not be made by anyone with a full head of hair!
[81] Shek. 4.1, 2; cf. also 7.5-7.
[82] Shek. 4.1. 'All produce of the Seventh Year was ownerless property and free to man and beast, Lev. 25.6-7. As the 'Omer and the Two Loaves had to be offered out of the new produce of the year, therefore in the Seventh Year guardians were set over a special field to guard its aftergrowths for the use of the 'Omer and the Two Loaves for that year, so that they might not be eaten by man or beast'; M. H. Segal (n. 8), p. 12 n. 6.
[83] 'Lit., "summer-fruit", eaten as dessert, a figurative name for the burnt-offerings which were offered after all the prescribed public and private offerings had been offered, to prevent the altar standing idle'; ibid., p. 14 n. 1.
[84] Shek. 4.4.
[85] Rabbi Ishmael maintained that the funds were to be used to speculate in produce, the profits from which economic ventures would then belong to the Sanctuary. This was rejected by others, however, as being improper and too risky: Shek. 4.3.
[86] Shek. 4.2: 'The viaduct for the (red) cow (cf. Num. 19.1-10; the viaduct was to protect the priest from unwittingly becoming unclean; cf. Segal, p. 13 n. 1) and the viaduct for the scapegoat (cf. Lev. 16.10, 21f.; this viaduct provided a private exit from Jerusalem: Segal, p. 13 n. 2) and the strip of scarlet which was between its horns, and (the maintenance of) the pool of water (within the Temple Court) . . . came out of the remainder in the chamber.'
[87] Ibid.: 'the wall of the city and the towers thereof and all the needs of the city (which, according to M. H. Segal, p. 13 n. 6, included: the maintenance of the water supply, the streets, the markets, etc.) came out of the remainder in the chamber.'

The Collection

by using funds from the Temple treasury to construct an aqueduct[88] resulted not so much from the use which was made of the money as from his impolitic high-handedness in arbitrarily designating the expenditure of funds for which the prerogative belonged by tradition and law to the Temple authorities.

G. *Temple tax became a Roman tax*

The half-shekel tax continued to flow yearly into the treasury of the Temple until it was destroyed by Titus in AD 70.[89] After that disaster the Emperor Vespasian converted the half-shekel Temple contribution into a Roman tax.[90]

H. *Jewish-Christians paid the Temple tax*

The young community of Christians in Jerusalem as well as Jewish-Christians throughout Palestine undoubtedly paid the half-shekel tax to the Temple. This may be inferred from their practice of continuing to participate in the Jewish cultic worship as reflected in Acts,[91] as well as from the necessity to maintain relationships of solidarity with the rest of Judaism for the sake of their mission.[92] It is confirmed by the account recorded in Matt. 17.24–27 in which Jesus was described as paying the Temple tax. This tradition was retained, not so much for the sake of the miraculous provision of the necessary money by a fish[93] but because the problem was timely for the Christian community.

It is intriguing to note that the use to which the tax money was applied[94] did not occupy a substantial role in their consideration. Rather the tax was regarded from the standpoint of being a symbol for the question of the relationship of the Christian faith

---

[88] Josephus, *Bel. Jud.* II, ix, 4; cf. *Antiq.* XVIII, iii, 2.
[89] Shek. 8.8: '(The laws of) the shekels ... have force only during the time of the existence of the Temple.'
[90] Josephus, *Bel. Jud.* VII, vi, 6: 'On all Jews, wheresoever resident, (Caesar) imposed a tax of two drachmas, to be paid annually into the Capitol as formerly contributed by them to the Temple at Jerusalem.' See below, pp. 144f.
[91] Acts 2.46; 3.1ff., etc.
[92] The proclamation of the faith to the 'Circumcision'; see above, pp. 42f. The Gospel of Matthew was particularly concerned with this mission.
[93] Cf. E. Klostermann, *Das Matthäusevangelium*, 2nd ed., Tübingen, 1927, p. 145, for a list of similar legends of treasure obtained from a fish, as well as related bibliographical material.
[94] The purchase of sacrifices for the Temple; see above, p. 75 n. 7. Compare the significance of the perfect priesthood of Christ for the cultic sacrifices as discussed in the Epistle to the Hebrews, espec. 5.1ff.; 7.11ff., 27; 8.1f.; 9.12ff.; 10.5ff.

Analogies to Paul's Collection in Contemporary Judaism

to cultic Judaism as a whole.[95] The conclusion reached was that they were no longer intrinsically bound to the cultic practices.[96] Nevertheless, 'not to give offence',[97] the tax was paid and the outward appearance of solidarity was maintained. Because of his expressed personal attitude to the requirements of the Law, it seems probable that Paul, as well as the majority of Jewish Christians in the Diaspora, also continued to pay the tax.[98]

It is of incidental interest to note that the shekel contribution has been recently reinstituted; not in connection with Temple sacrifices, it is true, but certainly as an expression of the solidarity among Jews.[99]

1. Parallels between the Temple tax and Paul's Collection

The parallels between the half-shekel Temple tax and the collection gathered by Paul for the Jerusalem community are too numerous to have been coincidental:

1. Jerusalem was the place to which the money was delivered. This was not the result of a geographical fortuity. Rather Jerusalem represented the centre of their respective interests: for Judaism the focal point of the cultic worship; for Christianity the historical nucleus of its faith and the location for the realization of its eschatological expectations.

2. Pentecost was an important date for the delivery.[100] To have been perfectly consistent, Paul should have chosen the Feast of the Tabernacles as the date for the delivery of his collection, corresponding to the delivery of the 'shekels' from the far

---

[95] Matt. 17.25b.
[96] Matt. 17.26. This is one of the clearest expressions within the Gospels that the Jewish Christian community considered itself to have been basically freed from the requirements of cultic Judaism. Compare Matt. 12.6; cf. Ernst Lohmeyer, *Das Evangelium des Matthäus* (Meyer Kommentar), Göttingen, 1956, p. 275; J. Munck, *Paul and the Salvation of Mankind*, London, 1959, pp. 249f.; A. Schlatter, *Der Evangelist Matthäus*, 2nd ed., Stuttgart, 1933, p. 539; cf. also on Matt. 12.6.
[97] Ἵνα δὲ μὴ σκανδαλίσωμεν αὐτούς, verse 27.
[98] Cf. espec. I Cor. 9.20: 'to the Jews I became as a Jew, that I might gain Jews'. This corresponds precisely to Jesus' attitude in paying the tax.
[99] 'The concept of the shekel was revived in modern times by the Zionist Organization, the members of which pay a small annual levy called a shekel, which entitles them to participate in elections to the World Zionist Congress. This shekel was introduced at the First Congress in 1897 to indicate support of the "Basle Program" and affiliation with the Zionist organizations', *The Standard Jewish Encyclopedia*, ed. Cecil Roth, Garden City, N.Y., 1959, col. 1704.
[100] Paul's intent to deliver the collection in Jerusalem at Pentecost is reflected in Acts 20.16, a portion of the 'we-source'.

The Collection

Diaspora.[101] Nevertheless the tax money delivered at Pentecost also came from outside Palestine, and the suitability of this date for the delivery of his collection was enhanced by the significance which the festival bore for the Church as the anniversary of its foundation.[102] Thus it was particularly fitting in view of the meaning which the collection had for Paul and the hopes which were connected with it that the delivery be made then.

3. Men were appointed in each of the local communities to accompany the funds to Jerusalem.[103] In both instances, this was not just for the sake of security, but also in order that the one sent could represent the entire community in Jerusalem.[104]

4. Central reception areas were established in which the contributions and representatives from the local communities were gathered together and from which the funds were forwarded to Jerusalem accompanied by the delegations.[105] The central gathering points which Paul appears to have used were Ephesus[106] and Corinth,[107] perhaps Philippi.[108]

5. Advantageous use was made of the protection provided under the special concessions granted to Judaism by the Roman Government.[109] If Paul had publicly differentiated between his collection and the other usual contributions sent to Jerusalem, his project would have been judged illegal[110] and he would either

---

[101] See above, p. 81.

[102] Cf. Acts 2.1ff. The festival of Pentecost as the celebration of the Feast of Weeks was closely associated with the harvest motif; a theme which was particularly meaningful for the Christian mission and was employed by Paul in his discussions of the collection (II Cor. 9.6ff; also I Cor. 16.2).

[103] See above, p. 83; compare above, pp. 15f., 68f.

[104] See above, n. 66, p. 83. On the significance of the delegates who accompanied Paul's collection, see below, pp. 138ff.

[105] Pp. 82f. above.

[106] This is conjectured from the length of his stay there (Acts 19.10), during which time he made concrete plans for the delivery of the collection (Acts 19.21). Compare also p. 69 and p. 83, n. 64.

[107] Rom. 16.23; cf. verse 16. These are references to the delegates from the various local Christian communities who accompanied Paul on his trip to Jerusalem with the collection; cf. Acts 20.4.

[108] Acts 20.6. It could be that some of the other localities at which they stopped on the trip to Jerusalem had been previously arranged by Paul to serve the same purpose; see pp. 68f.

[109] See pp. 83f. above. W. L. Knox (n. 3 above), p. 298, suggested that Paul's choice of Ephesus as a base of operations for his collection project was motivated by his desire to take advantage of the protection afforded the Jews there.

[110] Cicero, *Pro Flacco* 28.67; cf. J. Juster (n. 2 above), vol. I, p. 379. This may have been the cause of the suppression by the author of Acts of any clear, explicit reference to Paul's collection; see below, pp. 148ff.

Analogies to Paul's Collection in Contemporary Judaism

have had to covertly dispatch it to Jerusalem or risk possible confiscation. Because of his concept of the Church as the 'true Israel', he would have had no compunctions about taking advantage of such official protection.

6. The prudent practice of regularly setting aside money for the contribution was encouraged.[111]

7. Special care was taken to ensure that no opportunity might be provided for the personal vilification of those directly connected with the funds.[112] In this connection it is indicative that Paul's language reflects dependence upon the same proverb as was used to justify the elaborate care exercised at the appropriation from the Temple treasury.[113]

8. The contributions manifested a tangible expression of unity and solidarity. Although this aspect was peripheral to the primary purposes[114] of both contributions, yet in both instances it achieved an importance which in many respects tended to eclipse the overt objective.

For the Jews scattered throughout the world in the Dispersion, the Temple tax was one of the few means available for them to maintain contact with, personally participate in, and express their sense of identity with cultic Judaism as it was exemplified in the Temple worship.[115]

One is inclined to suspect that it was this aspect of the Temple tax which led Paul to include so many of its features in the structure of his collection project. He was undoubtedly aware of this potential in regard to his collection from his earlier experience with the famine relief from Antioch.[116] As the relationship of Jerusalem to his missionary work seriously deteriorated, this aspect acquired fundamental importance.[117]

---

[111] See p. 80 above; I Cor. 16.2.
[112] See pp. 84f. above; II Cor. 8.20f.
[113] Prov. 3.4.
[114] The half-shekel tax: provide the Temple sacrifices; Paul's collection: 'remember the poor'.
[115] W. Bousset (n. 9), pp. 81f., who listed the following practices as contributing to this sense of solidarity: delivery of the Temple tax, the pilgrimages to Jerusalem, synagogue worship on the Sabbath, observance of a common calendar of holy days, maintenance of communication between Jerusalem and the Dispersion.
[116] See pp. 26ff.; above.
[117] Paul's collection as an expression of the unity of the Church is discussed more fully below, pp. 59f.

The Collection

J. *Differences between the Temple tax and Paul's Collection*

In view of the attempt to interpret Paul's collection for Jerusalem as a tax imposed upon him and his Gentile communities by the leaders of the Jerusalem church, which has been made to bring into sharp profile his and all other Christians' subordinate dependency on the Jerusalem authority,[118] it is of some worth to consider here the points of variance between Paul's collection and the Temple tax. It should be noted that they are concerned, for the most part, with precisely those elements which determined the character of the act of participation:

1. It was specified that the half-shekel tax was to be paid for the purpose of purchasing the sacrifices which were offered daily in the Temple for the whole nation.[119] The tax was thereby directly related to the very nucleus of Jewish cultic worship. It was paid to the Temple authorities who handled it in strict accordance with recorded procedure,[120] and who were able to dispose of it only within certain well-defined limitations.[121] Because it was bound to a specific location, the tax became superfluous to the cult when that place no longer existed.[122]

Paul's collection, however, was not directly related to the worship of the Church. It was instigated to help provide the funds necessary to care for the poor.[123] In so far as the Jerusalem community continued to distribute succour at the time of the common meals,[124] which was accompanied by liturgical elements, his collection could be regarded as correlative to formal Christian worship. In his organization of the collection Paul recommended that money be set aside on the 'first day of the week',[125] certainly a liturgical reference; but it was to be done at home and not during worship. In his three most extensive discussions of the collection[126]

[118] The most vigorous exponent of this view was Karl Holl, 'Der Kirchenbegriff des Paulus in seinem Verhältnis zu dem der Urgemeinde', *Gesammelte Aufsätze*, vol. II, Tübingen, 1928, pp. 44–67; cf. also F. Rendall, 'The Pauline Collection for the Saints', *The Expositor*, 4th Series, Vol. VIII, London, 1893, p. 322; W. Mundle, 'Das Kirchenbewusstsein der ältesten Christenheit', *Zeitschrift für die neutestamentliche Wissenschaft und die Kunde der älteren Kirche*, Vol. 22, Giessen, 1923, p. 26.
[119] See pp. 75f., 84f. above.
[120] P. 81f. above.
[121] Pp. 84f. above.
[122] See above, p. 86, n. 89.
[123] Gal. 2.10.
[124] Acts 2.44ff.; 6.1ff.
[125] I Cor. 16.2.
[126] Rom. 15.25ff.; I Cor. 16.1ff.; II Cor. 8–9.

Analogies to Paul's Collection in Contemporary Judaism

Paul did not even mention the Jerusalem leadership. That they were mentioned at all was the result of contextual accident.[127]

2. It could be claimed of the Temple tax that the authority for its institution went back to Moses himself, and furthermore, to that precise time of the foundation of the cult of the Tabernacle.[128] Thus it was based on a very authoritative scriptural precedent and as such became one of the basic obligations of the pious Jew, undergirded with the strength which the importance of the law lent to such an institution.

Although there was sufficient scriptural basis and established precedent within Judaism for the legal foundation of charitable contributions,[129] Paul did not employ it. His use of Old Testament references in connection with the collection were for the purpose of illuminating his argument rather than to authenticate it.[130] Certainly Paul's concern for the plight of the poor, as well as that of the Jerusalem community, was in response to Jesus' own attitude as expressed in his ministry,[131] which in turn reflected a strong current in contemporary Jewish piety,[132] but there was no attempt to legalize or regulate this.

3. Because of the factors mentioned in 1 and 2 above, the procedure for collecting and receiving the Temple tax was highly organized with detailed written specifications for each related phase.[133]

The instructions which Paul gave for organizing the contributions[134] could hardly be regarded as detailed specifications regulating each phase of the collection. Rather they were the result of his concern to provide his communities with some practical suggestions to facilitate their participation in the project.

4. The Temple tax was a contribution made annually and was due to be paid and delivered at definite times within the liturgical year.[135]

There is no evidence to indicate that Paul intended to institute

---

[127] In Gal. 2.10 the collection was mentioned as one aspect of the agreement reached between Paul and the Jerusalem 'Pillars'.
[128] Ex. 30.11ff.
[129] See below, pp. 93f.
[130] Cf. the numerous allusions to OT passages in II Cor. 8–9.
[131] See below, p. 101.
[132] See below, pp. 94f.
[133] See the tract, 'Shekalim', as a whole.
[134] I Cor. 16.1ff.
[135] Neh. 10.32; p. 81 above.

The Collection

a practice which was to be regularly repeated.[136] Rather the length of time which he took to implement it[137] as well as the general tone of his language in discussing it indicate that this was to be an isolated project.[138] When it proved necessary or beneficial, he deferred delivery for a while.[139] He did single out a specific time of the year for delivery,[140] but this was an expression of the symbolic significance which the collection bore rather than a necessary terminal date.

5. The amount of the Temple tax was a legislated amount which, however obscure it may seem now, was apparently regarded then as specific and rigid.[141]

Paul was very careful not even to suggest a possible norm for the contributions. Instead he made the opposite emphasis of intense stress on the motivations for giving[142] while the secondary concern of the amount of the gifts went practically unmentioned.[143]

6. Because the half-shekel contribution was a legally established compulsory tax, the Temple authorities considered themselves justified to force payment from those who were obligated and accordingly made provisions to do so.[144] Related to this was the

---

[136] Against F. Rendall (n. 118 above), pp. 334ff.; V. Weber, *Die antiochenische Kollekte*, Würzburg, 1917, pp. 58f.; J. Knox, *Chapters in a Life of Paul*, Nashville, 1950, p. 56.

[137] About eight years.

[138] This is not to say that Paul considered that the obligations of Christians to be concerned for each other was finally discharged with his project. He would have been the last one to maintain that any human device could exhaust this concern.

[139] J. Jeremias, in his article, 'Sabbathjahr und neutestamentliche Chronologie', *Zeitschrift für die neutestamentliche Wissenschaft*, Vol. 27, Giessen, 1928, has made the very plausible suggestion that just as the famine aid from Antioch was delivered in AD 48 to relieve the increased distress accentuated by the lack of harvests in the Seventh year (see above, pp. 31f), so also Paul intended to deliver his collection to Jerusalem at the time of the next Sabbath year (AD 55), when the need for financial assistance in Jerusalem would again become particularly acute (pp. 102f.). If so, it seems that this intent was frustrated by two factors: (*a*) the unexpected desire to participate of the Macedonians (II Cor. 8.1ff.), (*b*) the unfulfilled commitment of the Corinthian community (II Cor. 8.6f., 10ff., 24; 9.2ff.). Because of these Paul postponed his trip to Jerusalem until the next year (AD 56).

[140] Pentecost; cf. Acts 20.16; and above, pp. 87f.

[141] Pp. 76ff.   [142] Rom. 15.27; II Cor. 8.4f., 7ff., 14f., 24; 9.5ff.

[143] I have rejected the interpretation of I Cor. 16.4 that makes Paul's willingness to go to the trouble of personally accompanying the collection to Jerusalem dependent upon the richness of the contributions; see above, p. 16. Paul implicitly alluded to the amount to be given in II Cor. 8.12ff. and 9.6ff., but this was apparently motivated by a desire to counteract those who had used the fear of self-impoverishment as an excuse for their lack of participation. Comp. the phrase, 'as he may prosper', I Cor. 16.2.

[144] Pp. 79f.

Analogies to Paul's Collection in Contemporary Judaism

distinction which was made between those who were obligated to pay the tax, those who could pay it as an act of freewill, and those from whom the tax money was to be refused if they offered it.[145]

Paul took precisely the opposite direction in his work with the collection. Repeatedly he stressed the voluntary character of the contributions and urged graciously volitional participation of the Gentile Christians.[146] In contrast to the Temple tax there was no discrimination drawn between those expected, those allowed, and those prohibited to contribute. Because of his vivid awareness that in Christ there were no valid distinctions,[147] Paul undoubtedly considered participation in the collection to be a privilege open to all.[148]

2. CHARITABLE PROVISIONS FOR THE POOR

A. *Old Testament provisions*

Another feature which lay in the background of Paul's collection was the concern within Judaism to provide for the needs of the poor.[149] Although the responsibility of the pious individual to respond spontaneously to the needs of the impoverished had been long recognized,[150] there are evidences of an early inclination to legislate provisions for relief of the poor to supplement such private charity.[151] In addition this concern found negative expression in the strong condemnation which was levied against those who oppressed and exploited the indigent.[152]

B. *Mandatory charity in local communities*

'Basket' for residents

By the first century AD the legislation of charity for the poor

[145] P. 79.   [146] Rom. 15.26, 27a; II Cor. 8.2ff., 8, 10ff.; 9.2, 5, 7; Gal. 2.10b.
[147] Cf. Gal. 3.28; 5.6; I Cor. 7.19, etc.
[148] Cf. the phrase, 'each one of you', I Cor. 16.2.
[149] Although 'the poor' was a designation which bore overtones of other connotations well known to Paul, yet in the first instance his collection was instigated for the purpose of providing relief for 'the poor' in an economic sense (Rom. 15.26; II Cor. 8.14; 9.12; Gal. 2.10). Paul was well aware of the real need which existed, both from his association with the Antioch famine relief and from his discussions with the Jerusalem leaders, and clearly considered it to be not just a legitimate but also a worthy project. See below, pp. 100ff.
[150] Numerous OT passages articulate this concern. See especially Job 22.6ff.; 29.12f., 15f.; 31.16ff.
[151] Ex. 23.10f.; Lev. 19.9f.; 23.22; Deut. 14.28f.; 24.19–22; Ruth 2.2ff., etc.
[152] Ex. 21.2ff.; 22.21ff.; Lev. 25.10, 25ff.; Deut. 15.2, 7ff.; 23.19f.; 24.6, 10ff., etc.; also Amos 2.6ff.; Isa. 5.8ff.; 10.1ff.; Jer. 5.26ff., etc.

The Collection

had been extended into the local communities.[153] Every week the inhabitants of the community were required[154] to pay a tax for the 'basket' collection. This tax was collected by two local officials appointed for the purpose, the proceeds of which were distributed on Friday. At that time, any impoverished person resident in the locality received enough funds to provide two meals a day for the next week.

'Tray' for transients

Provision was also made for any travellers passing through who were in need. Three officials daily canvassed the dwellings in the community and gathered obligatory donations of basic staples to be distributed from the 'tray'. The transients normally received from these supplies enough food to provide them with two meals.[155] In addition a supply of clothing was available to both local and wandering poor; although in the case of the latter, proof of need was required before they could receive any articles of apparel.[156]

Provision for the poor within the Jerusalem Christian community appears, according to the Acts 6.1ff. account, to have been organized somewhat as a combination of the two programmes discussed above.[157]

c. Spontaneous charity of pious

Although charitable concern within Judaism had become legalistically controlled by the time of Paul, this was not intended as a replacement for private gifts of the pious for charitable purposes. Rather it complemented the inclination to support the less fortunate which had developed into a cherished expression of personal righteousness.[158]

---

[153] On these regular provisions for charity which were established in the local communities, see Strack-Billerbeck, II, pp. 643ff.; G. F. Moore, *Judaism*, Cambridge, 1930, vol. II, pp. 174ff.

[154] The ones in charge of making the collection had the authority to compel payment.

[155] If they were staying overnight or over the Sabbath they were allowed to receive correspondingly more.

[156] In the case of food, they were supplied rations without question, although it was assumed that if they possessed enough for two meals they would not apply for aid.

[157] Cf. E. Haenchen, *Die Apostelgeschichte* (Meyer Kommentar), Göttingen, 1959, p. 215.

[158] Cf. W. Bousset (n. 9), pp. 161ff., who stressed the Jewish propensity to charitable works as 'the most essential concrete positive expression of Jewish ethics'.

Analogies to Paul's Collection in Contemporary Judaism

Many extravagant statements were made concerning the acceptability which an act of charity won for the giver in the eyes of God. Thus,[159] charity was one of the hall-marks of the Israelite nation; it was the purpose of creation; whoever did a charitable act was doing the work of God and thereby filled the world with the love of God; charity was greater than sacrifice; it made God a debtor to man; and man was thereby equal to God; it fulfilled all other commandments; it was a giving back to God of what was already his.

Every possible type of good fortune was promised as a reward for charity,[160] while those who were negligent in charitable works were guaranteed severe personal misfortune as a punishment.[161] Such unqualified approbation of charity as a pious work resulted in the propagation of a large element of professional beggars to take advantage of the proffered free maintenance.[162]

It was found necessary to legislate the maximum amount of a person's wealth which could be thus expended. This was done to prevent the overzealous from impoverishing themselves in a moment of enthusiasm, and subsequently becoming a burden for the charity of others.[163] Paul evidently drew upon this strain of thought when he was attempting to convince the Corinthian Christians that participation in his collection need not result in their subsequent destitution.[164]

Jewish concern for the poor as such appears to have been exclusively reserved for other members of the Jewish nation.[165] This is particularly clearly revealed in those regulations designed to protect the needy from exploitation. Thus, as a result of the vivid awareness within Judaism that it constituted a special people called out and separated by God, charity served to maintain and symbolize its solidarity as a nation.

[159] The following were selected from the extensive rabbinical citations listed in Strack-Billerbeck, 'Die altjüdische Privatwohltätigkeit', IV, Part I, p. 537.
[160] Ibid., p. 552; compare Paul's discussion of the blessings which he expected to result from the collection, II Cor. 9.8ff.
[161] Ibid., p. 557. [162] Ibid., p. 546.
[163] Ibid., p. 457; the limit set was 20 per cent. This was further specified to mean; initially 20 per cent of the individual's aggregate wealth, and subsequently 20 per cent of his yearly income, to prevent him from giving away 20 per cent of his total worth each year and thereby dissipating his capital assets.
[164] II Cor. 8.11ff.; 9.6ff.
[165] Cf. RGG³ I, 'Armenpflege', II, 3, col. 618. This provided the dramatic shock value to the reversed example related by Jesus in the parable of the 'Good Samaritan' (Luke 10.30ff.).

The Collection

3. THE 'APOSTLES' AND THE PATRIARCHAL TAX

The function of the 'apostles of the churches' who were appointed by the Jerusalem community to assist Paul in his project[166] had its roots within Judaism also. The legally authorized representation by an individual of the person or institution empowering him was a post-exilic development.[167] It was employed in the various spheres of economic, legal, social and religious life within Judaism.[168] It also provided a designation for those men who were considered to have been commissioned by God to fulfil functions normally understood to be his sole perogative.[169] The Christian community appropriated this designation with its various nuances and extensively broadened it to include those specially commissioned and 'sent out' by Christ to proclaim the Gospel.[170]

A. *Function of 'apostles' in Judaism*

A very important function which the 'apostles' fulfilled within Judaism was to provide a means of communication between Jerusalem and the Jewish communities in the Diaspora.[171] This became particularly important after the disastrous rebellion against Rome which resulted in the destruction of the Temple in AD 70. To fill in the vacuum created by the loss of the focal point of cultic Judaism and the authority it represented, permission was obtained from the Romans to establish a school for the study of the law at Jamnia (Jabneh).[172] Around this centre a council of scholars in the law, the Patriarchy, developed into the dominant ruling body, thereby providing Judaism with a new central authority.

B. *Voluntary contribution for scholars*

To support this central body a contribution was gathered throughout Judaism by 'apostles';[173] rabbis of good repute sent

---

[166] II Cor. 8.23; see pp. 18ff. above.
[167] *RGG*³ I, col. 497.
[168] *ThWB* I, pp. 414ff.
[169] *Ibid.*, pp. 419f.
[170] Primarily for the Twelve, and Paul; then also for a larger number, cf. I Cor. 15.7.; Rom. 16.7; Acts 14.4, 14; cf. II Cor. 11.13.
[171] Cf. E. Schürer (n. 2), vol. III, p. 77; J. Juster (n. 2), vol. I, pp. 388ff.
[172] Cf. R. Pfeiffer (n. 9), p. 44.
[173] It was in this sense of 'those commissioned for work in connection with financial contributions' that the men appointed to assist Paul with his collection were

Analogies to Paul's Collection in Contemporary Judaism

out from Jamnia in pairs to collect the funds. This contribution was at first voluntary. To encourage generosity, a list of the contributors was made, with those who contributed the most in each locality being placed first. This was supposed to ensure their reception of a special blessing from God.[174]

c. *Legislated tax*

Later this voluntary contribution was transformed into a legally recognized assessment; the 'aurum coronarium'.[175] In many respects this levy for the Patriarchy served as a substitute for the defunct Temple tax. Except for isolated instances,[176] it enjoyed the protection of imperial sanction. Eventually, in the fifth century, it suffered the same fate as its predecessor for the support of the Temple; it was converted into a Roman tax.[177]

4. THE EVIDENCE FROM QUMRAN

The Qumran community, which in all probability corresponded to the sect of the Essenes, constituted a special element within the Judaism contemporary with early Christianity. The remarkable number of aspects in their communal life which coincided with the New Testament account testify to the unique influence which

---

called 'apostles' (II Cor. 8.23). This restricted use of the term was also used by Paul to refer to Epaphroditus, who had delivered financial support to him from the Philippians (Phil. 2.25). Compare the use of the verb in Acts 11.30 in connection with the Antioch relief.

It should be noted that there is no direct dependency of Paul's collection on the contributions collected for the Patriarchy. The latter was extensively organized only after the destruction of the Temple, and is discussed here only as an example of a development within Judaism which in this aspect paralleled Paul's collection. Related to this special function of the 'apostle' were the designations of monetary gifts as ἀποστολή attested to in the Apocrypha; cf. Strack-Billerbeck, III, p. 316.

[174] *Ibid.*, p. 317. There was a parallel concern for the provision of material support for teachers and missionaries within early Christianity; cf. I Cor. 9.4ff.; II Cor. 11.9; 12.13ff.; Gal. 6.6ff.; I Thess. 2.6, 9; also cf. II Thess. 3.8f.; I Tim. 5.17f. This appears to have been applied by Paul also to the debt in which the Gentile churches stood over against the Jerusalem church; Rom. 15.27; II Cor. 8.9, 14.

[175] On this tax, cf. J. Juster (n. 2), vol. I, pp. 385ff.; E. Schürer (n. 2), vol. I, pp. 657ff.; vol. III, p. 77; H. Graetz, *Geschichte der Juden*, 4th ed., Leipzig, 1908, vol. IV, n. 21, pp. 441ff. Juster and Graetz both present citations from the sources related to this tax.

[176] The collection was prohibited under Emperors Julian (middle of 4th century); his letter to the Jews is available in Graetz, vol. IV, pp. 457f.; German transl. pp. 340f.; Juster, vol. I, p. 387 n. 1) and Honorius (end of 4th century; Codex Theodosianus XVI, viii, 14 in Graetz, vol. IV, p. 442; Juster, vol. I, p. 386 n. 2).

[177] Codex Theod. XVI, viii, 29; Juster, vol. II, pp. 287f.

The Collection

they exerted on the environment in which Christianity developed.[178]

A. *Participation in Temple tax*

Although no specific reference is made to the Temple tax in the various documents dealing with their fellowship, one may conjecture that they did pay the tax. There are a number of passages which witness to a severely critical attitude toward the Jerusalem cultic worship.[179] Corresponding to this are passages evidencing a spiritualized understanding of sacrifice.[180] This has led to the assertion that the Essenes categorically rejected the prevailing cultic worship as it was centred in Jerusalem.[181]

The majority of these references were, however, levied against the vileness of sacrifices offered by a corrupt and unclean priesthood rather than against the cult as such. This is confirmed by their expectations of an elaborate restoration of pure cultic worship at the time of the eschatological conflict.[182] I am inclined to regard Josephus' description as being fairly accurate when he maintained that the Essenes sent gifts to the Temple in Jerusalem, but did not personally participate in the Temple worship.[183]

B. *Emphasis on charity*

Because the custom of the compulsory pooling of personal resources for the maintenance of the Qumran community was practised, the need for organized taxes for relief of the poor was abrogated. Nevertheless there was a strong emphasis on good

---

[178] Cf. the collection of essays in *The Scrolls and the New Testament*, ed. K. Stendahl, New York, 1957, also 'Qumran' 4, 5, RGG³ V, cols. 745ff.

[179] ZD 3.20–4.2; 6.11–7.6a; Bk of Hymns, cols. 15.23f.; Com. Mic. on 1.5f.; Com. Neh. on 2.11, 13; Com. Hab. on 2.5ff.; 12f., 15ff.; Com. 37 (Frag. C) on vv. 32f.; MD 8.1–19; cf. also 9.1–6. The interpretation of the last passage has been contested by P. Wernberg-Møller, *The Manual of Discipline* (= Studies on the Texts of the Desert of Judah, ed. J. van der Ploeg, vol. I), Leiden, 1957, p. 133 n. 9, who maintains that it is to be understood in the sense of a spiritual concept of sacrifice rather than as a rejection of cultic sacrifice.

[180] MD 6.4–5 (the table ceremony a substitute for participation in cultic sacrifices?); 8.9; 9.1–6 (cf. preceding note); also Hymn of Init. stanzas 7, 10.

[181] A recent exponent of this view is Yigael Yadin, *The Scroll of the War of the Sons of Light against the Sons of Darkness*, Oxford, 1962, pp. 198ff.; cf. Philo, *Quod omnis probus liber sit* XII, 75.

[182] Especially in the 'War of the Sons of Light and the Sons of Darkness' (2.36) full cultic ceremonies including burnt-offerings and sacrifices, incense, and rites of atonement were expected to be established.

[183] *Antiq.* XVIII, i, 5.

works, including concern for the destitute,[184] which corresponded to the high value placed upon charity in popular Judaism.

5. SUMMARY

From the foregoing material it is seen that, although Paul's collection reflected several aspects of contemporary Judaism, he borrowed most heavily for the organization of his collection from the Jewish Temple tax. This is evident both in the external elements and in the symbolic significance which that tax bore for dispersed Judaism. It was because the symbolism of the Temple tax corresponded so precisely with the hopes for the unity of the Church with which Paul had invested his project that he was led to borrow and use so many other aspects of that tax.

[184] MD 1.5; ZD 6.11-7.6a; 14.12-18; Bk of Hymns, col. 5: 20; cf. Josephus, *Bel. Jud.* II, viii, 6; Philo, *Quod omn. prob. lib. sit.* XII, 87.

IV

THE THEOLOGICAL SIGNIFICANCE OF THE COLLECTION

PAUL devoted a considerable amount of thought, time, and energy to his collection. If the events which resulted in the launching of this project are taken into account, the time involved spanned the entire period of his known public missionary activity from Antioch to Rome.[1] The extent of his efforts in implementing and completing the project would lead one to expect that he invested it with an equivalent theological significance.

Paul maintained in his discussions of his collection project for Jerusalem three perceptible directions of interest: (1) the realization of Christian charity, (2) the expression of Christian unity, (3) the anticipation of Christian eschatology. All three concerns were valid in their own right; yet in the collection they were so welded together that each was presented as essentially involved in the other. Correspondingly, the expressions employed to express each of these concerns often possessed overtones which also reflected the other interests.

1. THE COLLECTION AS AN ACT OF CHRISTIAN CHARITY

According to Paul, his collection project was instigated at the time of his meeting together with the 'Pillars' of the Jerusalem church for the purpose of providing financial assistance to relieve the pressing needs of the poor.[2] Many commentators have underemphasized this aspect in the interest of accentuating one of the other areas of significance for the collection. Some have regarded it as an attempt by Paul to camouflage the real purpose of the collection as being a shameful imposition which revealed his

---

[1] Chapters one and two above are devoted to an examination of those events in Paul's career which either led up to or were directly a part of his collection project.
[2] Gal. 2.10: 'they would have us remember the poor'; compare Rom. 15.26: 'the poor among the saints at Jerusalem'.

subservience to Jerusalem.[3] In reply it must be stressed that this was a valid endeavour for Paul which was a direct and necessary expression of the Christian faith.

A. Grounded on the teaching and the ministry of Jesus

As has been pointed out above,[4] concern for the poor was early recognized as an important responsibility within Judaism. By the time of Christ it was not only regulated but also occupied an honoured position as a highly valued means of voluntarily demonstrating personal piety. As such it was one of the leading manifestations of Jewish ethics.

A concern for the poor was a dominant and well-remembered element in the ministry of Jesus.[5] He himself lived in voluntary poverty[6] and so did his disciples.[7] His needs were supplied either miraculously[8] or through the unsolicited mediation of others.[9] He instructed his followers to expect the same provision in their missionary work.[10] His teaching evidenced a deep concern for the poor[11] and he encouraged others to assist them.[12] Although he did not condemn wealth in itself, he testified to the difficulty with which a wealthy person kept himself oriented to God.[13]

---

[3] See especially Karl Holl, 'Der Kirchenbegriff des Paulus in seinem Verhältnis zu dem der Urgemeinde', *Gesammelte Aufsätze zur Kirchengeschichte*, vol. II, Tübingen, 1928, pp. 40ff. Holl judged Paul's use of the phrase in Romans (see preceding note) to be a 'veiled manner of speaking' (p. 59) because he was ashamed to be involved in the attempt by the Jerusalem church to 'impose a "Temple tax" on the "second class half-citizen" Gentile believers' (p. 58); cf. also E. Meyer, *Ursprung und Anfänge des Christentums*, vol. III, Stuttgart, 1923, pp. 194f.

[4] Pp. 93ff.

[5] Gerhard Uhlhorn, *Die christliche Liebestätigkeit in der alten Kirche*, Stuttgart, 1882, pp. 52ff.; RGG^3 I, 'Armenpflege' IV, cols. 619ff.; $ThWB$ VI, 'πτωχός' D I, pp. 902ff.

[6] Matt. 8.20 and parallels.

[7] Mark 1.17ff. par.; 2.23ff. par.; 10.28ff. par.

[8] Mark 1.13 par.; 6.35ff. par.; 8.4ff. par.; Matt. 17.27.

[9] Luke 8.3; cf. Mark 15.40f. par., Mark 11.1ff. par.; 14.12ff. par.; 15.26 par.

[10] Mark 6.7ff. par.; Luke 10.4ff.

[11] Matt. 5.3 par. (an interesting parallel has come to light in the Dead Sea Scrolls which could represent the Aramaic expression behind this famous verse, in which case Jesus may have been referring to those who voluntarily became poor; cf. Kurt Schubert, 'The Sermon on the Mount and the Qumran Texts', *The Scrolls and the New Testament*, ed. K. Stendahl, New York, 1957, p. 122); Matt. 11.5 par.; Luke 4.18ff.; cf. Mark 12.41 par.

[12] Matt. 5.42 par.; 6.2; 25.34ff.; Mark 10.21 par.; Luke 19.2ff.; John 13.29 (cf. J. Jeremias, *The Eucharistic Words of Jesus*, 2nd and rev. ed., London, 1966, p. 54).

[13] Mark 10.21 par.; 10.23ff. par.; 12.13ff.; 12.41 par.; Luke 16.19ff.; cf. Mark 4.19; Luke 6.24. Also RGG^3 II, 'Eigentum' I, 3, col. 364.

The Collection

B. *The idealized arrangement in the Jerusalem community of Acts*

Such an explicit confirmation in the ministry of Jesus for an element which had already occupied an important position in Judaism provided a strong impetus in determining the form which the communal life of the newly founded faith assumed after Pentecost.[14] In an attempt to concretely implement the teaching of Jesus, augmented by their sensitivity to the imminence of the Eschaton, they sought to establish an idealistic economic relationship in which the surplus of some was used to meet the needs of others.[15] This was ordinarily accomplished during the common meals, which expressed their fellowship together in Christ and at the same time bore liturgical overtones.[16]

Unfortunately the disparity between the large number of needy and economically unproductive compared with the relatively few of substantial means within the fellowship strained their financial arrangements.[17] This was aggravated in time by the predictable results stemming from a fiscal policy of liquidating capital assets.[18] For the shaky economical situation of the Jerusalem community, the impact of the food-shortage which held Palestine in its grip[19] heightened by the shortages of the Sabbath Year[20] was immense.

C. *Charity as a natural consequence of Pauline theology*

Although Paul's first contact with the Jerusalem community was limited, he undoubtedly gained some information while he was there as to the manner and means of their daily life together.[21] During his second visit,[22] at which time he delivered the famine

---

[14] See pp. 23f. above. Cf. G. Uhlhorn (n. 5), pp. 51f.; 65ff.
[15] Acts 2.42, 44f.; 4.32, 34ff.; 5.1ff.
[16] Acts 2.42, 44ff.; 6.1ff.; cf. Bo Reicke, *Diakonie, Festfreude und Zelos*, Uppsala, 1951, pp. 25ff.
[17] See p. 24 above and the literature listed in n. 43 there.
[18] The enthusiasm of the Macedonian Christians evidently led them to contribute with the same sort of uncalculating attitude (II Cor. 8.2f.). Paul carefully assured the Corinthians that they were not expected to impoverish themselves in providing relief for Jerusalem (8.13ff.; 9.8ff.). Compare the phrase 'as he may prosper' (I Cor. 16.2).
[19] See p. 29 above.   [20] See p. 31 above.
[21] Gal. 1.18f. During this visit he apparently did not participate in any of the gatherings of the Christian community there. If he had done so, he would have met more of the apostles. Nevertheless, the two he did meet were precisely the two most responsible for the leadership of the Jerusalem church. It is inconceivable that during their conversations they did not discuss the daily life of their fellowship.
[22] Gal. 2.1ff.; cf. pp. 42ff. above.

The Theological Significance of the Collection

relief sent to the Jerusalem Christians by the church at Antioch,[23] Paul was made vividly aware of the crucial situation which existed and for which only very limited resources were available. It was during this visit that he agreed with the leaders of the Jerusalem church to gather additional funds for their assistance from among the Gentile areas into which he was planning to extend his missionary efforts.[24]

To Paul, such an undertaking was not simply a peripheral matter which received from him only incidental attention and energy. Rather, concern for the needs of the Christian brother was a direct expression of the peculiar organic fellowship which Christians enjoyed 'in Christ'.[25] The central constitutive factor of this fellowship was love.[26]

As God loved Jesus as a father his son,[27] so God's love for men is evidenced in his son who was delivered up for men to the cross.[28] Thereby those who believe in him become sons of God and can call him 'Father'.[29] The love of the Son for men corresponds to the love of the Father.[30] Those who are called by God in love are to love God in thanksgiving and obedience.[31] The ability to realize this love is given to them through the Holy Spirit.[32] Just as the relationship between God and men is established through love, so also are believers to love one another.[33] This love fulfils the law[34] and is the wellspring from which all acceptable ethical activity and all valid social relationships stem.[35]

Concern for the needs of the poor was one of the expressions of fellowship in Christ. Christian charity was motivated not by sympathy or self-righteousness but by Christian love which was the determinative force of that fellowship.[36] Such charity expressed

[23] See pp. 53ff. above for the identification of Paul's trip to deliver the Antioch relief funds to Jerusalem with the Gal. 2 account.
[24] Gal. 2.10.
[25] Rom. 12.5; I Cor. 12.12f., 27, etc.
[26] Rom. 12.9; I Cor. 13, etc.
[27] Rom. 15.6; II Cor. 1.3; 11.31, etc.
[28] Rom. 5.8; 8.31f., etc.
[29] Rom. 8.15ff.; Gal. 3.26; 4.4ff., etc.
[30] Rom. 8.35, 38f.; Gal. 2.20, etc.
[31] Rom. 8.28ff.; I Cor. 8.3; Gal. 5.6, etc.
[32] Rom. 5.5; 15.30; Gal. 5.22.
[33] Rom. 13.8; I Thess. 3.12; 4.9ff., etc.
[34] Rom. 13.8ff.; Gal. 5.13f.; cf. the numerous passages where Paul addresses his readers as 'beloved'.
[35] I Cor. 8.1ff.; 13; Philemon 16, etc.
[36] I Cor. 13.3; Rom. 12.13, cf. verses 9f.

The Collection

the bond of love between Paul himself and the churches he founded in that he reckoned himself as poor,[37] and received ministrations from them for his own needs.[38] It was an essential element within the life of the individual communities,[39] as well as an expression of Christian concern between churches.[40] Therefore it is to be expected that the vocabulary Paul used in speaking of charitable acts reflected this insight.

'Ἁπλότης

In writing to the Roman Christians concerning the various functions of the body of Christ,[41] Paul included in his list 'he who contributes', and exhorted such ones to do so 'ἐν ἁπλότητι'.[42] This phrase has often been translated 'with/in liberality'.[43] Although it is technically correct,[44] this translation is misleading.[45]

When Paul used the phrase in connection with charitable giving, it was to refer to the motivating attitude of concern for the Christian brother which gave impulse to the act, and not to the actual amount given.

This is clearly demonstrated by his use of the term in connection with his collection project.[46] He told[47] of the Macedonian Christians whose contributions, in an exceptionally adverse situation[48] and out of 'extreme poverty', 'overflowed in a wealth of ἁπλότητος'. Under the prevailing circumstances, Paul could hardly have been

[37] II Cor. 6.10; cf. 11.27; Rom. 8.35; I Cor. 4.11; Phil. 4.11f.
[38] II Cor. 11.8f.; Phil. 2.25; 4.15ff.; cf. I Cor. 9.4.
[39] Rom. 12.8, 13; I Cor. 16.15; cf. Gal. 6.9; Phil. 1.1.
[40] Mainly Paul's collection for Jerusalem: Rom. 15.25ff.; I Cor. 16.1ff.; II Cor. 8; 9; Gal. 2.10; cf. also Paul's involvement in the Antioch relief for Jerusalem, Acts 11.27ff.
[41] Rom. 12.4ff.
[42] Rom. 12.8.
[43] ASV; RSV. In the KJV, the phrase 'with simplicity' was used, which is also inadequate. By abandoning a word-for-word translation and resorting to paraphrase, the NEB offers the most accurate rendition: 'with all your heart'.
[44] Cf. the citations listed in A & G, 'ἁπλότης', sect. 2, p. 85.
[45] 'Liberality' (as has its synonym 'generosity'), when used with reference to a monetary contribution, has almost lost its original significance of reference to motivation or the volitional act of the person giving, and instead conveys information about the gift itself, particularly in reference to its amount, as 'large, rich, above average'.
[46] II Cor. 8.2; 9.11, 13.
[47] II Cor. 8.2.
[48] They were evidently suffering under severe persecution; cf. I Thess. 1.6f.; 2.14. Possible, but less likely, they were themselves suffering under famine conditions. Jean Héring, *La seconde épitre de saint Paul aux Corinthiens*, Neuchâtel, 1958, ad loc., speculated that Paul might be referring to earthquakes which had occurred during the reign of Claudius.

The Theological Significance of the Collection

referring to the extent of the performance itself.[49] Rather he was describing the attitude which elicited this performance, and in verse 5 proceeded to outline the manner in which this attitude came to govern their act.[50] Thus the term retained its original meaning of 'singleness, simpleness, sincerity'[51] as the predominant emphasis.

Paul was saying that because the Macedonians had given themselves unreservedly to Christ, so were they able, then, to give themselves with sincerity and openness, without hidden, self-centred motives, to the project intended for the relief of fellow Christians.

This is the case also in II Cor. 9.13.[52] Paul was anxious that the Corinthians should respond to the project as had the Macedonians. Under the assumption that they would do so, Paul predicted that it would result in the Jerusalem Christians' glorifying God for their unreserved lack of duplicity in supplying relief for the poor, which was evidence of their obedient confession of faith in Christ.[53]

Κοινωνία

Paul employed the noun κοινωνία three times[54] with reference to the collection, and the verb κοινωνέω once.[55] This word-group is discussed more fully later.[56] Let it suffice here to point out that the expression was one of Paul's preferred phrases for speaking of the life of the Christian community.[57] Furthermore, Christian fellowship as such was possible only as a result of the fellowship of believers with the resurrected Christ.[58]

---

[49] Neither can it be regarded as a special term for 'giving alms' (Hans Lietzmann, *An die Korinther I–II*, Tübingen, 1949, *ad loc.*) or 'charity' (J. Héring, see preceding note, *ad loc.*).
[50] 'First they gave themselves to the Lord and to us by the will of God.'
[51] So P. Bachmann, *Der zweite Brief des Paulus an die Korinther* (Kommentar zum Neuen Testament, vol. VIII), Leipzig, 1909; H. Windisch, *Der zweite Korintherbrief* (Meyer Kommentar), 9th ed., Göttingen, 1924. Cf. *ThWB* I, pp. 385f.; A & G, p. 85, also *s.v.* ἁπλοῦς and ἁπλόω; compare II Cor. 11.3; Eph. 6.5; Col. 3.22; also the variant reading to II Cor. 1.12.
[52] The use of the term in 9.11 appears to correspond to a further extension of the expression to describe the act itself = 'open-handedness, giving without reserve'; cf. verses 8b–10; cf. James 1.5.
[53] Cf. verse 14: 'because of the surpassing grace of God in you'.
[54] Rom. 15.26; II Cor. 8.4; 9.13; cf. Rom. 12.13; Gal. 6.6; Phil. 1.5; 4.15.
[55] Rom. 15.27.   [56] See below, pp. 122ff.
[57] Cf. H. Seesemann, *Der Begriff Κοινωνία im Neuen Testament* (= Beiheft 14, Zeitschrift für die neutestamentliche Wissenschaft), Giessen, 1933, pp. 24ff.; *ThWB* III, pp. 804ff. (by F. Hauck).
[58] I Cor. 1.9; 10.16ff.; Phil. 3.10; cf. II Cor. 13.13; Phil. 2.1.

The Collection

In this connection it is significant to note that κοινωνία had special significance both for Paul and for the early Church with reference to the celebration of the Lord's supper;[59] that climactic event in the liturgical life of the Church with which the ministry to the poor and needy was intimately connected.[60] Thus it was perfectly logical that the term was employed for the form in which concern for fellow Christians was expressed; especially for the supplying of their needs whether spiritual[61] or material.[62] In applying the term to his collection Paul was clearly emphasizing that it was as a direct expression of Christian fellowship that his churches were contributing relief funds to Jerusalem.

It is further striking that in the collection passages containing this term Paul also emphasized the enthusiasm with which the communities participated in the collection. In II Cor. 8.4 he declared that the Macedonians had 'earnestly begged' to be included in the project. The passage in 9.13 was written under the assumption that the Corinthians would emulate this enthusiasm in their response. In Rom. 15.26f. he gave double emphasis through repetition for the manner in which both Macedonia and Achaia 'were pleased' to participate.

Also significant in this connection is the fact that the collection project was instigated as a direct outgrowth of the agreement reached between Paul and Barnabas and the Jerusalem 'Pillars'[63] which culminated in their reciprocally giving 'the right hand of Christian fellowship'.[64]

Διακονία

The etymological development of διακονία began with the very concrete sense of 'waiting at table' and was then extended to 'providing the necessities of life'. From there it was generalized to mean simply 'service' in a variety of functions and circumstances.[65] It is indicative of the New Testament use of the term that all three nuances of meaning were utilized[66] and that they were often

---

[59] I Cor. 10.16; cf. Acts 2.42ff. (Reicke, n. 16 above, p. 25).
[60] See the following section, Διακονία.
[61] Rom. 15.27; cf. I Cor. 9.11ff., 23; II Cor. 1.5ff.; Phil. 1.7.
[62] Rom. 12.13; Gal. 6.6; Phil. 1.5; 4.14f.
[63] Gal. 2.1ff.; see above, pp. 44ff.
[64] Gal. 2.9f.
[65] Cf. ThWB II, pp. 81f.; A & G, p. 183.
[66] So, for instance, 'waiting at table': Luke 12.37; 17.8; 'provision of sustenance': Luke 8.3; 10.40; 'service' in extended sense: Matt. 25.42ff.

The Theological Significance of the Collection

intertwined. This was undoubtedly the result of the significance with which Jesus imbued the concept of service.

In contrast to the profane understanding, service within Judaism was a positive relationship untainted by the sense of degradation. For the Jewish outlook, the highest form of relationship of men to God was one of service (but this was expressed in the LXX by terms other than διακονία).[67]

Jesus radically reoriented the concept of service to be understood as both the highest expression of the relationship between men[68] and also as a key concept in his own self-understanding.[69] He taught that he who did service to the least reputable was thereby serving God.[70]

In the early Church there was apparently no fundamental distinction made between liturgical and more mundane service.[71] They were equally recognized as being essential to the service of the Risen Lord. The Apostles themselves in their role as leaders of the Jerusalem community fulfilled all the services necessary for the communal life.[72] Only when the press of tasks became too great was there a practical division of labour made.[73] Even then, no fundamental distinction was established, for the 'Seven' were invested with liturgical responsibilities.[74]

It was characteristic that at the common meals of the community during which the most intense liturgical service was rendered to Christ in the celebration of the Lord's Supper, the provision for the needs of the poor occupied an essential place.[75] It was simply a broadening of this function within a Christian community to extend to the charitable relief from one Christian community to another which resulted in the application of the term 'service' to a monetary collection.[76]

---

[67] Δουλόω, λειτυργέω, λατρεύω.   [68] Luke 9.48; 22.24ff.; John 13.4ff.
[69] Matt. 20.26ff.; Mark 10.43ff.   [70] Matt. 25.44f.
[71] This insight into the life and structure of the early Church has been especially emphasized by B. Reicke (n. 16), pp. 22ff., who concluded that 'diakonie was organically bound to the liturgical in the early Church' (p. 48).
[72] Acts 1.17, 25.
[73] Acts 6.1ff. It is not possible to see in this incident the founding of an ecclesiastical office. G. Uhlhorn (n. 5), pp. 7of., noted that they were never referred to as 'deacons' in Acts; only as 'the Seven'. He suggested that if any official position was created then it was the office of 'elder', which did appear later (Acts 11.30) to have responsibility for charitable distributions.
[74] Acts 6.8ff.; 8.4ff., 26ff.
[75] Acts 2.42 (cf. Reicke, *op. cit.*, pp. 25f.); 6.1ff.; I Cor. 11.22.
[76] Acts 11.29; 12.25.

The Collection

Although the limited original connotation of διακονία as 'table service' does not appear in Paul's writings, the two extended meanings were frequently employed. As the 'suffering servant of God' concept was central both to Jesus' own self-understanding and to the Christology of the early Church,[77] so Paul could speak of Jesus as a 'servant'[78] and of the 'service' of the Spirit.[79] It was a fundamental designation for his own ministry.[80] Within the life of the Christian community 'service' could refer to a single function in the body of Christ[81] as well as being a collective term for all such functions.[82]

When Paul used various forms of διακονία in reference to his collection project[83] he was employing a designation which was quite familiar to his readers. At the same time it was a term which was rich with meaning for them in relation to their understanding of the Christian faith, in that it had not yet been crystallized into a technical designation.[84]

Because of his frequent and varied use of the term, Paul was well aware of the depth of meaning which it bore, and intentionally employed it for his project to emphasize the importance with which he regarded it. This is particularly clear from the context in which the term appears in II Corinthians. When speaking of the enthusiastic response of the Macedonians[85] Paul combined διακονία with κοινωνία[86] and χάρις[87] to describe the collection.

In the communication which followed shortly after,[88] he used

---

[77] 'Ebed Yahweh = παῖς Θεοῦ; cf. espec. O. Cullmann, *The Christology of the New Testament*, London, 1959, pp. 51f., 66; J. Jeremias, *ThWB* V, pp. 709ff. R. Bultmann, *Theology of the New Testament*, vol. I, London, 1952, p. 31, rejected this as an element in Jesus' self-understanding.

[78] Rom. 15.8; cf. II Cor. 5.18; Gal. 2.17.   [79] II Cor. 3.8.

[80] Rom. 11.13; I Cor. 3.5; II Cor. 3.6; 4.1; 5.18; 6.3f.; 11.8, 23; cf. Acts 20.24; 21.19.

[81] Rom. 12.7; 16.1; I Cor. 16.15; cf. Heb. 6.10.

[82] I Cor. 12.5.

[83] Rom. 15.25; II Cor. 8.4, 19; 9.1, 12, 13; cf. Rom. 15.31, where the term occurs in what appears to be a later variant reading; see below, p. 134 n. 259.

[84] This is against the assertion that this had become for Paul a technical expression for his collection; so H. Windisch (n. 51), on II Cor. 8.4; W. Sanday and A. C. Headlam, *The Epistle to the Romans* (ICC), Edinburgh, 1902, on Rom. 15.25. The rich variety of ways in which Paul employed the term excludes such an understanding. For the same reason, the attempt of H. Lietzmann, *An die Römer* (Handbuch zum Neuen Testament), 3rd ed., Tübingen, 1928, p. 121, to see in these uses of the term a reference to 'the office of deacon' must be rejected.

[85] II Cor. 8.4.

[86] See above, pp. 105f.; below, pp. 122ff.

[87] See the following section and pp. 135ff. below.

[88] Chapter 9 of II Cor. in its present form.

The Theological Significance of the Collection

the term for the collection again as he was speaking of the results which he anticipated to follow from this service;[89] a passage which, as will be seen below,[90] is of exceptional importance for understanding the significance which the collection held for Paul. By designating his collection διακονία, Paul was regarding it as an essential act of Christian fellowship fulfilled in the service of the Lord.[91]

Χάρις

When Paul used the expression 'grace' in connection with his collection project,[92] he was employing a term which was endowed with rich significance from within the context of Judaism. Out of the various uses which are evidenced in the Old Testament, 'grace' achieved its deepest and most vital significance as a designation for the relationship of God to man as revealed in the covenant which God established with Israel.[93]

While Jesus chose to speak of this relationship in terms of the sovereignty of God,[94] Paul developed 'grace' into a fundamental concept of the Christian faith. The significance of this term in Paul's theology as it is related to his collection project is discussed below in greater detail.[95] It is sufficient here to note that if any one phrase could summarize Paul's theology, it would be 'the grace of God in Christ'.

As applied to the collection,[96] 'grace' was: (1) the divine gift which made genuine Christian participation in the collection

---

[89] II Cor. 9.12f.
[90] Pp. 127ff.
[91] Otto Michel, *Der Brief an die Römer* (Kritisch-exegetischer Kommentar über das Neue Testament), 10th ed., Göttingen, 1955, p. 333; cf. also T. Zahn, *Der Brief des Paulus an die Römer* (Kommentar zum Neuen Testament), Leipzig, 1910, p. 560 (on 13.6).
[92] I Cor. 16.3; II Cor. 8.1, 4, 6, 7, 9, 19; 9.8, 14; cf. verse 15.
[93] *RGG*³ II, cols. 1632ff. (E. Würthwein); cf. espec. the references to the prophets and in the Psalms which are listed there.
[94] Βασιλεία τοῦ Θεοῦ (τῶν οὐρανῶν in Matt.; but see Matt. 12.28; 21.31, 43); and the variant readings to 6.33; 19.24); cf. K. L. Schmidt, *ThWB* I, pp. 582ff. In view of the dominant position which the concept of 'grace' held both in the theology of Paul and throughout the Church after him, it is highly significant to note that the term was never used in its theological sense in any of the sayings of Jesus. Only in the prologue to the Gospel of John (1.14, 16f.) was the word used in a theological sense approaching the depth with which Paul endowed it. Cf. W. Manson, 'Grace in the New Testament', *The Doctrine of Grace*, ed. by W. T. Whitley, London, 1932, pp. 34, 40ff.
[95] Pp. 135f.
[96] Cf. H. Windisch (n. 51), on II Cor. 8.1.

possible,[97] (2) the act of participation in the collection;[98] (3) the result of such participation.[99] As incorporated in the collection it was (4) a direct expression of Christian brotherly fellowship[100] and (5) an integral component of Paul's ministry,[101] stimulated and justified by the example of the grace of Christ.[102]

Other pertinent phrases

Paul employed other phrases and expressions in his discussion of his collection for Jerusalem which confirm that he took quite seriously the dimension of Christian charity which was its overt purpose. When he spoke of 'others being eased' by the collection[103] there was clearly an awareness that the ones receiving the relief were in a strained financial position. In the following verse (v. 14) this state of affairs was explicitly mentioned in terms of 'their want', and was repeated in the later communication.[104]

The same sensitivity to the very real need which existed in Jerusalem is reflected in the Romans passage. The comparison[105] between the 'spiritual blessings' which were shared by the Jerusalem Christians with the Gentiles (by which the implication is present that the Gentiles lacked such blessings before[106]) with the 'material blessings' which the Gentile Christians were now sharing with Jerusalem implied that a definite lack of material substance was present within the Jerusalem community.

In summary, it has been seen that, on the basis of the teaching and ministry of Jesus, from the context of the life of the Jerusalem community, and within the framework of Pauline theology, Christian charity, of which Paul's collection project was an extensive effort, was an integral and honoured element within the Christian fellowship.

[97] II Cor. 8.1 (cf. H. Lietzmann, n. 49 above; J. Héring, n. 48 above); 9.8, 14; cf. 9.15.
[98] II Cor. 8.6.
[99] I Cor. 16.3; to equate the term with 'proof of good will' (J. Sickenberger, *Die briefe des heiligen Paulus an die Korinther und Römer*, Bonn, 1932, *ad loc.*) is not adequate.
[100] II Cor. 8.4, 7. Note that in the latter passage this 'grace' is listed along with faith, utterance, knowledge, earnestness, and love as the attributes of the life of a Christian community.
[101] II Cor. 8.19; cf. 9.1.
[102] II Cor. 8.9.
[103] II Cor. 8.13.
[104] II Cor. 9.12.
[105] Rom. 15.27.
[106] Cf. Rom. 1.18ff., etc.

The Theological Significance of the Collection

It is erroneous to regard the collection as an attempt by Paul to erect an instrument of political manipulation.[107] Rather, whether Paul used the specific term 'poor',[108] or omitted mention of the classification,[109] he well appreciated the economic need which oppressed the Jerusalem church and welcomed the opportunity to mobilize his Gentile communities to participate in this act of Christian sharing.

2. THE COLLECTION AND THE UNITY OF THE CHURCH

The problems relating to the question of the unity of the Church have occupied the attentions and energy of scholars in every century following the founding of the Christian faith.[110] This question has received particular emphasis in recent times.[111] It is, therefore, of singular interest that Paul so ordered the collection for Jerusalem among his Gentile congregations that it was at the same time both a charitable expression of Christian fellowship and a tangible witness to the solidarity of all believers within the Body of Christ.

The aspect of unity in Paul's collection has been recognized and emphasized by a great many scholars.[112] Because of this feature, the project has been described with justification as 'historically, the most important decision of the (Apostolic) Council'.[113] From an appreciation for the impact which Paul's collection had for Christian unity within the life of the early Church, Oscar Cullmann has used this project as a basis for his proposal that a reciprocal collection be instituted in our times between Protestants and

---

[107] B. Weiss, *Brief des Paulus an die Römer* (Meyer Kommentar), Göttingen, 1881, p. 642, correctly insisted on a categorical rejection of such an assertion.
[108] Rom. 15.26; Gal. 2.10.
[109] The 'poor' as a designation for the recipients does not appear in either I or II Corinthians; but cf. II Cor. 8.9, of Christ.
[110] For a concise synopsis of the various efforts made within the history of the Church, as well as valuable bibliographical material for the different periods, cf. 'Einigungsbestrebungen', *RGG*³ II, cols. 379ff.
[111] *Ibid.*, sections V–VII, cols. 394ff.
[112] Other than practically all of the commentaries to the NT passages involved, cf., for example, W. Paley, *Horae Paulinae*, London, 1822; F. Rendall, 'The Pauline Collection for the Saints', *The Expositor*, 4th ser., vol. VIII, London, 1893; V. Weber, *Die antiochenische Kollekte*, Würzburg, 1917; W. L. Knox, *St Paul and the Church of Jerusalem*, Cambridge, 1925; G. Schrenk, 'Der Römerbrief als Missionsdokument', *Studien zu Paulus* (= Abhandlung zur Theologie des Alten und Neuen Testaments, No. 26), Zürich, 1954; John Knox, *Chapters in a Life of Paul*, Nashville, 1950, p. 54, etc.
[113] R. Bultmann, *Theologie des Neuen Testaments*, 3rd ed., Tübingen, 1958, p. 97.

The Collection

Roman Catholics as a symbol of their solidarity under the lordship of Christ.[114]

A. *The conflict threatening the unity of the Church*

The Christian community at Antioch, under the leadership of Hellenist Christians from Cyprus and Cyrene,[115] directed its missionary endeavours to include the proclamation of the gospel to Greeks also.[116] When these efforts were rewarded with singular results,[117] they launched the new faith out in a basically unprecedented direction.[118] It was a step which had not been envisaged by the Jerusalem Christians as being taken so quickly,[119] and consequently for which they had made no provision. When they heard of the innovation at Antioch, they sent Barnabas to investigate,[120] being motivated by a highly critical reaction to the situation which had arisen there.[121]

Upon Barnabas's arrival he was so struck by the obvious evidence of the presence of God's grace among the Gentile Christians there that he abandoned his critical attitude and entered wholeheartedly into both their fellowship and their missionary work.[122] In addition he enlisted Paul, who, according to his own words,[123]

---

[114] This suggestion is mentioned in *Peter: Disciple, Apostle, Martyr*, 2nd ed., London, 1962, p. 46 n. 39, and is further developed in *Message to Catholics and Protestants*, Grand Rapids, Michigan, 1959. It was first made by Dr Cullmann in an address entitled, 'Das Urchristentum und das ökumenische Problem', delivered in 1957 in Zürich, Switzerland.

[115] Acts 11.20. Presumably these men had been connected with the Jerusalem Christian community and, because of their association with the Hellenist group there, were forced to flee with the other Hellenists to escape the persecution following the martyrdom of Stephen (cf. 11.19). Perhaps Mnason (21.16) was one of these men. The fact that Barnabas was from Cyprus (Acts 4.36) has given rise to the erroneous hypothesis that he, too, was really a Hellenist and was to be identified as one of these men (see p. 28 n. 54 above).

[116] Acts 11.20. It is curious that the author of Acts remembered the majority of these men to have been exclusively devoted to proclaiming the Gospel to the Jews (11.19); compare Stephen's speech, 7.2ff., and the charge against him, 6.13f.

[117] Acts 11.21.

[118] See pp. 26ff. above.

[119] Both from the OT understanding of the role Israel was to fulfil in the '*Heilsgeschichte*' as a blessing for the nations and from the teaching of Jesus there was no question that the salvation of God in Christ was to be proclaimed to all men. The question which had not been answered was *when* the beginning of this proclamation to Gentiles should be undertaken.

[120] Acts 11.22.

[121] Compare Acts 8.14; 11.1ff.

[122] Acts 11.23; compare there action of the Jewish-Christian missionaries to the reception by Cornelius and his household of the Holy Spirit (10.44ff.).

[123] Gal. 1.17f., 22f.

The Theological Significance of the Collection

was known only by hearsay to the bulk of the Jerusalem Christians at that time, to join with him in labouring in Antioch.[124] By the time of their trip to Jerusalem for the purpose of delivering the Antioch famine relief funds they were in the precarious position of having actively approved and strengthened a situation which was regarded by the Jerusalem church with critical uncertainty.[125]

The question of *at what point* within the '*Heilsgeschichte*' the gospel was intended to be proclaimed to the Gentiles was a matter demanding urgent attention when Paul and Barnabas arrived in Jerusalem. It accordingly provided the main topic in the discussions which took place there.[126]

The leaders of the Jerusalem church maintained that the gospel was first to be proclaimed to Israel. Only after this task was successfully accomplished would they direct their attention to the conversion of the Gentiles. Jesus was remembered to have considered himself as having been sent first of all to Israel.[127] He had even forbidden his disciples to preach to Gentiles.[128] This is not to say that Jesus rejected the Gentiles. On the contrary, he promised them participation in salvation.[129] But they were to be included within the scope of his redemptive activity at the eschatological time of the Last Judgment.[130] The newly founded Jerusalem community accordingly oriented and geared its missionary programme to be exclusively focused on the task of proclaiming the gospel to Israel.[131]

Paul insisted for his part that God was calling Gentiles to

---

[124] Acts 11.25ff.
[125] See pp. 26ff. above for a more detailed discussion of their viewpoint.
[126] The position has been developed above (pp. 42ff.) that this was the primary concern in the conversations which Paul and Barnabas held with James, Peter, and John, the 'Pillars' of the Jerusalem church. The question of the circumcision of Gentiles who believed was incidentally involved, but was magnified out of proportion to its essential significance by the demands of the 'false brethren' that Titus, a Greek Christian, be forced to accept circumcision (pp. 46ff. above). It did *not*, however, constitute the central problem.
[127] Cf. J. Jeremias, *Jesus' Promise to the Nations*, London, 1958, pp. 25ff.
[128] Matt. 10.5f., 23.
[129] J. Jeremias, *op. cit.*, pp. 46ff.
[130] *Ibid.*, pp. 55ff.; for the similar conception within Judaism of an eschatological incorporation of the Gentiles into Israel, cf. P. Volz, *Die Eschatologie der jüdischen Gemeinde im neutestamentlichen Zeitalter*, Tübingen, 1934, pp. 356ff.
[131] Cf. B. Reicke, *Glaube und Leben der Urgemeinde* (= Abhandlung zur Theologie des Alten und Neuen Testaments, No. 32), Zürich, 1957, p. 33; also 'The Risen Lord and His Church', *Interpretation*, vol. XIII, no. 2, 1959, pp. 159ff.

salvation in Christ right then, and that his mission to the Gentiles was therefore a valid and divinely led endeavour. He was concerned with the upbuilding of the new Israel of God,[132] which recognized no distinctions.[133] The force which compelled him to insist on the validity of this point was his confident certainty that he had been specifically called to be an Apostle precisely for the purpose of proclaiming the gospel to the Gentiles.[134]

He could support his view by the conviction which he shared with the Jerusalem Christians that they were living in the end times, that the Second Coming of Christ and the accompanying Last Judgement were at hand, and that therefore the time had come for the inclusion of the Gentiles into God's redemptive purpose as promised by Jesus. The conclusive support which he presented during the discussions with the 'Pillars' in corroboration of his position was the irrefutable evidence that his work among the Gentiles had been blessed with the grace of God. The relief funds which he brought provided very tangible testimony to the renewing work of the Spirit in the Antioch Christians.[135]

The Jerusalem Christians were just as convinced of the validity of their mission to Israel to which they felt they had been called and to which they were committed. Nevertheless, in the face of such undeniable proof as Paul had advanced in defence of his work, they recognized the mission to the Gentiles as being conducted in direct response to the lordship of Christ. They therefore agreed with Paul to maintain two simultaneous missionary programmes corresponding to the two equally valid commissions from Christ. They exchanged the 'right hand of fellowship' in recognition that they were acting in obedience to their common Saviour.

In this accord, the Jerusalem leaders requested that Paul continue to stimulate charitable concern among the Gentile Christians with whom he was to work, in view of the dire economic situation existing in Jerusalem.[136] If this atmosphere of agreement had continued undisturbed, the question of the unity of the Church would not have acquired such an urgent aspect in Paul's collection,

---

[132] Gal. 6.16; cf. Rom. 9.6ff.; Gal. 3.7, etc.
[133] I Cor. 12.13; Gal. 3.26ff., etc.
[134] Gal. 1.16; 2.7.
[135] Gal. 2.7, 9; cf. pp. 59f. above.
[136] Gal. 2.9f.

The Theological Significance of the Collection

and that project would have developed simply along the lines discussed in the first section of this chapter.[137]

But the situation did not remain the same. The conflict in Antioch between Peter and Paul, the leaders of the two respective missionary enterprises, caused a severe rupture in the concord which had been reached in Jerusalem and ceremoniously accepted with the 'right hand of fellowship'.[138] The occurrence in Antioch revealed that the leaders of the Christian faith had completely overlooked the delicate situation created by their agreement for communities composed of both Jewish and Gentile Christians. In addition the conflict brought into sharp relief the fundamental incompatibility of a Christianity committed to observance of the Jewish law, albeit voluntarily and without any tinge of its being considered a necessity for salvation, and a Christianity divorced from the confines of that law.[139]

The fracture in the solidarity of all Christian believers was deep and threatened to become permanent. Such a possibility violated Paul's conception of the inherently cohesive nature of the Christian fellowship.

B. *Centrality of the unity of the Church in Pauline theology*

It is not possible within the scope of this study to discuss in detail the importance which the unity of the Church held for Paul's theology. It has always commanded a great amount of attention from scholars of the New Testament. In the space available, it is only possible to indicate the pertinent conceptual lines which contribute to his doctrine.

Fundamental to Paul's conception of the unity of the Church was his use of the term 'church' itself.[140] It was directly related to

---

[137] I.e., as an uncomplicated act of charity expressing Christian fellowship and brotherly concern inspired by the love of Christ.
[138] For a discussion of the conflict in Antioch (Gal. 2.11ff.), see above, pp. 62ff.
[139] The agreement in Jerusalem involved the rather unrealistic implication that the Christian mission to the Jews under Peter and its counterpart to the Gentiles led by Paul would be developed as two essentially separate, self-contained enterprises. This was the only possible way in which the two divergently oriented missions could co-exist. It was, of course, made practically impossible by the overlapping which had already occurred in Antioch and which subsequently was to occur in the Christian communities yet to be founded. The Jewish settlement in the Diaspora was too extensive (and perhaps too enticing for Paul?) to be avoidable by the Apostle to the Gentiles.
[140] Cf. especially the thorough article by K. L. Schmidt, *ThWB* III, pp. 502ff. He considered it probable that the term was first applied to the Christian fellowship

The Collection

the Old Testament concept of the assembly of God's people.[141] As God had only one people, so did all those whom he called to faith constitute one fellowship in Christ. This held true whether Paul spoke of the church in a locality, churches in the plural, or the whole Church; whether he designated it 'of God', 'in Christ', or used the term without any further specification.[142] By insisting on the essential solidarity of the one people of God in Christ, Paul was maintaining precisely that understanding which had been constitutive for the Jerusalem Christians in the critical days of the foundation of their community, and from which they had subsequently deviated[143] out of concern for the success of their mission.

This conception found further expression by Paul in his designation of the Christian fellowship as the true Israel, the 'Israel of God'.[144] In using this expression, he was intentionally cutting across all the ethnic, social and cultic distinctions which were of such determinative importance for 'Israel after the flesh'. Related to this radical redefinition of 'Israel' as the people of God in Christ was his use of the designations 'called',[145] 'chosen',[146] 'saints',[147] 'Temple of God',[148] 'descendants of Abraham',[149] 'children of the promise',[150] as applied to all Christians. Consistent with this context was his insistence on the freedom of all believers from obedience to the requirements of the Law as a necessary requisite for salvation.[151]

For Paul, the unity of the fellowship of believers did not consist of an aggregate of individuals who happened to have the same opinion or spiritual inclination. Rather Christian unity was an organic solidarity which he characterized by the phrases 'one

---

by Hellenist, Jewish-Christians as a distinctive improvement on 'synagogue' by which the Jewish fellowship was known (pp. 519f.).

[141] The concept was Hebraic; the Greek term corresponding to it was mediated through the LXX; cf. Schmidt, pp. 505f., 517, 520.
[142] Ibid., pp. 507ff.
[143] Ibid., p. 511, lines 19ff.
[144] The specific phrase appears only in Gal. 6.16; but cf. Rom. 9.6ff.; 11.5; 17ff., I Cor. 10.18; Gal. 3.7; 4.28; Phil. 3.3, etc.
[145] I Cor. 1.9; 7.17ff.; Gal. 5.13, etc.
[146] Rom. 8.33; 16.3; I Thess. 1.4.
[147] Rom. 1.7; I Cor. 1.2; II Cor. 1.1; Phil. 1.1; Philemon 5, etc.
[148] I Cor. 3.16f.; II Cor. 6.16.
[149] Rom. 4.16; 9.7f.; Gal. 3.7ff., 29.
[150] Rom. 9.8; Gal. 4.28.
[151] Rom. 3.20ff. 28; 6.14f.; 7.4ff.; 8.2; 10.4, etc.

The Theological Significance of the Collection

Body in Christ',[152] 'the body of Christ'.[153] Corresponding to this was his frequent use of the phrase 'in Christ'[154] (also, 'in the Spirit').[155]

In using these phrases, Paul was not attempting to formulate a pedagogically illustrative analogy. On the contrary he employed the phrase in a literal sense: the Church *was* the Body of Christ. This was reflected in his theology of the sacraments. Baptism and the Lord's Supper were not simply cultic symbols or liturgical rituals but were real acts of participation in the Body of Christ.[156]

As the Church was the new Israel, the eschatological assembly of God in Christ, whose unity was possible only in Christ, so the concept of unity for Paul permeated every aspect of the life of the Church. The categories of distinction which held cardinal importance for the 'secular' world were meaningless within the Christian fellowship.[157] Although differing types of charismatic gifts and offices were granted to individual members to fulfil functions within the life of the community, this did not provide any basis for fundamentally distinguishing between such members.[158] Neither were factions or cliques to be tolerated, for they only caused dissension within the fellowship, thereby disrupting the unity in Christ by the disharmony they caused.[159] Just as there was one God[160] and one Lord Jesus Christ[161] and one Spirit,[162] so was there one gospel no matter who preached it.[163] Upon joining the one Body of Christ all were baptized by one Spirit[164] and accordingly partook of one Lord's Supper as the most intense experience of their oneness in and with Christ.[165]

[152] Rom. 12.5; I Cor. 10.17; 12.12f.; Gal. 3.28.
[153] I Cor. 12.27; cf. 1.13a; 6.15.
[154] Cf. A. Oepke, 'ἐν', ThWB II, sect. 3, pp. 537f.
[155] *Ibid.*, sect. 2, pp. 536f.
[156] Baptism: Rom. 6.3ff.; Gal. 3.27; Lord's Supper: I Cor. 10.16f.
[157] I Cor. 7.19; 12.13; Gal. 3.28; 5.6; etc.
[158] Rom. 12.7ff.; I Cor. 12.4ff., 27ff. Paul does list the gifts and functions in what appears to be a preferential order (cf. I Cor. 14.5). Yet the assessment is related to the functions themselves in terms of the contribution they made to the common life of the Body of Christ rather than to the person fulfilling the function. This is confirmed in the preceding chapter 13, when Paul located the *essential* valuation of all gifts and services expressed within the Christian community of their being fulfilled as acts of Christian love.
[159] I Cor. 1.13; 11.16, 18f.; II Cor. 12.20.
[160] Rom. 3.30; I Cor. 8.4, 6; Gal. 3.20.
[161] I Cor. 1.2; 8.6; 10.17; II Cor. 5.14f.
[162] I Cor. 6.17; 12.13.
[163] I Cor. 3.8, 11; II Cor. 11.4; Gal. 1.6ff.
[164] I Cor. 12.13.   [165] I Cor. 10.16f.

The Collection

C. *The Collection as an expression of the unity of the Church*

It is important for the following discussion of the significance of the collection for the unity of the Church to draw out from the preceding discussion the dominant theme. For Paul, the unity of the Church was directly and exclusively centred in the person of the Lord Jesus Christ. Christ gave unity, Christ maintained unity, only in Christ could unity be established and sustained. In this spirit Paul had come to agreement with the Jerusalem 'Pillars' and had given, as well as received, the 'right hand of fellowship'.[166]

It was precisely this awareness of the person of Christ as the exclusive source and foundation of Christian fellowship which Peter, in essence, rejected when he withdrew from the common table of the Antioch Christians because of the presence of Gentiles there. By his action Peter was saying that, although he did not consider the Law as being an essential requisite for the salvation of the Gentiles, yet for the sake of his Christ-commanded mission to the Jews it was necessary for him to disrupt the Christian fellowship. To Paul this involved a fundamental fallacy, for Peter's action asserted that the will of Christ (the proclamation to Israel) was destroying the will of Christ (the unconditional Christian fellowship). Therefore he judged Peter guilty of duplicity in regard to the gospel and accused him of a lack of personal integrity as evidenced by his inconsistency.[167]

Because Peter did not respond to Paul's remonstrances and thereby continued to perpetuate the serious schism which had suddenly been opened, three obvious possibilities presented themselves as a solution: (1) the Gentile Christians could voluntarily accept the requirements of the Mosaic Law upon themselves, become Jewish proselytes, and thereby restore the unity of the Christian fellowship, although it would then be based on faith in Christ *and* observance of the Law; (2) Paul and the Gentile Christians could leave things as they stood and accept the position of being inferior Christians and an embarrassing hindrance to the evangelization of Israel—this would mean that there could not be

---

[166] This appreciation of the nature and spirit of the agreement reached in Jerusalem suggests that the interpretation of the agreement as 'a piece of well-planned ecclesiastical strategy' which was pragmatically reached because both sides 'needed each other in difficult times ahead' (Holmes Rolston, *Stewardship in the New Testament Church*, Richmond, 1946, p. 69) must be rejected.

[167] Gal. 2.14.

The Theological Significance of the Collection

any direct relationship either with the Jewish Christians in Palestine or with any Jews in the Diaspora who were won to the new faith; (3) Paul could make a clean break with the Jewish Christians and organize his own independent Gentile Church, thereby creating two Bodies in Christ. All, of course, contradicted the basic fundamentals both of Paul's personal faith and of his sense of mission, and therefore had to be categorically rejected.

Instead, Paul chose a more difficult and less certain approach which, he earnestly hoped, would restore positive relations on an acceptable theological basis and at the same time be a witness to the whole civilized world of the genuineness of the Christian fellowship. The relief funds which had been sent from Antioch had served once as a clear and tangible testimony to the presence of the grace of God working in and through him among the Gentiles.[168] Paul decided to invest the collection project which he had agreed to undertake at the Jerusalem meeting with the same purpose. If, in spite of the adverse light in which his labours were regarded in Jerusalem, he could motivate his Gentile churches to contribute to the needs of the Jerusalem community out of single-minded, unadulterated, sincere love for the Jerusalem Christians, stimulated by the love of Christ in them, he could present their efforts in Jerusalem as unequivocal testimony, which for the latter to reject would require their denial also of the Lordship of Christ over his Church.[169]

The Gentile Christians as debtors to Jerusalem

When informing the Roman Christians of his collection project, of which the delivery to Jerusalem was the last task to be accomplished before he could come to them,[170] he described the participation of the Gentiles as being only just, in that they were debtors to the Jerusalem Christians.[171] From a superficial reading, this could appear to mean that he was subordinating Gentile to Jewish Christianity. But this is not the case.

It has been seen that Paul made a clear distinction between the

[168] See pp. 59f.
[169] This suggests that a deeper dimension was present in Paul's expression of anxiety over the possible rejection of his collection by the Jerusalem community (Rom. 15.31b). Not only would it mean that the fellowship of Paul and his Gentile Christians was thereby rebuffed, it would involve the Jerusalem Christians in a serious act of disobedience to Christ.
[170] Rom. 15.24f.
[171] Rom. 15.27.

The Collection

value of functions contributing to the life of the community and the persons fulfilling these functions.[172] The same evaluating criteria applied to contributions made to the Body of Christ by various segments of believers. Undoubtedly the function of the Jerusalem Christian community in serving as the source from which the gospel was disseminated to the rest of the Empire was worthy of higher valuation in terms of its contribution to the Body of Christ than the monetary support which the Gentile Christians were sending to Jerusalem in return.[173] But the motivating force behind both actions was the same: the impulse of Christian love.[174] Paul was using the term 'debtors' here as an expression for the responsibility of voluntary reciprocal sharing which to him was the essence of the communal relationship in the Christian fellowship.[175]

That this is the correct understanding of Paul's use of the term in connection with his collection project is even more clearly shown by his mention of Christ as a prototype for the participation of the Corinthians.[176] When he referred to the complete self-giving of Christ he was not urging them to reproduce the function which Christ had already accomplished once and for all, but rather they were to emulate the selflessness of their Lord.[177] From such a viewpoint, a mechanistic computation of the extent of debt in which one group of Christians stood in relation to another was irrelevant. Furthermore, Paul could imply that in the future such reciprocal sharing would continue,[178] for the debt of love was

---

[172] See n. 158 above.

[173] The same sort of reciprocity of gifts which were unequal in substance appears in I Cor. 9.10f., 14; Gal. 6.6; cf. Rom. 4.4; II Cor. 12.14.

[174] Compare the preceding verse, lit. 'to make a sharing'. In this context, cf. espec. Rom. 13.8: 'Owe no one anything, except to love one another,' in which the same Greek root word as is in 'debtors' is used.

[175] Paul's use of the word-group containing the idea of 'debt, owe' is restricted to (1) a statement concerning a person's obligation to God: Rom. 1.14 (of his own ministry); 8.12; 13.7 (of taxes to the State as God's servant); or, (2) of the responsible relationship of Christians to each other: Rom. 13.8f. (the opposite of trusting in the love of Christ is to trust in the Law whereby one is then obligated to the Law, Gal. 5.3); Rom. 11.7, 10 (in regard to orderly worship); 15.1; I Cor. 7.3, 36; 9.10 (cf. Rom. 4.4; II Cor. 12.14); II Cor. 12.11. Only in Philemon 18 is it directly related to money.

[176] II Cor. 8.9; cf. Rom. 15.3, 7 ff.; Phil. 2.4ff.

[177] H. Windisch (n. 51), *ad loc.*, considered that this verse interrupted Paul's line of thought. On the contrary, in verse 8 he had just spoken of 'genuine love' and in verse 9 he gave the most obvious illustration of the type of love he meant. Paul was here referring to the incarnation and humiliation of Jesus; cf. H. Lietzmann (n. 49), *ad loc.*

[178] II Cor. 8.14; 9.8, 10f.

The Theological Significance of the Collection

never fulfilled. So the Corinthians were assured that they would continue to share in the 'spiritual blessings' of the Jerusalem Christians.[179]

Because the common source and the definitive factor of all Christian sharing was love,[180] the sharing of the Jerusalem Christians and of the Gentile Christians, as viewed from the determinative perspective of motivation, was equal. There was no qualitative difference in the act. So Paul could consider the material contributions sent by his congregations to Jerusalem to be a source of blessing just as that which had been sent out from Jerusalem to them.

He expressed this conviction in his designation of the collection as εὐλογία.[181] Overwhelmingly in the New Testament the word-group to which this term belongs is oriented vertically to reflect the relationship between God and men.[182] The sense of 'blessing' must be retained in Paul's collection references.[183]

---

[179] II Cor. 8.14 hardly refers to future material support sent from Jerusalem to the Gentiles. The existing economic situation which existed there as well as the lack of any internal prospects for a significant improvement in the future excluded that (against J. Héring, n. 48 above, *ad loc.*; H. Windisch, *op. cit.*, *ad loc.*, but see his extensive discussion of the possibilities; H. Lietzmann, *op. cit.*, *ad loc.*). It could simply mean a further and deeper growth in the faith of the Corinthians, but Paul seemed to have had something more active on the part of the Jerusalem Christians in mind (J. Sickenberger, n. 99 above, *ad loc.*, suggested that Jerusalem would continue to supply spiritual blessings in the form of 'advice and deed, word and example, and intercession').

Probably Paul was making an eschatological reference to the Last Judgement (cf. Matt. 16.19; 19.28f.; Luke 22.29f.). Cf. P. Bachmann (n. 51), *ad loc.*, who pointed out that the phrase 'in the present time' in the first clause requires a counterpart ('in the end time'?) in the second (cf. Rom. 8.18). Cf. 9.6 where the 'reaping' is clearly eschatological (Windisch; Lietzmann).

It is significant that the riches Christ bestowed (v. 9) were also eschatological blessings of salvation, both already received and expected in the future. So Windisch, who, however, in commenting on the reciprocation which Paul encouraged the Corinthians to expect from Jerusalem, considered this interpretation but rejected it because the quotation in verse 15 did not fit. But within Paul's argumentative line, verse 15 belongs with verse 12, while 13f. constitutes a related remark inserted into the main flow of thought.

[180] See pp. 103f. above.

[181] II Cor. 9.5f. (three times).

[182] Only in dependence on Jesus' exhortation to 'bless those who curse you' (Luke 6.28; cf. Matt. 5.44 var.) does the term refer to a relationship between men: Rom. 12.14; I Cor. 4.12; cf. I Peter 3.9. Elsewhere it is an attribute of the Godhead, or an act of God to man, or an act of worship from man to God; cf. *ThWB* II, pp. 759ff. (by H. W. Beyer).

[183] Both Windisch (n. 51) and Lietzmann (n. 49) have correctly insisted on the retention of the original sense of the word as essential to a correct interpretation of Paul's statements. Literally it should be rendered 'gift of blessing'. Cf. also, H. L. Strack and P. Billerbeck, *Kommentar zum Neuen Testament aus Talmud und Midrasch*,

The Collection

He was using it in regard to the motivation with which the Corinthians contributed. Only if their participation was a free act of Christian love could their gift be a vehicle for the blessings of God. Furthermore, the blessings resulting from their action would flow both from themselves[184] and from Jerusalem to God[185] as well as from God to them.[186] The most urgently needed blessing which Paul foresaw was their reconciliation with the Jewish Christians and the restoration of the unity of the Body of Christ.[187] This was the 'fulness of the blessing of Christ' within which Paul anticipated arriving to visit the Roman church.[188]

Κοινωνία

Because Paul understood the fellowship of the Church to be an organic unity with and in Christ, κοινωνία and its related forms was an important term used in his writings to express the intimate relationship both of believers with Christ and of believers with

---

vol. III, on II Cor. 9.5. The prevailing translation is 'bounty' (KJV; ASV; NEB; RSV at 9.6) or 'willing gift' (RSV at 9.5).
Although the antithesis of 'sparingly' used in 9.6 appears to provide some substantiation for the above translations, it must again be insisted that Paul was *not* concerned with the *amount* of the collection. What he *was* concerned about was the *motivation* with which they gave. This is supported by the preceding verse where the antithesis to εὐλογία is πλεονεξία (= greediness, insatiableness, avarice, covetousness: A & G, p. 673). Paul was insisting that the act of giving be an ungrudging act of selflessness rather than one tainted by avaricious self-interest. Beyer, *op. cit.*, p. 761, emphasized that this term could be used for the collection 'because it proceeded from such unconditional love'. The following verse (v. 7) confirms this interpretation.

[184] II Cor. 9.13.   [185] II Cor. 9.11f.
[186] II Cor. 9.8ff.   [187] II Cor. 9.14.
[188] Rom. 15.29. This verse does not refer to a result of Paul's impending visit to Rome (so Sanday and Headlam; H. Lietzmann, both n. 84 above; P. Althaus, *Der Brief an die Römer*, 2nd ed., Göttingen, 1935; C. K. Barrett, *The Epistle to the Romans*, London, 1957). Neither is it adequate on the basis of Rom. 1.11 to interpret it as a personal ministration by Paul to the Romans (J. Sickenberger, n. 99 above; O. Michel, n. 91 above; Lietzmann, *op. cit.*).
The repetition of the verb 'come' testifies that the phrase 'in the fulness of the blessing of Christ' is a clause of accompanying circumstance. So also the grammatical structure (v. 28: *when* . . . accomplished, I shall go; v. 29: *when* I come, I shall come, etc.). The 'fulness of the blessing of Christ' is grammatically associated with the delivery of the collection in verse 28.
Furthermore Paul's implication in speaking of the '*fulness*' of the blessing of Christ is that, at the time of writing, the blessing of Christ was incomplete. The prevailing deficiency was indicated further on in verse 31, of which the second part is pertinent to this stage of the study. That is, Paul was counting on the testimony of his collection to impel the Jewish Christians to recognize the Gentiles as genuine Christian brothers, thereby closing the breach in the unity of the Church. (See below, pp. 141f. for further discussion of this important phrase.)

The Theological Significance of the Collection

each other. In every use which he made of the word-group, this theological orientation was retained.[189] It is therefore highly significant for the purpose of establishing the interpretation of his collection project as an expression of the unity of the Church that he used this term in connection with and as a designation for that project.[190]

Three distinct nuances have been discerned in Paul's use of this word-group: (*a*) participate in, have a share in; (*b*) give a share, 'communicate'; (*c*) fellowship, communion.[191] The term expressed the state of the Christian relationship (*c*) as well as the reciprocity inherent in the relationship (*b*, giving; *a*, receiving).

The most determinative use of the term for the sense of the other Pauline applications was in the context of his discussion of the sacrament of the Lord's Supper.[192] In this passage the term expressed the relationship of believers with Christ and with each other, significantly welded together in the momentous liturgical expression of the Christian fellowship.

Against this background of organic fellowship in and with Christ are to be understood the other Pauline uses. Christians are called to participation in and with Christ,[193] to share in the blessings of the gospel,[194] to participate in the Spirit.[195] Also expressive of sharing in and with Christ are the expressions Paul employed of verbs compounded with 'with'.[196]

As fellowship with Christ inseparably comprehends fellowship with other Christians,[197] so Paul used κοινωνία to underline the aspect of mutual fellowship between Christians in various situations within the life of the Church. He applied it to the ceremonial handclasp with which he and the Jerusalem 'Pillars' formally

---

[189] The only exception in which the term appears in Pauline literature without this theological reference is II Cor. 6.14, which is probably not of Pauline origin; cf. H. Windisch (n. 51), pp. 211f.; H. Seesemann (n. 57), p. 99.
[190] Rom. 15.26f.; II Cor. 8.4; 9.13.
[191] Cf. H. Seesemann, *op. cit.*, pp. 24ff., 99; F. Hauck, *ThWB* III, pp. 804ff.
[192] I Cor. 10.16ff.; cf. Hauck, pp. 805f. Seesemann, p. 103, suspected this use by Paul to be the point of origin for his singular use of the term elsewhere.
[193] I Cor. 1.9; cf. Seesemann's interpretation of the use of the term here with a genitive of person: pp. 47ff. Cf. also, 'share in his suffering', Phil. 3.10; cf. II Cor. 1.5, 7; Phil. 1.7; 4.14.
[194] I Cor. 9.23. This involves at the same time a sharing with others in the faith; cf. Phil. 1.5; Philemon 6.
[195] II Cor. 13.13; Phil. 2.1. Not 'fellowship implemented by the Spirit', cf. Seesemann, pp. 56ff.; Hauck, p. 807.
[196] Rom. 6.4ff.; 8.17; II Cor. 7.3.
[197] I Cor. 10.17 in the context of verses 16ff.

The Collection

certified their agreement to embark the missionary enterprise in two directions.[198] On the other end of the spectrum it expressed the close, personal relationship between Paul and another individual, which (in keeping with the consistent theological emphasis by Paul) was at the same time a fellowship in the gospel.[199] Within the Christian fellowship, sharing the burdens and ministering to the needs of others had its honoured place.[200]

The most significant factor in the above discussion is that no matter to what situation, function, or relationship within the life of the Church this term referred, κοινωνία was always inseparably bound to and directly expressive of the fellowship of Christ.

This held true for Paul's collection also. Whether he used the term to refer to the act of involvement (participate, have a share in),[201] or to the act of imparting (give a share, communicate),[202] or to the expression of the relationship (fellowship),[203] it was always solidly anchored in the fellowship of Christ and reflected that context. The use of such a concept to refer to the relationship between congregations was a logical extension of Paul's profound appreciation of its significance for the dynamic relationship between the believer and Christ. His application of it to the collection project testifies to the deep concern he felt about the tense and suspicious relationship existing between the two branches of the Church and to his ardent longing that the fissure be eliminated.

This is undoubtedly the cause behind two constructions he used which are grammatically intricate. In Rom. 15.26 he used the noun modified by an indefinite pronoun in connection with the infinitive of the verb 'to make' which produces the singular literal result: 'they were pleased to make a certain communicativeness'.[204]

---

[198] Gal. 2.9.
[199] Philemon 17; cf. II Cor. 8.23; cf. also the designation, 'fellow worker' (συνεργός) II Cor. 8.23; Philemon 1, 24, et al.
[200] Rom. 12.13; Gal. 6.6. The first passage is an exhortation to share in the needs of the saints, whereby not just sympathy but material assistance is certainly intended; the second deals with the sharing of sustenance (good things) with the teachers in the community. Yet both really belong together, for whether the situation involved reciprocal sharing or one-sided charity both instances were to be met within the controlling context of fellowship in Christ. Such was the case with Paul and the Philippian Christians. They shared in his burdens and needs (Phil. 1.7; 4.14f.; cf. 2.25) which was an essential expression of their fellowship in the faith (Phil. 1.5).
[201] Rom. 15.27; II Cor. 8.4.
[202] Rom. 15.26; II Cor. 9.13.
[203] Gal. 2.9f.
[204] That the accent is on active 'sharing' is confirmed by contrast to the passive 'have shared' in the next verse. The linguistic difficulty is that the verb 'to make'

The Theological Significance of the Collection

Paul's animated discussion of the enthusiastic response of the Macedonians produced one sentence in which he heaped so many theologically significant terms together (grace, 'fellowship', ministry, saints) that the cumulative effect is one of critical import.[205]

Since Paul's use of κοινωνία was consistently controlled by his appreciation of the fellowship of all believers in and with Christ, his use of the term in connection with his collection was an expression of the legitimate Christian character of the Gentiles' sharing. They were valid Christians who themselves were caught up in the fellowship of Christ, and from this context were sending aid to Jerusalem out of genuine Christian concern for other Christians. It was therefore a tangible insistence on their solidarity with the Jewish Christians in the Body of Christ in spite of the reservations which the latter felt towards them.[206]

The emphasis on free will

Because the collection was to testify in Jerusalem to the genuineness of the incorporation of the Gentiles into the people of God, it was essential for Paul that their participation in the collection be of their own free will. Only then would the gift exemplify their Christian love and concern for the Jerusalem Christians motivated by the love of Christ for them. Just as Paul had voluntarily agreed to initiate the project,[207] so were they voluntarily to fulfil it.

The instructions which Paul wrote in I Cor. 16.1ff. do not contradict this emphasis. He was not establishing a rigid technique which was intended to control their participation. Rather he was

---

requires a concrete object, which has led both Seesemann, pp. 28f., 67, and Hauck, p. 809, to suggest that Paul used the term in a concrete sense (= collection), but without surrendering the religious significance which it conveyed. Cf. O. Michel (n. 91); E. Gaugler, *Der Römerbrief*, Zürich, 1952.

[205] II Cor. 8.4. The meaning of κοινωνία in this verse is dependent on the interpretation of 'grace' with which it is connected. If grace retains its primary theological significance of the free gift of God' (as it probably does, cf. v. 1; see below, pp. 135f.), then Paul was saying that they considered the opportunity to help the Jerusalem Christians to be a gift of God's grace to them, and κοινωνία has the sense of 'fellowship' with the accent on 'sharing in'. Cf. Seesemann, pp. 67f.; cf. Hauck, p. 809, who lists it under the general heading of 'giving a share'; also H. Windisch (n. 51); H. Lietzmann (n. 49).

[206] With reference again (see also n. 188 above) to Paul's expression of anxiety over the acceptance by the Jerusalem Christians of the collection (Rom. 15.31b), their rejection of the collection would involve rejection of the person of Christ as the sole source and basis of Christian fellowship.

[207] Gal. 2.10. The collection was instigated within the context and atmosphere of the agreement reached there, which in turn was an expression of mutually recognized Christian fellowship (Gal. 2.9).

The Collection

recommending to them measures which he knew, from his experience with the Galatian Christians, would facilitate their contributing. The instructions were intended to be a means to help them plan wisely and in advance, so that when the time came to accumulate the individual contributions for transportation to Jerusalem, no one would have to decimate the funds necessary for his own subsistence in order to participate. By using the phrase 'as he may prosper', Paul was clearly leaving the decision as to the extent of their participation up to them.[208]

In II Corinthians Paul waxed eloquent on the subject of freewill participation, necessitated undoubtedly by the need to counteract any wrong impression which might result from his expressions of concern over the hitherto poor response to the collection in Corinth. The real value of the Macedonians' performance lay in their enthusiastic, spontaneous, sincere[209] response[210] which was a direct result of and witness to their commitment to Christ.[211] So the self-giving love of Christ was to be the controlling motivation also for the response of the Corinthian Christians.[212]

It was this desire to emphasize the motivation and not the amount of the performance which resulted in Paul's illogical approbation of their 'willing' over their 'doing'.[213] The initial reaction of the Corinthians had been an enthusiastic response of Christian love,[214] but their subsequent indolence in advancing the project indicated that they had lost this initial perspective. Accordingly, Paul exhorted them to let their initial enthusiasm again become dominant and to embody it with tangible results.[215]

---

[208] Cf. A. Robertson and A. Plummer, *First Epistle of St Paul to the Corinthians* (ICC), 2nd ed., Edinburgh, 1914, ad loc.; O. Schmitz, *Urchristliche Gemeindenöte*, Berlin, 1939, p. 215.
[209] ʽΑπλότης, II Cor. 8.2; cf. above, pp. 104f.
[210] II Cor. 8.5.   [211] II Cor. 8.5.   [212] II Cor. 8.9.
[213] II Cor. 8.10. Cf. H. Windisch (n. 51); also J. Héring, (n. 48); P. Bachmann (n. 51). Against H. Lietzmann (n. 49), who held that Paul considered the doing more important and simply expressed himself clumsily here; W. L. Knox (n. 112), p. 339, n. 13, who maintained that 'In order to avoid saying anything which might lead to soreness of feeling among the Corinthians he expresses himself *as though* the first enthusiasm was the really important thing' (Italics mine).
[214] Cf. 9.2; cf. I Thess. 4.9f.
[215] II Cor. 8.11f. In verse 11, the 'readiness to will' (ASV) is the initiating impulse, the 'doing' is the completion, the fulfilment. Both are incorporated within the motivation, 'to will'. Verse 12 again emphasizes that the worth of the performance is in the motivation and not in the external amount which resulted. From Paul's point of view the will to do something and the doing (in so far as it was possible) were inseparable within the context of the Christian fellowship.

The Theological Significance of the Collection

The same emphasis is evident in the following chapter. The previous zeal which the Corinthians had evidenced in response to the collection project had been so great that, by its example, the enthusiasm of the Macedonians had been stimulated.[216] Paul was himself partly responsible for this in that he had boasted of their Christ-inspired enthusiasm.[217] He therefore sent his associates in the project to them to revitalize their commitment to Christ in order that their participation in the collection would be a sincere expression of the love of the Lord[218] rather than grudgingly given by them because they felt they had to.[219] In addition he assured them that as their sincere, wholehearted participation in this project reflected their total commitment to the love of Christ, so God in his loving providence would not only supply their own needs but also the means for them to continue such tangible expressions of Christian love and concern in the future.[220]

Because it was only by the volitionary participation of his churches that the collection would testify to the genuineness of their faith in Christ and thereby confront the Jerusalem Christians with the undeniable fact of the legitimacy of their membership in the Body of Christ, it was of the utmost importance to Paul that the Gentiles contributed sincerely and of their own free will.

The Collection as proof

Paul explicitly expressed the significance which he hoped the collection would bear as testimony to the Jerusalem Christians of the genuine participation of the Gentiles in the salvation of the gospel. He urged[221] the Corinthians to use this opportunity as a means of demonstrating their love and of verifying Paul's boasting on their behalf.[222] Those to whom they were to show their love were the three associates whom Paul was sending to them. Two

---

[216] II Cor. 9.2. This is to be understood as a complementary and not contradictory element to their primarily God-inspired enthusiasm as described in 8.1ff.
[217] II Cor. 9.3.
[218] II Cor. 9.5, cf. the interpretation of this verse above, n. 183. On this basis one may conclude that the primary task of those whom Paul sent was to revive the half-hearted faith of the Corinthians (cf. 8.6, 16f., 23f.), and, as an outgrowth of that, to resurrect the defunct collection project.
[219] II Cor. 9.6f.
[220] II Cor. 9.7bff.
[221] II Cor. 8.24.
[222] He boasted of the zeal with which they had responded to the collection project out of their earlier deep appreciation of the love of Christ, II Cor. 8.11f.; 9.2.

The Collection

of these three were official representatives of the Jewish Christians.[223] That he was referring to the collection and not to their personal relationship with his fellow workers is established by an earlier remark made when he was citing the exemplary performance of the Macedonians. As the Corinthian Christians excelled in every other spiritual expression of the Christian life, so were they to excell in this 'grace' also. The way to prove that their Christian love was genuine was, as the Macedonians had already done, to enter sincerely and earnestly into the collection.[224]

Later he more specifically related the effect which the collection was intended to have on the Jewish Christians.[225] When the delivery was made to Jerusalem the Christians there would not only have their financial plight relieved[226] but would also be moved to profusely praise God. That which would provoke these thanksgivings would be their recognition of the 'proof', as conveyed in the collection, of (*a*) the genuine faith in the gospel of Christ to which the Gentiles had been called; and (*b*) the reality and sincerity of the Christian fellowship existing between the two segments of the Body of Christ as evidenced by the ingenuousness of the Christian concern of the Gentiles for their Jewish partners in the faith. It would also evoke the response in them of cherished appreciation and intercession for their Gentile brothers.

It was from this context that Paul made the somewhat obscure figurative statement about 'sealing to them this fruit' in Romans.[227] His intent is clear. He was saying, 'When I have com-

---

[223] See above pp. 18ff. H. Windisch (n. 51), correctly noted that, for Paul, the 'churches' were present in the person of those whom they had sent.

[224] II Cor. 8.7f. H. Lietzmann (n. 49) considered it grammatically possible to translate the verse, 'proving through your earnestness for others . . .', which does give added clarity to the statement.

[225] II Cor. 9.13ff. Cf. P. Bachmann; H. Windisch (both n. 51).

[226] This would be the source of any gratitude which they might feel toward the Gentile Christians. It is significant that gratitude on this level plays almost no role in Paul's discussions of his project. He was not interested in making the Jewish Christians feel beholden or dependent for support upon the Gentile Christians and thereby use their indebtedness as a lever to force an appearance of solidarity which did not flow directly from the love of Christ.

[227] 15.28 (ASV). The opaqueness of the imagery which Paul used has produced much consternation in commentators trying to explain what he meant. Least probable of the explanations is that the passage should be interpreted literally as an act to ensure safe delivery (E. Barnikol, *Römer 15—Letzte Reiseziele des Paulus: Jerusalem, Rom und Antiochien*, Kiel, 1931, p. 22; cf. C. K. Barrett, n. 188 above). On the interpretation followed above, cf. T. Zahn (n. 91) *ad loc.*; R. Schumacher, *Die beiden letzten Kapiteln des Römerbriefs* (= Neutestamentliche Abhandlungen, Vol. XIV, No. 4), Münster, 1929, pp. 45f.

The Theological Significance of the Collection

pleted delivery of the collection, I will stop by you on my way to Spain.' But the vocabulary he chose indicates that implicitly he had something deeper in mind. The term 'fruit' was used by Paul predominantly in a figurative sense,[228] of which three instances refer to the result of Paul's ministry,[229] which is the sense it bears in this passage also. This interpretation is supported by the expression 'seal', which Paul used elsewhere to affirm that his ministry was authenticated by God[230] of which his Gentile Christians were the confirmation.[231] In this passage is reflected Paul's hope that the collection would move the Jerusalem Christians to recognize the full and present validity of his mission to the Gentiles.

In brief, by organizing the collection and insisting that participation in it be a volitionary act of Christian love expressing the reciprocal concern inherent to the Christian fellowship, Paul relied on it to testify to the Jerusalem Christians of the real and full inclusion of Gentile believers into the Body of Christ. He further trusted that this testimony would be so unequivocal that they would be moved to restore complete and unconditional bonds of fellowship with the Gentiles.

3. THE ESCHATOLOGICAL SIGNIFICANCE OF THE COLLECTION

There is no way to determine what the monetary results of Paul's collection were. However, in two of the main areas involved circumstances existed which indicate that the amount given was not great. Macedonia was itself suffering under severe poverty, aggravated by the persecution to which the Christians there were being subjected. Corinth, the chief city of Achaia, probably gave a meagre contribution, as it had finally implemented the project only a relatively short time before Paul himself arrived to organize the delivery trip to Jerusalem. Therefore, one may assume that the

---

[228] Of the nine instances in which it occurs (Rom. 1.13; 6.21f.; 15.28; I Cor. 9.7; Gal. 5.22; Phil. 1.11, 22; 4.17), only once (the Cor. passage) does it have the literal sense of botanical produce. In Rom. 6.21f.; Gal. 5.22; Phil. 1.11 the reference is to the new orientation of life from faith in Christ and its expressions.
[229] Rom. 1.13; Phil. 1.22; 4.17.
[230] II Cor. 1.22.
[231] I Cor. 9.2. The only other use Paul made of the term was in reference to the circumcision of Abraham as the confirming sign of his justification by faith, Rom. 4.11.

actual sum of money was not extraordinarily large, although any amount would undoubtedly have been welcomed by the Jerusalem Christians as relief for their crucial financial situation.

It is all the more amazing that Paul took with him such a large retinue of delegates from the contributing churches[232] to deliver the collection in Jerusalem. Such an endeavour not only demanded much of the Apostle's time and energy to organize but also involved a sizeable outlay of money for travel and sustenance at the expense of an already slender collection. Such an undertaking could only be assessed as an unjustifiable extravagance unless Paul had some other, overriding reason, which was of such paramount importance that these disadvantages were nullified.

The factor of providing protection to ensure secure delivery, while perhaps being a secondary consideration, was not sufficient in itself to warrant the expense of the large group. It has been seen above[233] that those accompanying Paul corresponded to men appointed in local Jewish communities in the Diaspora to accompany the delivery of the Temple tax to Jerusalem. The latter were not appointed primarily for security reasons[234] but to represent their community at the sacrifices offered in the Temple for the nation.

It is in this capacity of serving as representatives for their communities in Jerusalem that the envoys accompanying Paul are to be understood. This function was not, of course, to be fulfilled at the focal point of cultic Judaism, the Temple. Therefore the import of their representation must be sought elsewhere. Johannes Munck[235] has shown the direction that such an inquiry must take, by establishing that this delegation directly proceeded from Paul's understanding of the role his mission to the Gentiles was to fulfil in God's redemptive economy, particularly with regard to the salvation of Israel.

A. *The position of Gentiles within Jewish eschatology*

As understood by the Old Testament writers,[236] the position in which the 'nations' stood over against Israel was twofold. In so

[232] On the delegates, cf. pp. 68f. above.
[233] No. 3, p. 88.
[234] The official evaluation of their capabilities as guards against banditry was rather low; cf. p. 83 above, n. 65.
[235] *Paul and the Salvation of Mankind*, London, 1959.
[236] Cf. A. Jepsen, 'Eschatologie im AT', *RGG*³ II, espec. 2c, col. 657; 3b, cols. 659f.

The Theological Significance of the Collection

far as they composed the hostile forces seeking to hinder and destroy the Divine Will with regard to his Chosen People, Israel looked to their eventual annihilation as political powers and their utter condemnation before God's Judgement Seat. The dominating concept which found especially strong emphasis in the prophetic literature was, that as God was the God not just of a nation but of his whole creation, so was his salvation ultimately intended for all men. The '*heilsgeschichtlich*' sequence by which this was to be accomplished was, first, that Israel was to repent and be restored in the divinely intended relationship with God, and then, through Israel, God's call to repentence and salvation would be mediated to the Gentile nations.[237] With their response, the distinctive differentiation between Israel and the Gentiles would be eradicated.

The same two elements were present within the eschatological expectations of first-century Judaism, but the emphasis was reversed. Relatively seldom does one meet unconditionally positive attitudes towards the participation of the nations in God's salvation.[238] The dominant opinion, made even more acute by Jewish resentment of long years of oppression under the various heathen political powers, was that of the complete destruction of the nations through the terrible wrath of God as revenge for Israel's suffering. The only possibility of escape for Gentiles was through their becoming a part of Israel, whereby their position was one of being inferior servants to God's Chosen People.[239] It was this view, prevalent in the Judaism out of which the Christian faith developed, that was in the background of the Jewish hostility which was alienating the Jerusalem church from Paul's mission to the Gentiles.[240]

In his ministry and teaching Jesus rejected the predominant Jewish attitude concerning the eschatological fate of the Gentiles. Instead he revitalized the emphasis prevailing in the Old Testament that the Kingdom of God was to include all men, and he laid

[237] Cf. F. Hahn, *Mission in the New Testament*, London, 1965, p. 19, and the literature and biblical citations there. But cf. R. Chasles, *Israel und die Weltvölker*, Stuttgart, 1945.
[238] Cf. P. Volz (n. 130), pp. 358f.; F. Hahn, *op. cit.*, p. 21.
[239] Volz, pp. 357f.; cf. W. L. Knox (n. 112), pp. 24, n. 51; 26, n. 57.
[240] I.e. the 'false-brethren', Gal. 2.3ff., see pp. 46ff. above; the 'men from James', Gal. 2.12, see pp. 64ff. above; the 'different gospel' of Paul's opponents in Galatia, Gal. 1.6; cf. 3.1ff., 10, 28f.; 4.12, 21, 31; etc.

particular weight on the participation of the Gentiles in redemption.[241] Nevertheless, he retained and adapted the Old Testament scheme of, first, the conversion of Israel, and then, through redeemed Israel, the conversion of the nations. It was this expectation which moulded the direction of his own ministry[242] and prompted his limiting instructions to his disciples.[243] Accordingly this persuasion governed the form and direction of the missionary task of the early Church, and it was against such authority that Paul had to contend to validate in their eyes his mission to the Gentiles which they regarded as premature.

B. *Paul's apostleship to the Gentiles*

Paul's self-awareness of having been directly called by God to the specific task of proclaiming the gospel to the Gentiles was inseparably connected with his own conversion experience.[244] His conversion involved a radical reorientation from a trust in the efficacy of the fulfilment of the Law to gain righteousness to an unconditioned dependence on the freely-given grace of God in Christ apart from the Law.[245] This perception of salvation coming to men solely through the unlimited grace of God in Christ remained constant as the fundamental thrust of Paul's proclamation throughout his missionary activity. The direction which Paul took in proclaiming the gospel of salvation to the Gentiles, unrestricted by the requirements of the Law which would have, to all practical purposes, excluded them, was a natural consequence of his own encounter with the Risen Lord.

But Paul considered his mission to the Gentiles to have been based on something more explicit than just a logical extension of his own conversion experience. His apostleship was the result of a specific commission from God to carry the good news of salvation to the Gentiles. This God-given direction to his efforts was not simply a pragmatic ordinance but was of essential significance in

[241] Cf. J. Jeremias (n. 127), pp. 46ff. In the famous 'cleansing of the Temple' account (Mark 11.15-17, par.) Jesus cleared the Court of the Gentiles for the eschatological influx when the nations would come to worship God; cf. E. Lohmeyer, *Lord of the Temple*, Edinburgh, 1961, pp. 36ff.; F. Hahn, (n. 237), p. 36.

[242] J. Jeremias, *op. cit.*, pp. 25ff.

[243] *Ibid.*, pp. 19ff.

[244] Espec. Gal. 1.15f.: 'But when he who had set me apart before I was born, and had called me through his grace, was pleased to reveal his Son to me, in order that I might preach him among the Gentiles. . . .'

[245] Phil. 3.7ff.; cf. G. Bornkamm, 'Paulus', 2b, c, *RGG*³ V, cols. 171ff.

The Theological Significance of the Collection

the consummation of God's redemptive intent. His awareness that his task comprised an indispensable element within the '*Heilsgeschichte*' was reflected in his application in reference to his apostleship of a mode of expression employed by the prophets to depict their sense of being chosen to a special task by God.[246]

c. The Gentile Christians in the 'Heilsgeschichte'

In Rom. 9–11, Paul developed his understanding of the role to which the Gentile Christians had been appointed in the divine economy of salvation. His understanding was based on an element in the Old Testament which, although subsidiary to the dominant emphasis,[247] was none the less clearly set forth. It was the articulated reversal of the order in which God's redemption would be received. Because Israel was so stubborn and self-reliant, God would take from them the ability to hear his Word.[248] Only after it had found response from a people strange to the promises to Israel[249] would it then be again proclaimed to Israel.

Further, the instruments God would use to proclaim his salvation to Israel would be those Gentiles for whom, originally, Israel was to have been the instrument of blessing.[250] In the prophets this view resulted from a desire to stress the awfulness of the judgement of God on Israel for its unfaithfulness. But for Paul it provided the touchstone which gave unique direction, vigour, and purpose to his labours.

The discussion which Paul presented in Rom. 9–11 shows that the question of the meaning behind his successful apostleship to the Gentiles over against the relatively unsuccessful mission of the Jewish Christians to Israel was a problem to which he had devoted much contemplation. He could not accept the apparent exclusion of Israel from the salvation of God as being final.[251] He was much

---

[246] Gal. 1.15; cf. espec. Isa. 49.1ff., where the phrase is immediately associated with the proclamation of salvation to the nations; also Jer. 1.5. Munck (n. 235), pp. 36ff., found additional support for this aspect of his study in II Thess. 2.6f., based on an article by O. Cullmann: 'Le caractère eschatologique du devoir missionaire et de la conscience apostolique de S. Paul. Étude sur le κατέχον (-ων) de II Thess. 2.6–7', *Revue d'Histoire et de Philosophie religieuses*, Strasbourg, 1936, who developed the thesis that the 'one restraining' the anti-Godly forces whose active hostility and destruction was to herald the End was Paul himself.
[247] See above, pp. 130f.
[248] Rom. 9.33 (cf. Isa. 28.16); 10.21 (cf. Isa. 65.2); 11.8 (cf. Isa. 29.10).
[249] Rom. 9.25f. (cf. Hos. 2.23; 1.10); 10.20 (cf. Isa. 65.1).
[250] Rom. 10.19 (cf. Deut. 32.21); cf. 11.11ff.
[251] Rom. 11.1, 11f., 29.

The Collection

too concerned for them[252] and was convinced that the destiny of his work among the Gentiles was to ultimately effect the conversion of the Jews.[253] So he summarized his argument by writing, 'a hardening has come upon part of Israel, until the full number of the Gentiles come in, and so all Israel will be saved'.[254]

D. The Collection project and the conversion of Israel

It must be insisted that Paul's announcement in Romans[255] of his impending trip to Jerusalem to deliver the collection did not comprise an abrupt shift from lofty to mundane matters. Rather it is directly connected to the preceding 'theological' material of the whole epistle, and refers particularly back to the discussion of the role of the Gentile mission for the conversion of Israel in chapters 9-11.[256]

This is substantiated by the fact that Paul took up the theme of the '*heilsgeschichtlich*' significance of his ministry once again in the material immediately preceding his discussion of his project.[257] From his standpoint the gospel had been preached to the nations from Jerusalem to Rome.[258] His 'priestly service' in preparing the 'offering of the Gentiles' was completed in this area.[259] He was therefore free to make the long-desired visit to Rome on his way to the virgin mission field of Spain at the edge of the Empire.[260] But before he could enter on this last phase, it was necessary to convey the collection and the representatives of the Gentile

---

[252] Rom. 9.1ff.; 10.1ff.
[253] Rom. 11.13ff., 23f.
[254] Rom. 11.25f.
[255] Rom. 15.25ff.
[256] Cf. K. Barth, *The Epistle to the Romans*, London, 1933, p. 534; G. Schrenk (n. 112), pp. 99ff.; J. Munck (n. 235), pp. 287ff.; F. Hahn (n. 237), p. 107.
[257] Rom. 15.14ff.
[258] Rom. 15.19, 23.
[259] Rom. 15.16. This corresponded to the 'full number of the Gentiles' in 11.25. On the basis of the understanding that the Gentile collection and the delegates accompanying its delivery represented the 'full number of the Gentiles' resulting from Paul's ministry, which he described as a sacrificial offering, it is possible that the variant reading in 15.31 of δωροφορία (in the Western MSS group: B, D, G) was the original (so B. Weiss, n. 107 above, *ad loc.*). The term was apparently associated with gifts dedicated for cultic sacrificial purposes (cf. O. Michel, n. 91 above, *ad loc.*). Although a later copier may have understood the collection as an embodiment of 11.25 and 15.16 and therefore made the change to emphasize it, it seems more likely that the sacrifical term was original and was replaced by 'ministry', a more familiar designation which Paul had repeatedly used with reference to his project (Rom. 15.25; II Cor. 8.4; 9.1, 12, 13).
[260] Rom. 15.22ff. K. Barth (n. 256), p. 534, described the whole scheme as sketched out by Paul here to be 'more apocalyptic than rational'.

The Theological Significance of the Collection

Christian churches back to Jerusalem as the irrefutable evidence to Israel that the 'Gentiles who did not pursue righteousness have attained it, that is, righteousness through faith.'[261]

Χάρις

The key concept in Paul's understanding of why Israel, who had received the promises, was caused to reject the salvation of God, while the Gentiles, who were 'not God's people', received salvation, was the χάρις of God.[262] It is therefore highly significant that precisely this same term was so often used in his discussion of his collection.[263]

The Pauline concept of the 'grace of God' stands primarily over against the concept of the 'wrath of God'. As God's wrath is not a hostile disposition but is the *act* of a divine judgement, so the 'grace of God' is not a friendly disposition which overcomes that hostility but an *act* of God which saves man from the present reality of God's wrath.[264] The 'love of God' and 'the mercy of God' are complementary concepts which also retain the predominant sense of a divine act.

The grace of God is given through the cross of Christ.[265] It is this gracious act of God in Christ which was determinative for Paul's use of the word, and in terms of which all other Pauline references to grace must be understood.[266] Through the Spirit, this act of God in Christ is made comprehensible to men[267] who, when they have received it,[268] live freed from bondage to this world and particularly to the Law.[269] Thus the grace of God constitutes a new orientation in which they stand and which controls their common life together[270] and the functions which they, individually, contribute to it.[271]

As the grace of God in Christ possessed Paul himself completely,

---

[261] Rom. 9.31; cf. also 10.12; see F. Hahn (n. 237), p. 109.
[262] Cf., e.g., Rom. 11.5f.; cf. 3.21ff.; 5.15ff.; etc.
[263] I Cor. 16.3; II Cor. 8.1, 4, 6, 7, 9, 19; 9.8, 14.
[264] R. Bultmann (n. 113), pp. 387ff.
[265] Rom. 3.24ff.
[266] W. Manson, 'Grace in the New Testament', *The Doctrine of Grace*, ed. by W. T. Whitley, London, 1932, pp. 44f., 59f.
[267] I Cor. 2.12; in the context of chapter 2 the reference is clearly to the crucifixion.
[268] II Cor. 6.1.
[269] Rom. 4.4; 5.16ff.; 6.14f.; 11.6; II Cor. 1.12; etc.
[270] Rom. 5.2; Gal. 5.4.
[271] Rom. 12.6; I Cor. 1.4f.; 12.1ff.

The Collection

so was it the source, power, and direction of his ministry.[272] This found its most concrete expression with reference to his mission to the Gentiles.[273]

Although Paul used 'grace' in a variety of ways in connection with his collection project,[274] it was always closely related to the free gift of redemption in Jesus Christ. As proof of 'the surpassing grace of God' in the Gentiles,[275] the collection was an unmistakable witness to the fact that salvation had come to the Gentiles, for those who had eyes to see and ears to hear. The collection was not only a verification of the grace of Paul's ministry and evidence that the grace of God had been given to the Gentiles. It was even more than an incorporation of this grace as expressed through their Christian fellowship and concern for the Jewish Christians, inspired by the grace of Christ. It was, itself, a conveying instrument of the saving grace of God to Israel in that, through it, they would become members of the Israel of the promise. The collection as a 'blessing gift'[276] was equal, both in motivating intent and functional contribution in the Body of Christ, to the 'spiritual' things for which the Gentiles were indebted to Jerusalem.[277]

The anticipated results of the project

The sequence of events initiated by the delivery of the collection, as Paul expected them to occur, may be reconstructed as follows: The testimony of the collection to the genuine Christian love and concern in the Gentiles for the Jewish Christians instigated by the love of Christ would remove all reservation from the attitudes of the latter and an unqualified reconciliation would occur. At the same time, the witness of the Gentile delegates to the reality of their reception of redemption would, by provoking jealousy among the Jews, revitalize the hitherto ineffectual mission to Israel and prompt their acceptance of the gospel. In the meantime Paul would have gone on to Spain and proclaimed Christ at that edge of the civilized world. Thus the presuppositions for the consummation of the End, in so far as men were instrumentally involved, would be fulfilled.

[272] I Cor. 15.10; II Cor. 12.9. Cf. W. Manson, *op. cit.*, pp. 46f.
[273] Rom. 1.5; 12.3; 15.15; I Cor. 1.4; 3.10; Gal. 1.15f.; 2.7ff.
[274] See pp. 109f. above.
[275] II Cor. 9.14.
[276] II Cor. 9.5f.; cf. pp. 121f. above.
[277] Rom. 15.27.

The Theological Significance of the Collection

That Paul had embodied his desire for the conversion of Israel within his collection project and expected its delivery to be of cardinal import in the realization of that desire is reflected in two references which he made to Old Testament passages in II Cor. 9.10: 'He who supplies seed to the sower and bread for food will supply and multiply your sowing and increase the harvest of your righteousness.' The first half of the verse was taken from Isa. 55.10. That portion of Isaiah is concerned with the participation of the nations in the redemptive purpose of God.[278] Furthermore, the quotation itself is there used to illustrate the effective fruitfulness of the Word of God that does not return empty, but 'it shall accomplish that which I purpose, and prosper in the thing for which I sent it.'[279] The second half of Paul's verse was taken from Hos. 10.12. Again the context is significant. Hosea 10 speaks of the proportionate increase in the unfaithfulness of Israel to God as their land and nation prospers. Judgement of destruction and desolation is therefore proclaimed against them. Within this context they are exhorted to 'sow for yourselves righteousness, reap the fruit of steadfast love; . . . for it is the time to seek the Lord, that he may come and rain salvation upon you'.[280]

The combination of the two quotations in II Cor. 9.10 exactly corresponded to Paul's conviction that the effectiveness of the Word of God among the Gentiles was of instrumental significance for the conversion of Israel. In that verse Paul was referring not to an increase in funds, but was assuring the Corinthian Christians that their involvement in the project would be used by God to produce an abundant harvest in connection with the proclamation of the gospel of redemption among Israel.

It was this factor which Paul expected to result in the offering of 'many thanksgivings to God'.[281] The thanksgivings would be called forth not simply because the Jerusalem Christians had received financial assistance,[282] but much more, through its witness to the salvation of the Gentiles, their mission to convert Israel would prosper. The thanksgivings to God would flow not only from them but from those previously 'disobedient',[283] who

[278] Isa. 55.4f.
[279] Isa. 55.10f.
[280] Hos. 10.12.
[281] II Cor. 9.11f.
[282] Mark the intensification of 'not only . . . but also' in verse 12.
[283] Rom. 15.31.

The Collection

were impelled to faith out of jealousy, and thereby shared in the salvation of God.

The role of the delegates

The delegates from the contributing Gentile churches, who accompanied Paul to deliver the collection to Jerusalem, were the first-fruits of an expectation long associated in Judaism with the coming eschatological judgement of the world.[284] This was the expectation that all the nations would stream to Zion to worship the true God, the God of Israel.[285] The Jewish conception was constructed around the assumption that the Gentiles would come to be assimilated into Israel, the Chosen People of God, and would only then be admitted to the 'new Jerusalem'. Israel was intended to mediate the salvation of God to them.[286]

Jerusalem was important for Paul, too, as it was there that the Christians expected their Lord to appear at the Second Coming.[287] Much has been made of the fact that Paul's project among his Gentile churches displayed a particular acknowledgement of the Jerusalem church.[288] Without doubt there is evidence to bear out this assertion. The title 'saints' was a self-designation employed by the Jerusalem Christians. Paul's use of the title in connection with his collection reflected that special application.[289] The same is perhaps true of 'poor'.[290]

---

[284] So J. Munck (n. 235), pp. 302ff. C. K. Barrett (n. 188), p. 279, judged that the collection project was 'intended to play a vital part among the events of the last days'.
[285] Cf. J. Jeremias (n. 127), pp. 57ff., who discerned five stages to this expectation: (1) the epiphany of God—the nations wait, (2) the call of God to the nations, (3) the procession of the nations to Zion, (4) the nations worship God, (5) the participation of the nations in the messianic banquet on God's holy mountain.
[286] See above, pp. 130f.
[287] This was strongly influenced by Jewish apocalyptic conceptions. Cf. Gal. 4.25f.; Rom. 9.26 (Sanday and Headlam, n. 84 above, *ad loc.*); compare the many references in Rev.
[288] See espec., Karl Holl (n. 3); also, Hans Lietzmann, *An die Galater*, Tübingen, 1932; H. Schlier, *Der Brief an die Galater*, Göttingen, 1949; P. Bonnard, *L'épitre de saint Paul aux Galates*, Neuchâtel, 1953 (all on Gal. 2.10); O. Michel, *ThWB* IV, p. 686.
[289] Rom. 15.25f.; II Cor. 8.4; 9.1, 12. Cf. K. Holl, *op. cit.*, pp. 59f.; H. J. Cadbury, 'Names for Christians and Christianity', *Beginnings* V, pp. 380f.; R. P. Shedd, *Man in Community*, London, 1958, pp. 131f.; cf. E. Schweizer, *Church Order in the New Testament*, London, 1961, n. 96.
[290] K. Holl, *op. cit.*, p. 60; R. Bultmann (n. 113), p. 41; K. L. Schmidt, *ThWB* III, p. 510; E. Bammel, *ThWB* VI, pp. 908ff.; W. L. Knox (n. 112), p. 190 n. 20. The name 'Ebionite' used by the later Jewish-Christian sect leaves little doubt that at some earlier time the term was employed as a self-designation (cf. O. Cullmann, *RGG*³ II, cols. 297f.). Paul only used the designation twice, Rom. 15.26 and Gal. 2.10, of which the former ('the poor among the saints at Jerusalem') indicates that

The Theological Significance of the Collection

Also indicative of this recognition was the permission which Paul gave to the Macedonian Christians to participate, even though they were in the same situation and suffering under the same need as the Jerusalem community.[291] Such an honouring could not, from Paul's standpoint, have been substantiated by the position of the persons who were members of the Jerusalem fellowship.[292] On the other hand, the fact that Jerusalem was the base of operations for the mission to Israel, coupled with the position their fellowship held as the Church of God in the locality where their Lord was expected to reappear, provided ample grounds for special honour.

From his understanding of the role that the Gentiles were to fulfil in the scheme of redemption, Paul made an audacious alteration in the prevalent Jewish conception of the eschatological role of Jerusalem. The Gentile Christians, represented by the delegates from the churches, were to stream to Jerusalem, but not as the seekers and petitioners of Israel. They were coming as the true Israel of God, those already chosen by his grace to participate through faith in Christ in salvation. Further, they were coming to fulfil the function in the '*Heilsgeschichte*' assigned by the prophets to Israel. That is, they were coming to proclaim the salvation of God instead of to receive salvation through the mediation of Israel. Thus in the collection and the delegation which accompanied it Paul envisaged the culmination of the mystery that Israel was hardened while the nations responded to the proclamation of salvation, and its resolution, in the acceptance by Judaism through their witness of God's promise of salvation fulfilled by his free grace in Christ. By believing they would join with the Gentiles in the fellowship of Christ, the Israel of the promise.

---

he had the economic situation primarily in mind. Nevertheless, if the Jerusalem Christians had already become accustomed to referring to themselves as 'the poor' Paul would certainly have been aware of it and would have had to take it into account in his use of the term.

[291] Cf. H. Windisch (n.15), on II Cor. 8.4. The same factor held true in the earlier collection which Antioch sent as famine relief to Jerusalem. If the 'famine' was a food shortage which stretched out well over two years, the Christians in Antioch were certain to have suffered want also.

[292] Paul's attitude toward the apostles and leaders of the Jerusalem church illustrates this quite adequately. He was not overawed by their reputation based on their past physical association with Jesus (Gal. 2.6) or their present activity as leaders of church and mission (I Cor. 15.10).

The Collection

Paul's failure to mention the delegates

Although the eschatological significance which the collection project had for Paul is clearly intimated in II Corinthians and is obvious when the Romans 15 passage is considered as an inherent part of his discussion in the rest of the epistle, it is necessary to ask why Paul did not explicitly say that he anticipated it to result in the conversion of Israel. More specifically, why did he not mention the function which he expected the representatives of the churches to perform?

One may explain his failure to mention this aspect in the letters to his Gentile communities (I and II Cor., Gal.) on practical grounds. To have made this factor seem reasonable to them, he would have had to develop his understanding of the '*Heilsgeschichte*' much in the way he did in Rom. 9–11. But all three of the epistles involved were written in response to situations which had called into question the relationship of Paul to his Gentile churches. In such an atmosphere, for him to have so vehemently expressed his concern for his countrymen[293] and his conviction that the Gentiles were to be the means to Israel's salvation[294] might have led them to think he was only secondarily interested in his work among them. Therefore to avoid any such possible misunderstanding he simply refrained from bringing up the subject.

Those particular extenuating circumstances were not involved when Paul wrote to the Romans. Earlier in the letter he had expressed himself with warmth and vigour concerning the instrumentality of Gentile Christians for the conversion of Israel.[295] Certainly he was hoping to spend a time of refreshment[296] with them and if possible enlist their help for his trip to Spain,[297] but should they consider his attitude presumptuous it would not seriously threaten any field for his ministry.

Closer to the mark, perhaps, was his fear that the delegation would be misunderstood from another perspective. The group accompanying him to Jerusalem could be judged a premature attempt to force the consummation of the End, instigated by Paul

[293] As he did in Rom. 9.1ff.; 10.1.
[294] Rom. 10.19; 11.11ff.
[295] Rom. 9.11.
[296] Rom. 1.12; 15.32.
[297] Rom. 15.24.

The Theological Significance of the Collection

because he blamed the Jerusalem Christians for the ineffectiveness of their mission to the Jews.[298] Should the erroneous news that Paul regarded their efforts in a deprecating light somehow get back to Jerusalem it would only add fuel to the flame of an already smouldering antagonism. In addition the Roman Christians would gain the misconceived notion that Paul regarded his apostleship and his mission work to be superior to that of the Jerusalem Christians.

However, I believe that the reason he failed to mention the function invested in the delegation is to be sought back at the Jerusalem meeting in which the collection project was first decided upon.[299] The agreement reached there was that Peter would lead the mission to the 'circumcision', while Paul would labour among the Gentiles.[300] The ceremonious 'right hand of fellowship' certified that this division[301] was made in the understanding that basically the gospel of salvation in Christ was offered to all without distinction.

Although the subsequent conflict with Peter in Antioch[302] illustrated that, in practice, this division raised some unforeseen and not immediately soluble difficulties, yet nevertheless, Paul's apostleship to the Gentiles had not been repudiated. The basic agreement was still in force.

It would have been a disaster of the worst irony if the project, which Paul expected to weld the two wings of the Church into an inviolable solidarity, had been misinterpreted as an indication that he was commandeering Peter's mission to Judaism as his sphere of labour also. This would have appeared as an abrogation of the agreement reached in Jerusalem and a repudiation of the Jerusalem church, its leaders, and its fellowship. Thereby the basic accord upon which Paul was counting so heavily would be violated and a permanent schism in the Body of Christ would result.

Thus it was of the utmost importance that Paul first 'seal this fruit'[303] of his ministry before the Christian community in Jerusalem. Only after they had accepted it as it was offered, as the valid

---

[298] I Cor. 15.10 evidenced that Paul was well aware of the discrepancy existing between the success which God had granted to his labours and ineffectiveness of the Jerusalem mission.
[299] Gal. 2.1ff.   [300] Gal. 2.7f., 9b.   [301] Gal. 2.9a.
[302] Gal. 2.11ff.   [303] Rom. 15.28; cf. 128f. above.

and genuine expression of the grace of God in the Gentile Christians which had moved them to uncomplicated love and concern for their Jewish Christian brothers, would the unity of the Body of Christ be restored. Only then would it be possible to move to the next phase in the '*Heilsgeschichte*', the conversion of Israel through the witness of the Gentiles.

All of this was involved in Paul's expression of hope that when he came to Rome he would arrive in the 'fulness of the blessing of Christ'.[304] Certainly the peace and accord of a unified fellowship of believers living in a harmony generated from a singleness of mind and will was an essential factor to this fulness. But for Paul, who longed so earnestly for his countrymen to respond to the gospel, the blessing of Christ could not be complete until they accepted the grace of God in Christ, thereby making the Israel of the flesh an integral part of the Israel of God. When Paul had seen these two goals being realized, then he could come to Rome in the fulness of the blessing of Christ, share with them the good news of these additional signs that the Second Coming was at hand, and be refreshed with them in this joy made real through the will of God.[305]

4. SUMMARY

In this chapter three levels of significance have been distinguished in the collection project which Paul organized among his Gentile communities for the relief of the Jerusalem church: (1) an act of Christian charity among fellow believers motivated by the love of Christ; (2) an act expressing the solidarity of the Christian fellowship by presenting irrefutable evidence that God was calling the Gentiles to faith; (3) an eschatological pilgrimage of the Gentile Christians to Jerusalem by which the Jews were to be confronted with the undeniable reality of the divine gift of saving grace to the Gentiles and thereby be themselves moved through jealousy to finally accept the gospel. In view of the tremendous importance with which Paul invested his project, his concern as to the reception it would receive is understandable.[306] Also it lends

---

[304] Rom. 15.29.
[305] Rom. 15.32. 'Joy' in this verse corresponds exactly to the expectation in the OT of eschatological joy connected with the fulness of salvation; cf. Ps. 126.2, 4f.; Isa. 12.3, 6; 51.3; 61.7, 10; 65.18; etc.
[306] Rom. 15.31. The request for intercession that he might be delivered from the disobedient Jews was evoked by Paul's awareness that the jealousy, which his col-

The Theological Significance of the Collection

credence to the account presented in Acts of the trip[307] which Paul insisted on completing in spite of plots, threats, and warnings,[308] in that Paul's insistence is seen as evidence of his strong singleness of purpose.[309] The author of Acts was quite correct in portraying this trip as the culmination and embodiment of Paul's entire apostleship when he had Paul say to the Ephesian elders with reference to his trip, after alluding to the warnings which he had received, 'I do not account my life of any value nor as precious to myself, if only I may accomplish my course and the ministry which I received from the Lord Jesus, to testify to the gospel of the grace of God.'[310]

---

lection project and its accompanying delegation would excite in the Jews, was a negative reaction. Although it was the necessary prelude to their acceptance of the gospel, yet when added to the active hostility with which they already regarded Paul, this jealousy could produce a situation of intense personal danger for him. It is notable that in the account of Paul's arrest and imprisonment in Acts, he is described repeatedly as blaming his situation on his earnest hope for the conversion of Israel; cf. Acts 23.6ff.; 24.21; 26.6f., 17f., 20ff., 29; 28.20, 23ff.

[307] Acts 19.21–21.16.
[308] Acts 20.3, 23; 21.4, 10ff.
[309] The warnings through the mediation of the Holy Spirit (cf. the last three refs. in previous note) were apparently understood as 'neutral forecasts' of what was to occur. However, it is possible that the author of this portion of Acts did not know of the importance which Paul attached to his project or did not agree with it, and regarded Paul's insistence as simple stubbornness (cf. 21.12). At any rate, these are the only instances in Acts where Paul is pictured as acting contrary to the Spirit; cf. 11.28; 13.2, 4, 9; 16.6f.; 19.21.
[310] Acts 20.24.

V

THE COLLECTION AFTER PAUL

WITHIN the intended scope of this study there remains to be considered the influence which Paul's collection project had upon the life of the Church in the period up to AD 150. As the analogy between the Pauline collection and the Jewish Temple tax was so striking,[1] the eventual fate of that tax will be briefly discussed as compared to the fate of Paul's project. Then evidence in the writings of the period will be examined for the three theological concerns of the collection: Christian charity, church unity, and the conversion of Israel.

1. THE DESTRUCTION OF JERUSALEM AND THE TEMPLE TAX

When Jerusalem fell in AD 70 to Titus and his legions, the Temple was destroyed. This event heralded the termination of Jewish cultic worship as it had been centred in the sacrifices offered at the Temple. Correspondingly, the religious purpose for which the half-shekel Temple tax[2] had been gathered was removed. From the standpoint of the Jewish religious leaders the obligation of Jews to pay the tax was thereby severed.[3]

The Emperor Vespasian took advantage of the already established practice, and converted the Temple tax into a Roman tax of two drachmas to be paid to the temple of Jupiter Capitolinus in Rome.[4] The tax, called the 'fiscus Judaicus',[5] was levied on all Jews, whether slave or free.[6] Possibly the Jewish Christians also

[1] See pp. 87ff. above.
[2] On the Temple tax, see above, pp. 74ff.
[3] Shek. 8.8; quoted above, p. 86 n. 89.
[4] Josephus, *Bel. Jud.* VII, vi, 6; quoted above, p. 86 n. 90.
[5] Cf. J. Juster, *Les Juifs dans l'empire Romain*, Paris, 1914, vol. II, pp. 282ff., on this tax; also E. Schürer, *Geschichte des Judischen Volkes im Zeitalter Jesu Christi*, 3rd ed., Leipzig, 1898, vol. II, pp. 259f.; vol. III, pp. 74f.
[6] This in contrast to the Temple tax which regarded the payment by slaves as voluntary, cf. p. 79 above. Juster, *op. cit.*, pp. 282f. n. 6, argued that women and children were still exempt, while R. H. Pfeiffer, *History of New Testament Times*, New York, 1949, p. 178, maintained that they also had to pay the tax.

144

The Collection after Paul

were required to pay the tax.[7] Since the funds received from this tax went to the support of a pagan temple, it was particularly odious both to the Jew and to the Jewish Christian.[8] In addition, the imposition of the tax created an atmosphere conducive to the harassing of Jews in other ways. Nerva forbade the condoning of such abuses by the authorities, but nevertheless continued to collect the Jewish tax.[9] There is evidence that the tax was collected well into the third century.[10]

Although the destruction of the Temple was a severe shock to Judaism, yet the consequences were not as disastrous as one might have expected. There had been an element gaining strength within Judaism for some time which insisted on the primary importance of the study and observance of the law, and consequently reduced emphasis on Temple worship.[11] Following the destruction of the Temple a group of Jewish scholars founded in Jamnia a school for the study of the law. Soon a Patriarchy of scholars developed there to provide a new central authority for Judaism to replace the function eliminated with the loss of the Temple. Eventually an assessment was collected from all Jews to support the Patriarchy and its work.[12] This tax was, in reality, the corresponding successor to the Temple tax, although a radical external reorientation of Judaism was necessary for it to become so.

2. THE COLLECTION IN THE POST-PAULINE CHURCH

It has been asserted above[13] that Paul's collection project was favourably received by the Jerusalem Christian community. Certainly the economic support which the collection provided for

[7] Cf. W. M. Ramsay, *The Church in the Roman Empire before A.D. 170*, 9th ed., London, 1907, p. 265; but cf. Juster, *op. cit.*, p. 284 n. 4.
[8] Hadrian's order (AD 130) to build a temple to Jupiter Capitolinus on the site of the temple in Jerusalem certainly intensified this feeling; cf. R. H. Pfeiffer, *op. cit.*, p. 45.
[9] In *A Dictionary of the Bible*, ed. J. Hastings, Edinburgh, 1902, 'Tribute', vol. IV, p. 813, it is erroneously asserted that Nerva 'made (the tax) less offensive to the Jews by disassociating it from the heathenish use (of supporting the temple of Jupiter Capitolanus)'. Both Schürer, vol. II, p. 295, vol. III, p. 75, and Juster, vol. II, p. 285 (both n. 5 above), understood his measures as dealing with abuses committed against the Jews.
[10] Cf. Juster, vol. II, p. 286; Schürer, vol. III, p. 75.
[11] Cf. R. H. Pfeiffer (n. 6), pp. 48f.
[12] On this tax, see above, pp. 96ff.
[13] Pp. 70ff.

their strained financial situation was gratefully accepted. But of more importance, the project also resulted in the wholehearted acceptance by the Jewish Christians of the Gentile Christians as true brothers in Christ. It thereby created the context in which steps were taken to make the fellowship of Gentile and Jewish believers in Christ a practical reality, acceptable even to those Jewish Christians still weak in the freedom of the grace of God.[14]

A. *The notable lack of direct references*

In view of the importance with which Paul regarded his collection project and the far-reaching consequences which he expected to result from it, the absence of references to the collection outside of the Pauline literature is conspicuous. Other than in Acts,[15] the only New Testament passage in which an allusion to the collection may be conjectured is Heb. 6.10: 'For God is not so unjust as to overlook your work and the love which you showed for his sake in serving the saints, as you still do.' As the verse stands, it expresses approbation for a willingness to share with other Christians. However, in the phrase, 'your work and the love which you showed for his sake in serving the saints', it is possible that previous participation in Paul's collection is to be understood as included.[16]

B. *Reasons why the Collection was not mentioned*

The absence of any direct reference to Paul's collection in the later Christian writings was the result of several factors.

There is no evidence to indicate that Paul anticipated the repetition of his project. On the contrary, one gains the impression from his discussions that he intended the collection to be a solitary endeavour. Consequently there was no basis for a later attempt to organize such a project as a reiteration of his effort.

With the outbreak of the revolt against Rome which resulted

---

[14] I am of the opinion that as a result of the reconciling effect of the collection project the 'Apostolic Decrees' were formulated as a guide to the Gentile churches for the ordering of their fellowship so that Jewish Christians, conditioned to avoid ritually unclean foods, could without compunction share the liturgical meals of the community; see p. 54ff. above.
[15] See below, pp. 148ff.
[16] Cf., in this connection, the association of the verse with the metaphor of the fruitful land which receives the Word of God (v. 7; cf. II Cor. 9.6, 10), and the eschatological hope (v. 11).

The Collection after Paul

in the destruction of Jerusalem, the Jewish-Christian community was forced to abandon the city and disperse. Although a few may have returned to Palestine after the war, a large segment settled in Pella.[17] Because they were no longer associated with Jerusalem, they forfeited the special recognition they had received as the true people of God within the Holy City.[18] They continued to exist as a sect, on the periphery of the growing Gentile Christian Church[19] and rejected by their own countrymen.[20] In contrast to the adjustment which occurred within Judaism after the destruction of the Temple, no community or institution within Christianity developed in the period up to AD 150 as the replacement of the Jerusalem community.

The Christian mission to the Jews had aborted. The enthusiasm generated by the rapidly developing militant nationalistic movement within Judaism posed a serious challenge to the mission to Israel from the outset. It was an appreciation of this threat which had moved Peter to react in such a contradictory manner to the problem of fellowship with Gentile Christians in Antioch.[21] During the intervening years until Paul delivered his collection the popularity and influence of the Zealots mounted. The basic cleavage between their aims and the goals of the Christian proclamation became increasingly evident, and the hostility with which they regarded the Jewish Christians became correspondingly more intense. The result was that the Christian mission to the circumcision was brought, to all practical purposes, to a standstill.

In spite of Paul's high hopes[22] the delivery of the collection project only served to aggravate an already tense and explosive situation. The uproar which led to his arrest and the agitation caused by his extended presence as a Roman prisoner in Palestine directed much unfavourable attention toward the Jewish Christians. When the Jerusalem Christians were forced to flee at the

---

[17] Cf. W. G. Kümmel, 'Judenchristentum im Altertum', *RGG*³ III, col. 969.
[18] See above, pp. 138f. Although it is practically certain that they continued to suffer from poverty, there is no evidence whatsoever that the Gentile churches, or even Antioch, sent any further aid to relieve their distress.
[19] Cf. O. Cullmann, 'Ebioniten', *RGG*³ II, col. 297f.
[20] W. G. Kümmel, *op. cit.*, mentions the Jewish curse against 'heretics and Christians' which came into use at the end of the first century.
[21] Gal. 2.11ff.; cf. above, pp. 62ff.
[22] See above, pp. 136ff.

The Collection

beginning of hostilities with Rome they abandoned what had developed into a sterile mission field. From this standpoint Paul's project failed, and any reference either to his collection or to a subsequent Gentile representation would have been highly unrealistic.

But from another standpoint, that of the goal of the unity of the Church,[23] Paul's project was a success. Its vivid witness to the grace of God which had been given to the Gentile Christians, corroborated by the testimony of the delegates from the contributing churches who accompanied its delivery, resulted in the warm acceptance by the leading Jewish Christians of the Gentiles as full brothers in the fellowship of Christ. From that moment on there was no question of the possibility of the rejection, subjugation or segregation of the Gentile in relation to the Jewish believer. Any further attempt to accomplish this goal by means of a similar project would have been superfluous.

c. *The Collection in Acts*

The author of Acts included in his narrative a reference to the delegation of representatives from the Gentile churches who accompanied Paul to Jerusalem,[24] the account of the trip itself,[25] and the decision concerning the mixed fellowship of Jewish and Gentile Christians which resulted from it.[26] It is therefore remarkable that the collection appeared only in one distorted reference[27] and one allusion.[28] One can speculate over the reasons which led to the almost complete suppression of references to the project itself. From the various possibilities the choice made would depend to a large extent on the understanding of the one choosing as to the time and purpose of the composition of Acts.

One possibility is that the author of Acts simply knew nothing

[23] See above, pp. 111ff.
[24] Acts 20.4; cf. above, pp. 68f.
[25] Acts 19.21; 20.1-21.16.
[26] It was, however, erroneously recorded as having been reached in the earlier meeting (Acts 15.1ff.) between Paul and the Jerusalem leaders, at which time the collection project alone was actually instigated (Gal.2.1ff.); cf. pp. 54ff. above.
[27] Acts 24.17.
[28] Acts 20.33ff. J. N. Sanders, 'Peter and Paul in the Acts', *New Testament Studies*, vol. 2, no. 1, September 1955, p. 136, suggested that the Acts account of the famine relief sent to Jerusalem from Antioch (Acts 11.27ff.), from which he disassociated Paul and Barnabas, was possibly written in because of the suggestion in the incident to Paul's later project; cf. also J. Knox, *Chapters in a Life of Paul*, Nashville, 1950, pp. 69ff.

The Collection after Paul

about the collection project. This would assume a relatively (but not impossibly) late date for the composition of the work as we know it. It would also require the supposition that all specific references to the collection project had, at some previous time, been eliminated from the 'we-source' account for information on the collection was certainly originally included there.[29] The variant reading which maintained that the delegates accompanied Paul only as far as Asia[30] could have arisen only out of ignorance concerning the project and the relationship of the delegates to it. Evidently, therefore, the Pauline collection did drop for a time into oblivion.

The more probable explanation for the scant references to the collection in Acts is that the author intentionally suppressed any obvious mention of it. Various reasons have been suggested by scholars to explain this. The collection project was inconsequential to the author and to those for whom he was writing.[31] It conflicted with the author's description of a 'secret' arrival of Paul in Jerusalem.[32] Mention of the collection was omitted because it did not contribute to the author's description of the basic point of conflict between Paul and Jerusalem.[33] It detracted from the author's presentation of Paul's independent authority by portraying him as a subservient alms-collector for the Jerusalem community.[34] It was not particularly satisfactory for proving 'either the inspiration of the Church or the legal innocence of Paul'.[35] The delivery of the collection actually resulted in an intensification of the Jews' molesting of the Jerusalem church.[36]

If one of the main concerns of the author of Acts in compiling his document was to present Christianity in a favourable light to Roman officialdom, then this may well supply the most satisfactory explanation for his suppression and distortion of the project.

---

[29] E. Schwartz, 'Zur Chronologie des Paulus', *Nachrichten von der königlichen Gesellschaft der Wissenschaften zu Göttingen-Philologish-historische Klasse*, Berlin, 1907, p. 290, correctly pointed this out.
[30] Acts 20.4; attested to by A, D, H, L, S, P, etc.
[31] So E. Barnikol, *Römer 15 — Letzte Reiseziele des Paulus: Jerusalem, Rom und Antiochien* (Forschung zur Entstehung des Urchristentums, des Neuen Testaments und der Kirche, n. IV), Kiel, 1931, p. 7.
[32] E. Schwartz, *op. cit.*
[33] E. Meyer, *Ursprung und Anfänge des Christentums*, vol. III, p. 194; cf. also J. Knox (n. 28), pp. 71f.
[34] W. L. Knox, *Saint Paul and the Church of Jerusalem*, Cambridge, 1925, p. 295.
[35] K. Lake and H. J. Cadbury, *Beginnings* IV, p. 303.
[36] W. Schmithals, *Paul and James*, London, 1965, p. 83, n. 11.

The Collection

He was writing at a time when the Christian Church had already become separated from any direct association with Judaism. The Roman government had become aware by this time of the fundamental distinction between the two. The collection delivered by Paul to Jerusalem would therefore have been regarded by the Roman authorities as an illegal operation. To have described it in detail would have provided valid legal grounds for increased official suspicion of the Christian faith. Because the clear-cut distinction between Christianity and Judaism had not existed at the time of the project, and because the author was aware that for Paul the Church was the true Israel of God and therefore entitled to benefit from the special concessions made by Rome to Israel, he tersely portrayed the collection in Acts 24.17 as the delivery of religious contributions recognized as legally permitted.

There are other elements present in the Acts account of Paul's imprisonment by the Roman officials in Palestine which support the probability of this explanation. In 25.8 the author listed the charges brought against Paul.[37] Apparently it was on the basis of the charge that he had offended against Caesar that he appealed to Caesar to judge his guilt.[38] Yet nowhere else in the Acts account was any further reference made to this aspect of the case; and this in spite of the fact that the collection project could have been urged as evidence that he had broken the law of the Empire.

Although Felix was aware that Paul had access to available funds,[39] and had heard Paul testify that he had brought contributions to Jerusalem,[40] this factor was ignored in the ensuing deliberations. The Jews who accused Paul were present when he supposedly described his collection project as a delivery of Jewish cultic contributions,[41] yet they did not contradict him. Neither did the author of Acts describe them as making that specific charge at any of the opportunities given to them to accuse Paul before the Roman authorities.[42] On the contrary his description of the investigations which followed Paul's arrest was constructed to support the assertion that those Roman officials most intimately

[37] Compare the preceding verse; also verses 10f.
[38] Acts 25.11f.
[39] Acts 24.26.
[40] Acts 24.17.
[41] Acts 24.1ff., 22.
[42] Acts 21.33f.; 22.21f., 30ff.; 24.1ff.; 25.2, 7.

informed about the case judged the conflict to be only a dispute within the framework of Judaism and not sufficient to justify the condemnation of Paul.[43]

D. *Evidence of other Christian collections*

The responsibility assumed by local Christian communities to provide for the necessities of their poorer members resulted in a certain amount of organization.[44] In I Tim. 5.9, 11, lists of widows are mentioned. Although the passage reflects the official function which widows were then fulfilling within the Christian community,[45] the lists were originally intended to certify those entitled to relief, and were still closely associated with that original purpose.[46] There were apparently 'common funds' set aside in the communities to provide such assistance.[47] The Didache attests to the practice of itinerant prophets who collected money for charitable purposes.[48] There are echoes of the association of charity with the Christian liturgy in the New Testament[49] but the specific mention of a collection taken during the worship service did not appear until much later.[50]

Eusebius included in his *Ecclesiastical History* a singular account he had found in Hegesippus[51] which may reflect that collections for Christian charity were being raised in the churches during the reign of Domitian. In the course of the persecution of Christians which that Emperor had instigated two Christians, who were descendants of Judas the brother of Jesus, boasted of their belonging to the lineage of David. They were taken before Domitian, who feared that in the name of Christ a revolt would be mounted against his reign.[52] After they had admitted their descent

---

[43] Acts 23.28f.; 24.22; 25.18f., 24ff.; 26.24, 28, 31f.
[44] According to Acts, such organizing began in the early days of the Jerusalem Christian community; cf. Acts 6.1ff.
[45] Cf. I Tim. 5.10ff.
[46] I Tim. 5.3ff.,16.
[47] Ignatius, *ad Polyc.* 4.3; cf. Sanday and Headlam, *The Epistle to the Romans* (ICC), Edinburgh, 1902, on Rom. 15.26.
[48] Did. 11.12; the verse contains the warning that if a prophet, supposedly speaking in the spirit, asked for money for himself (instead of for others) his demands were to be rejected and he was to be regarded as a false prophet; cf. Did. 11.4ff.
[49] Acts 2.42; 6.1ff.; Heb. 13.10ff.; James 1.27; cf. Bo Reicke, *Diakonie, Festfreude und Zelos*, Uppsala, 1951, pp. 25ff.
[50] Justin, *Apol.* I, 67; cf. H. Lietzmann, *An die Korinther I–II*, Tübingen, 1949, on I Cor. 16.2; B. Reicke, *op. cit.*, pp. 42f.
[51] Eusebius, *Hist. Eccl.* III, 20, 1ff.
[52] Cf. the comment that he feared the appearance of Christ just as Herod had done.

from David he inquired, strangely enough, as to the amount of their possessions. Apparently he had received information that the Christians were collecting money and he suspected that it was to be used to finance an uprising led in the name of Christ by these two distant relations of his. By exhibiting the hard skin and calluses on their hands, the two men were able to persuade him that, far from being the recipients of revolutionary funds, they were simple folk who earned their living by manual labour in the fields.[53]

3. THE THEOLOGICAL IMPACT OF THE COLLECTION ON THE LATER LIFE OF THE CHURCH

Three different levels of significance have been defined in this study as having been present in Paul's collection project.[54] Traces of the further development of each of these concerns are contained in the other New Testament writings and in the works of the Apostolic Fathers. The paucity of direct references to the Pauline collection itself renders it impossible to determine the exact extent of influence which his project exerted on these elements in the life of the Church. Nevertheless certain general tendencies are discernible.

A. *Charity in the post-Pauline Church*

As was true within the Christian fellowship prior to Paul's collection,[55] so after him Christian charity played an important role in the life of the Church.

Both the non-Pauline New Testament literature and the Apostolic Fathers placed a high value on acts of charity among Christian brethren.[56] Because such charity gave rise to those who took

---

[53] The account goes on to relate that Domitian then questioned them concerning the Lordship of Christ and was so relieved to learn that not a worldly but a spiritual kingdom was to be established at the end of time that he ordered the cessation of the Christian persecution. The two men were released and, because they had not only confessed their faith before the Emperor during a persecution but also were physically related to the Lord, they served various Christian communities in positions of leadership.
[54] Cf. above, pp. 100ff.
[55] See p. 102 above.
[56] Eph. 4.28; II Thess. 3.13; I Tim. 5.3, 16; 6.18f.; Titus 3.8, 14; Heb. 6.10; 13.16; James 1.27; 2.2ff., 15; I Peter 4.9; I John 3.17f.; III John 5ff. In the Apostolic Fathers: Did. 1.5f.; 4.5ff.; 12.2; 13.1ff.; 15.4; Barn. 19.5, 8ff.; I Clem. 33; 34; Ign., *ad Smyrn.* 6.2; *ad Polyc.* 4.1; Polyc., *ad Phil.* 6.1; 10.2, etc.

advantage of the free support, warnings and promises of punishment were expressed against the unworthy recipients of charity.[57] Within this context an increasingly sharp criticism of wealth developed, reminiscent of the Old Testament identification of the wealthy as the oppressors of God's people.[58] Accordingly all believers, and especially church officials, were to be free of greed and avarice.[59] Furthermore one of the pragmatic tests of a wandering prophet was whether he asked for money. If he did, then he was a false prophet.[60]

It becomes clear that Christian charity, as did the whole question of the relationship of the Christian to material wealth, proved to be a much more intricate problem for the post-Pauline Church than it had been for Paul. Although the language which he employed in his discussions of the collection project may have helped shape the terms by which charity was later described, no direct dependence upon the collection appears as a factor for their understanding of Christian charity.

B. *The conversion of Israel*

The interest of the Church in the mission to convert Israel through the proclamation of the gospel was not readily surrendered,[61] yet circumstances forced its eventual abandonment. The increasingly sharp hostility which the surging Jewish nationalism had provoked against the Jerusalem church, augmented by the sense of outrage and revulsion stimulated in the Jews at the audacity of Paul in bringing Gentiles to Israel to preach to Jews, effectively removed any vestige of hope that the Jews would enthusiastically respond in obedience to the gospel in the near future. After the Jerusalem Christian community was forced to flee in the face of the impending conflict with Rome, the central base of operations necessary for a revival of the Jewish mission

---

[57] II Thess. 3.10ff.; I Tim. 5.8, 16. In Apostolic Fathers: Did. 4.5; Barn. 19.9; Ign., *ad Polyc.* 4.3; Polyc., *ad Phil.* 4.3; Herm., 2nd Comm. 5.
[58] I Tim. 6.9f., 17; II Tim. 3.2; James 2.6f.; 5.1ff.; Rev. 3.17. Cf. the numerous references in Herm.; Barn., etc.
[59] Eph. 5.15; Col. 3.5; I Tim. 3.3, 8; 6.6ff., 17ff.; Titus 1.7; Heb. 13.5; James 4.2ff. Did. 2.6; 3.5; 15.1; Barn. 19.6; 20.1; Polyc., *ad Phil.* 2.1; 4.1, 3; 5.2; 6.1; 11.1f.; etc.
[60] Titus 1.11; II Peter 2.3, 14f. Cf. espec. Did. 11.4ff.; also Herm., 11th Comm. 1.11.
[61] The positive attitude toward this mission is retained in Matthew, Hebrews, James, I Peter, etc.

The Collection

was eliminated. At the same time the Gentile mission of the Church continued to prosper. The vast field for labour among the Gentiles and the increased demands on their efforts required by the crystallizing of official Roman opposition to the new faith directed the attention of the Gentile Christians away from the Jewish nation.

In the post-Pauline New Testament literature, evidences of a growing antagonism toward Jews and Jewish influence within the Church began to appear.[62] In Ignatius this attitude received particularly sharp exposition.[63] That such an attitude should find expression at all indicates the rapidity and thoroughness with which the Christian faith freed itself from the close association to Judaism with which it had begun.

Of more direct relevance to this study, the antagonism of the Christian Church towards Judaism signified a fundamental repudiation by the Gentile Christians of Paul's conception of the sequence of events in which the '*Heilsgeschichte*' was to unfold. No longer was there a burning concern for the proclamation of the gospel to Israel. No longer was the instrumentality of Gentile believers for the conversion of Israel offered as justification for their reception of the grace of God in Christ. The origin of Christianity within the context of Judaism came to be regarded as an historical fact divorced of eschatological significance.

c. *The unity of the Church*

Paul's collection achieved its most spectacular success as an expression of the solidarity of all believers in the one Body of Christ. Through this project his insistence that God was electing Gentiles by his grace to become members of his people solely through faith was recognized as valid. Consequently the Jewish Christian community in Jerusalem welcomed them as full brothers in the faith. This aspect of Paul's collection and the theological conviction that it represented was influential for the later reflection of the Church.[64] But already in the later New Testament

[62] Cf. Col. 2.16ff., 20ff.; II Thess. 1.8f.; I Tim. 1.3f., 6f.; 4.7; Titus 1.10, 14ff.; 3.9; Rev. 2.9; 3.9.
[63] Ign. *ad Magn.* 8.1; 9.1; 10.3; *ad Philad.* 6.1; 8.2; 9.1. The Epistle of Barnabas also expressed strongly anti-Jewish sentiments.
[64] Cf. Eph. 3.4ff.; 4.1ff., 11ff.; 5.23ff.; Col. 1.4ff., 17ff., 24ff.; 2.2f., 19; 3.9ff., 14f.; James 2.21ff.; I Peter 2.9f.; 3.8; cf. the participation of the nations in God's salvation in Rev. 15.4; 21.3, 24, 26; 22.2. Cf. Ign., *ad Smyrn.* 1.2.

The Collection after Paul

writings the concurring development of the emphasis that the unity of the Church was maintained not solely through exclusive and single-minded obedience to the Lord of the Church but also through holding fast to the apostolic tradition by means of correct teaching,[65] especially as vested in the church functionaries,[66] was becoming the dominant motif.

The unconditional reconciliation of the two wings of the Church which resulted from his project is clearly reflected in Eph. 2.11–22.[67] Whereas Paul's insistence on the lack of distinctions in the fellowship of Christ was written from a more polemic standpoint, in this passage the solidarity of Gentile and Jewish believers is described as a recognizable fact of their fellowship. Through the grace of God (cf. vv. 8f.) in Christ, the Gentiles have become members of the Israel of God (vv. 12ff., 19ff.), in whom all of the factors which had previously distinguished them from the Chosen People have been abolished (vv. 14f.). Thus Christ has 'reconciled us both to God in one body through the cross, thereby bringing the hostility to an end' (v. 16).

4. SUMMARY

The collection project was only partially successful in fulfilling the aspirations with which Paul had endowed it. As a work of Christian charity it provided a dramatic expression of an essential element in the life of the Christian fellowship. As an embodiment of the unity of the Church it effected through its witness to the genuine Christian faith of the Gentiles a concord between the two missionary wings of the Church. From this unanimity the harmony of the Christian fellowship could become tangible in the mixed fellowship of the local communities without violating Jewish compunctions or subjugating Gentile involvement. But as an instrumental event of the '*Heilsgeschichte*', intended to prod the unbelieving Jews to profess faith in Christ, Paul's project was a crashing failure. Instead of supplying the critical break-through which would bring the Jews streaming to Christ, the project not

---

[65] Cf. II Thess. 2.15; 3.6, 14f.; I Tim. 1.3ff.; 4.16; 6.3ff., 14, 20; II Tim. 1.13f.; 2.16ff.; 3.14ff.; 4.2ff.; Titus 2.1, 7f., 15; James 3.1ff.; II Peter 3.15f.; II John 9ff.; Rev. 2.6, 15; 22.18f.
[66] Cf. I Tim. 2.4f.; II Tim. 2.23ff.; Titus 1.9; I Peter 5.1ff.
[67] Cf. also Col. 1.17ff., 25ff.; 2.11ff.; 3.11; I Tim. 2.5ff.; Titus 3.3ff.; James 1.1.

The Collection

only supplied the *coup de grâce* to the faltering mission to the Jews, but also resulted in the frustration of Paul's plans for his future missionary activity and required him to reorient his apostleship to that field of limited labour available to him as a Roman prisoner.[68]

Yet from the perspective of its influence on the later life of the Church, Paul's collection was immensely fruitful. If the threat posed by the conflict in Antioch had not been raised, the collection would not have been endowed with the weighty purpose of testifying to the unity of all believers in Christ. But the threat was raised, Paul was required to devote much effort and thought to the unity of the Church, and his collection proved that this theological necessity could also be a substantial reality. Consequently, in the succeeding centuries of the history of the Church, Christians have turned to Paul again and again in guilt because of their disunity; for instruction that this is the necessary, given nature of the fellowship of believers; for hope that the unity of the Body of Christ may once again acquire a corporeal manifestation.

[68] Phil. 1.7, 12ff., 16ff., 20ff., 29f.; 2.17; 3.8ff.; Philemon 1, 23 (the applicability of these references depends upon which imprisonment of Paul is meant here); cf. Acts 23.11; 26.28f.; 27.24; 28.30f.

BIBLIOGRAPHY

WORKS CITED

Allo, E. B., 'La portée de la collecte pour Jerusalem dans les plans de s. Paul', *Revue Biblique*, no. 45, 1936
Althaus, P., *Der Brief an die Römer* (Das Neue Testament Deutsch), 2nd ed., Göttingen, 1935
Bachmann, Philipp, *Der erste Brief des Paulus an die Korinther* (Kommentar zum Neuen Testament), Leipzig, 1905
——*Der zweite Brief des Paulus an die Korinther* (Kommentar zum Neuen Testament), Leipzig, 1909
Barnikol, Ernst, *Römer 15—Letzte Reiseziele des Paulus: Jerusalem, Rom und Antiochien* (Forschung zur Entstehung des Urchristentums, des Neuen Testaments und der Kirche, no. 4), Kiel, 1931
Barrett, C. K., *The Epistle to the Romans* (Black's New Testament Commentaries), London, 1957
Barth, Karl, *The Epistle to the Romans*, transl. by E. C. Hoskyns, London, 1933
——*A Shorter Commentary on Romans*, London, 1959
Beyer, H. W., *Apostelgeschichte* (Das Neue Testament Deutsch), 2nd ed., Göttingen, 1935
——*Der Brief an die Galater* (Das Neue Testament Deutsch), 2nd ed., Göttingen, 1935
Bonnard, Pierre, *L'épitre de saint Paul aux Galates*, Neuchâtel, 1953
Bornkamm, G., 'The History of the Origin of the So-called Second Letter to the Corinthians', *New Testament Studies*, vol. 8, n. 3, London, April 1962
Bousset, Wilhelm, *Die Religion des Judentums im neutestamentlichen Zeitalter*, 2nd ed., Berlin, 1902
Bruce, F. F., *The Acts of the Apostles*, London, 1951
Buck, C. H., Jr, 'The Collection for the Saints', *Harvard Theological Review*, vol. XLIII, no. 1, Cambridge, Mass., 1950
Bultmann, R., *Theologie des Neuen Testaments*, 3rd ed., Tübingen, 1958
——Engl. trs. of 1st ed., *Theology of the New Testament*, vol. I, London, 1952
Burrows, Millar, *The Dead Sea Scrolls*, New York, 1956
Burton, E. D., *The Epistle to the Galatians* (International Critical Commentary), Edinburgh, 1921

Bibliography

Chasles, R., *Israel und die Weltvölker*, 4th ed., Stuttgart
Cullmann, Oscar, *The Christology of the New Testament*, transl. by S. C. Guthrie and C. A. M. Hall, London, 1959
—— *Message to Catholics and Protestants*, transl. by Joseph A. Burgess, Grand Rapids, Mich., 1959
—— *Peter: Disciple, Apostle, Martyr*, transl. by Floyd V. Filson, 2nd (revised) ed., London, 1962
Deissmann, A., *Light from the Ancient East*, transl. by L. R. M. Strachan, new ed., London, 1927
—— *Paul: A Study in Social and Religious History*, New York, 1957
Dibelius, Martin, *Studies in the Acts of the Apostles*, London, 1956
Dibelius, Otto, *Die Werdende Kirche*, 4th ed., Berlin, 1941
Dodd, C. H., *The Epistle of Paul to the Romans* (The Moffatt New Testament Commentary), London, 1932
Filson, Floyd V., *Three Crucial Decades*, Richmond, 1963
Gaugler, Ernst, *Der Römerbrief*, vol. II, Zurich, 1952
Goguel, M., *Les premiers temps de l'Église* (Manuels et Précis de Théologie, 28), Paris, 1949
Graetz, H., *Geschichte der Juden*, 4th ed., Leipzig, 1908
Haenchen, Ernst, *Die Apostelgeschichte* (Meyer Kommentar), Göttingen, 1959
Hahn, Ferdinand, *Mission in the New Testament* (Studies in Biblical Theology, 47), London, 1965
Hengel, Martin, *Die Zeloten*, Leiden, 1961
Herford, R. Travers, *The Pharisees*, London, 1924
Héring, Jean, *La première épitre de saint Paul aux Corinthiens*, Neuchâtel, 1949
—— *La seconde épitre de saint Paul aux Corinthiens*, Neuchâtel, 1958
Holl, Karl, 'Der Kirchenbegriff des Paulus in seinem Verhältnis zu dem der Urgemeinde', *Gesammelte Aufsätze zur Kirchengeschichte*, vol. II, Tübingen, 1928
Jackson, F. J. Foakes, *The Acts of the Apostles* (The Moffatt New Testament Commentary), London, 1931
—— and Lake, Kirsopp, editors, *The Beginnings of Christianity, Part I, The Acts of the Apostles*, London, 1920–33
Jeremias, J., 'Sabbathjahr und neutestamentliche Chronologie', *Zeitschrift für die neutestamentliche Wissenschaft*, vol. 27, Giessen, 1928
—— *Jesus' Promise to the Nations* (Studies in Biblical Theology, 24), London, 1958
—— *The Eucharistic Words of Jesus*, 2nd ed. (transl. of 3rd Ger., with revisions), transl. by N. Perrin, London, 1966
Juster, J., *Les Juifs dans l'empire Romain*, Paris, 1914

Bibliography

Klostermann, E., *Das Matthäusevangelium*, 2nd ed., Tübingen, 1927
Knox, John, *Chapters in a Life of Paul*, Nashville, 1950
Knox, Wilfred L., *The Acts of the Apostles*, Cambridge, 1948
—— *St Paul and the Church of Jerusalem*, Cambridge, 1925
Lagrange, M. J., *Saint Paul épitre aux Galates*, Paris, 1950
—— *Saint Paul épitre aux Romains*, Paris, 1950
Leenhardt, Franz J., *L'épitre de saint Paul aux Romains*, Neuchâtel, 1957
Lietzmann, Hans, *A History of the Early Church*, London, 1961
—— *An die Galater* (Handbuch zum Neuen Testament), Tübingen, 1932
—— *An die Korinther I–II*, Tübingen, 1949
—— *An die Römer* (Handbuch Zum Neuen Testament), 1928
—— *Der Sinn des Aposteldekret* (Biblische Zeit- und Streitfragen, no. 5), Berlin, 1911
Lightfoot, J. B., *Saint Paul's Epistle to the Galatians*, London, 1892
Lohmeyer, Ernst, *Das Evangelium des Matthäus* (Meyer Kommentar) Göttingen, 1956
—— *Lord of the Temple*, London, 1961
Lüthi, Walter, *Die Apostelgeschichte*, Basle, 1958
Manson, W. M., 'Grace in the New Testament', in *The Doctrine of Grace*, ed. by W. T. Whitley, London, 1932
Meinertz, Max, *Theologie des Neuen Testaments*, Bonn, 1950
Meyer, E., *Ursprung und Anfänge des Christentums*, Stuttgart, 1923
Meyer, W., *Der erste Brief an die Korinther*, pt 2, Zürich, 1945
Michel, Otto, *Der Brief an die Römer* (Kritisch-exegetischer Kommentar über das Neue Testament), 10th ed., Göttingen, 1955
Moore, G. F., *Judaism*, vol. II, Cambridge, 1930
Munck, Johannes, *Paul and the Salvation of Mankind*, transl. by Frank Clarke, London, 1959
Mundle, W., 'Das Kirchenbewusstsein der ältesten Christenheit', *Zeitschrift für die neutestamentliche Wissenschaft und die Kunde der älteren Kirche*, vol. 22, Giessen, 1923
Nygren, Anders, *Commentary on Romans*, transl. by C. C. Rasmussen, Philadelphia, 1949
Oehler, W., *Ein Missionar kämpft um seine Gemeinden*, Neukirchen, 1960
Oepke, Albrecht, *Der Brief des Paulus an die Galater* (Theologischer Handkommentar zum Neuen Testament), 2nd ed., Berlin, 1957
Paley, William, *Horae Paulinae*, London, 1822
Pallis, Alexander, *To the Romans*, Liverpool, 1920
Pfeiffer, R. H., *History of New Testament Times*, New York, 1949
Ramsay, W. M., *The Church in the Roman Empire before A.D. 170*, 9th ed., London, 1907
—— *St Paul the Traveller and the Roman Citizen*, 10th ed., London, 1908

Reicke, Bo, *Diakonie, Festfreude und Zelos*, Uppsala, 1951
—— 'The Risen Lord and His Church', *Interpretation*, vol. XIII, no. 2, Richmond, Va, April, 1959
—— 'Der Geschichtliche Hintergrund des Apostelkonzils und der Antiochia-Episode, Gal. 2.1-14', *Studia Paulina*, Haarlem, 1953
—— *Glaube und Leben der Urgemeinde* (Abhandlung zur Theologie des Alten und Neuen Testaments, no. 32), Zürich, 1957
Rendall, F., 'The Pauline Collection for the Saints', *The Expositor*, 4th series, vol. VIII, London, 1893
Ricciotti, Giuseppe, *Der Apostel Paulus*, Basle, 1950
Richter, Julius, *Die Briefe des Apostels Paulus als missionarische Sendschreiben*, Gütersloh, 1929
Robertson, Archibald and Plummer, Alfred, *First Epistle of St Paul to the Corinthians* (International Critical Commentary), 2nd ed., Edinburgh, 1914
Rolston, Holmes, *Stewardship in the New Testament Church*, Richmond, 1946
Sanday, W., and Headlam, A. C., *The Epistle to the Romans* (International Critical Commentary), Edinburgh, 1902
Sanders, J. N., 'Peter and Paul in the Acts', *New Testament Studies*, vol. 2, no. 1, Cambridge, September 1955
Schlatter, Adolf, *Die Apostelgeschichte*, Stuttgart, 1948
—— *Die Briefe an die Galater und Epheser*, 3rd ed., Stuttgart, 1920
—— *Paulus, der Bote Jesu: Eine Deutung seiner Briefe an die Korinther*, Stuttgart, 1956
Schlier, Heinrich, *Der Brief an die Galater* (Meyer Kommentar), Göttingen, 1949
Schmitz, Otto, *Urchristliche Gemeindenöte*, Berlin, 1939
Schoeps, Hans-Joachim, *Paulus*, Tübingen, 1959
Schmithals, Walter, *Paul and James* (Studies in Biblical Theology, 46), London, 1965
Schrenk, Gottlob, *Studien zu Paulus* (Abhandlung zur Theologie des Alten und Neuen Testaments, no. 26), Zürich, 1954
Schürer, Emil, *Geschichte des Jüdischen Volkes im Zeitalter Jesu Christ*, 3rd ed., Leipzig, 1898
Schumacher, Rudolph, *Die Beiden Letzten Kapitel des Römerbriefs* (Neutestamentliche Abhandlungen, vol. XIV, no. 4), Münster, 1929
Schwartz, E., 'Zur Chronologie des Paulus', in *Nachrichten von der königlichen Gesellschaft der Wissenschaften zu Göttingen—Philologisch-historische Klasse*, Berlin, 1907
Schweitzer, Albert, *The Mysticism of Paul the Apostle*, trans. by W. Montgomery, London, 1931

Bibliography

Schweizer, Eduard, *Church Order in the New Testament* (Studies in Biblical Theology, 32), London, 1961

Seesemann, H., *Der Begriff Κοινωνία im Neuen Testament* (Zeitschrift für die neutestamentliche Wissenschaft, Suppl. 14), Giessen, 1933

Shedd, Russell Philip, *Man in Community*, London, 1958

Sickenberger, Joseph, *Die Briefe des Heiligen Paulus an die Korinther und Römer*, 4th ed., Bonn, 1932

Steinmetz, Rudolph, *Das Aposteldekret* (Biblische Zeit- und Streitfragen, no. 5), Berlin, 1911

Stendahl, K., ed., *The Scrolls and the New Testament*, New York, 1957

Tresmontant, Claude, *Paulus in Selbstzeugnissen und Bilddokumenten*, Hamburg, 1959

Uhlhorn, Gerhard, *Die christliche Liebestätigkeit in der alten Kirche*, Stuttgart, 1882

Volz, P., *Die Eschatologie der jüdischen Gemeinde im neutestamentlichen Zeitalter*, 2nd ed., Tübingen, 1934

Weber, Valentine, *Die antiochenische Kollekte*, Würzburg, 1917

—— 'Der Heilige Paulus vom Apostelübereinkommen bis zum Apostelkonzil', *Biblischen Studien*, vol. VI, Freiburg, 1901

Weiss, Bernhard, *Brief des Paulus an die Römer*, Göttingen, 1881

Weiss, Johannes, *Der erste Korintherbrief* (Meyer Kommentar), 4th ed., Göttingen, 1910

—— *Earliest Christianity*, 2 vols, New York, 1954, 1959

Wellhausen, J., 'Noten zur Apostelgeschichte', in *Nachrichten von der königlichen Gesellschaft der Wissenschaften zu Göttingen—Philologisch-historische Klasse*, Berlin, 1907

Windisch, Hans, *Der zweite Korintherbrief* (Meyer Kommentar) 9th ed., Göttingen, 1924

Zahn, Theodor, *Der Brief des Paulus an die Galater*, Leipzig, 1905

—— *Der Brief des Paulus an die Römer* (Kommentar zum Neuen Testament), Leipzig, 1910

SOURCES AND REFERENCE WORKS CONSULTED

Arndt, W. F., and Gingrich, F. W., ed., *A Greek-English Lexicon of the New Testament*, Cambridge and Chicago, 1957 (cited in text as A & G)

Bihlmeyer, Karl, *Die Apostolischen Väter*, Tübingen, 1956

Eusebius, *Kirchengeschichte*, ed. by Ed. Schwartz, 5th ed., Berlin, 1952

Galling, Kurt, et al., *Die Religion in Geschichte und Gegenwart*, 3rd ed., Tübingen, 1957–63 (cited in text as RGG^3)

Bibliography

Gastor, Theodor H., transl., *The Dead Sea Scriptures*, Garden City, N.Y., 1956
Goodwin, W. W., and Gulick, C. B., *Greek Grammar*, Boston, 1930
Hastings, James, ed., *A Dictionary of the Bible*, Edinburgh, 1902
Josephus, *Works*, transl. and ed. by H. St. J. Thackeray and Ralph Marcus (The Loeb Classical Library), London, 1926–
——*Flavii Iosephi Opera*, ed. by B. Niese, Berlin, 1890
Kittel, Gerhard, and Friedrich, Gerhard, ed., *Theologisches Wörterbuch zum Neuen Testament*, Stuttgart, 1933– (cited in text as *ThWB*)
Nestle, D. Eberhard, *Novum Testamentum Graece*, 20th ed., Stuttgart, 1952
Philo, *Works*, transl. and ed. by F. H. Colson and G. H. Whitaker (The Loeb Classical Library), London, 1929–62
Rabin, Batya and Chaim, transl., *The Scroll of the War of the Sons of Light against the Sons of Darkness*, Oxford, 1962
Rahlfs, Alfred, *Septuaginta*, 5th ed., Stuttgart, 1952
Roth, Cecil, ed., *The Standard Jewish Encyclopedia*, Garden City, N.Y., 1959
Segal, M. H., transl. 'Shekelim', *The Babylonian Talmud*, Seder Mo'ed, ed. by I. Epstein, vol. IV, London, 1938
Strack, H. L., and Billerbeck, Paul, *Kommentar zum Neuen Testament aus Talmud und Midrasch*, vol. III, München, 1926
Wernberg-Müller, *The Manual of Discipline* (= Studies on the Texts of the Desert of Judah, ed. J. van der Ploeg, vol. I), Leiden, 1957

ENGLISH TRANSLATIONS OF THE BIBLE

The Holy Bible, Authorized King James Version (cited in text as KJV)
The Holy Bible, The American Standard Version, New York, 1901 (cited in the text as ASV)
The Holy Bible, Revised Standard Version, New York, 1946–52 (cited in the text as RSV)
New English Bible, New Testament, Oxford and Cambridge, 1961 (cited in the text as NEB)

INDEXES

INDEX OF AUTHORS

Italic page numbers indicate that the reference is in the text; all others are in footnotes.

Althaus, P., 122

Backmann, Philipp, 15, 16, 17, 18, 19, 105, 121, 126, 128
Bammel, E., 138
Barnikol, Ernst, 128, 149
Barrett, C. K., 122, 128, 138
Barth, Karl, 14, 134
Beyer, H. W., 32, 49, 53, 55, 121, 122
Bonnard, Pierre, 40, 42, 43, 46, 53, 138
Bornkamm, G., 17, 55, 58, 132
Bousset, Wilhelm, 66, 76, 82, 84, 89, 94
Braun, H., 53, 58
Bruce, F. F., 29, 37, 52, 68
Buck, C. H., jun., 17, 52, 68
Bultmann, R., 108, 111, 135, 138
Burton, E. D., 39, 41, 42, 43, 46, 49, 51, 59, 64, 65

Cadbury, H. J., 23, 36, 138, 149
Chasles, R., 131
Cicero, 82, 84, 88
Conzelmann, H., 39, 55, 58, 108, 111f., 133, 138
Cullmann, Oscar, 37, 55, 64, 66, 75, 147

Deissmann, A., 82
Dibelius, Martin, 25, 37, 51, 53
Dibelius, Otto, 24, 68
Dodd, C. H., 24

Emmett, C. W., 52
Eusebius, 151, 151

Filson, Floyd V., 43, 46, 51, 55

Gaugler, Ernst, 125
Graetz, H., 97

Haenchen, Ernst, 23, 25, 28, 30, 31, 37, 39, 55, 68
Hahn, Ferdinand, 26, 32, 42, 131, 132, 134, 135
Harnack, A. von, 37
Hauck, F., 105, 123, 125
Hengel, Martin, 66
Herford, R. Travers, 66
Héring, Jean, 16, 17, 18, 20, 104, 105, 110, 121, 126
Holl, Karl, 43, 75, 90, 101, 138

Jackson, F. J. Foakes, 23, 25, 29, 37, 51
Jackson and Lake, 23, 24, 29, 37, 66, 68
Jepsen, A., 130
Jeremias, J., 25, 31, 31, 39, 53, 75, 92, 101, 108, 113
Josephus, 25, 77, 79, 82, 83, 84, 86, 98, 99, 144
Juster, J., 25, 74, 76, 82, 83, 84, 88, 96, 97, 144, 145

Kennedy, A. R. S., 76, 77
Klostermann, E., 86
Knox, John, 41, 51, 58, 61, 92, 111, 148
Knox, Wilfred L., 18, 21, 23, 25, 29, 32, 35, 36, 37, 41, 46, 50, 52, 57, 75, 83, 88, 111, 126, 131, 138, 149

Index of Authors

Kümmel, W. G., 147

Lagrange, M. J., 14, 40, 51
Lake, K., 23, 29, 37, 48, 50, 53, 55, 57, 58, 83, 149
Lake and Cadbury, 29, 34, 35, 37, 68
Leenhardt, Franz J., 69
Lietzmann, 14, 16, 17, 18, 19, 20, 37, 40, 42, 44, 46, 49, 53, 55, 59, 64, 65, 68, 105, 108, 110, 120, 121, 122, 125, 126, 128, 138, 151
Lightfoot, J. B., 40, 43, 51, 59, 65
Lohmeyer, Ernst, 87, 132
Lüthi, Walter, 37, 50

Manson, W. M., 109, 135, 136
Meinertz, Max, 75
Meyer, E., 25, 53, 101, 149
Meyer, W., 16
Michel, Otto, 29, 109, 122, 125, 134, 138
Moore, G. F., 94
Munck, Johannes, 15, 37, 43, 46, 71, 87, *130*, 133, 134, 138
Mundle, W., 90

Nygren, Anders, 39

Oehler, Wilhelm, 41
Oepke, Albrecht, 40, 43, 44, 46, 53, 117

Paley, William, 111
Pallis, A., 14
Pfeiffer, R. H., 66, 76, 96, 144, 145
Philo, 25, 76, 76f., 79, 82, 83, 84, 98, 99

Ramsay, W. M., 26, 31, 37, 40, 52, 145
Reicke, Bo, 53, *65*, 102, 106, 107, 113, 149
Rendall, F., 90, 92, 111
Ricciotti, Giuseppe, 31

Richter, Julius, 50
Robertson, Archibald and Plummer, Alfred, 15, 16, 24, 126
Rolston, Holmes, 16, 118
Ropes, J. H., 35, 37

Sanday, W. and Headlam, A. C., 24, 108, 122, 138, 151
Sanders, J. N., 25, 26, 55, 148
Schlatter, Adolf, 10, 15, 19, 29, 46, 51, 87
Schlier, Heinrich, 40, 42, 43, 44, 46, 51, 64, 65, 138
Schmithals, Walter, 16, 25, 44, 45, 50, 64, 71
Schmidt, K. L., 109, 115, 116, 138
Schmitz, Otto, 15, 16, 126
Schoeps, Hans-Joachim, 45, 67, 75
Schrenk, Gottlob, 111, 134
Schubert, K., 101
Schumacher, Rudolph, 128
Schürer, Emil, 66, 74, 76, 77, 82, 96, 97, 144, 145
Schwartz, E., 15, 26, 34, 39, 53, 58, *71*, 71, 149
Schweitzer, Albert, 45, 75
Schweizer, Eduard, 138
Seesemann, H., 105, 123, 125
Segal, M. H., 76, 77, 85
Shedd, Russell Philip, 138
Sickenberger, Joseph, 15, 16, 69, 110, 121, 122
Steinmetz, Rudolph, 37, 51
Strack-Billerbeck, 55, 74, 76, 78, 79, 80, 81, 82, 83, 84, 85, 94, 95, 97, 121

Tresmontant, Claude, 75

Uhlhorn, Gerhard, 101, 102, 107

Volz, P., 113, 131

Weber, Valentine, 25, 26, 31, 52, 66, 75, 92, 111
Weiss, Bernhard, 16, 111, 134

Index of Authors

Weiss, Johannes, 15, 16
Wellhausen, J., 25, 37, 53, 58
Windisch, Hans, 16, 17, 18, 19, 20, 53, 105, 108, 109, 120, 121, 123, 125, 126, 128, 139
Wernberg-Møller, 98

Wurthwein, E., 109

Yadin, Yigael, 98

Zahn, Theodor, 15, 41, 43, 51, 61, 68, 109, 128

INDEX OF BIBLICAL REFERENCES

Italic page numbers indicate that the reference is in the text; all others are in footnotes.

OLD TESTAMENT

Exodus
21.2ff.	93
22.21ff.	93
23.10f.	93
30.11ff.	91
30.11–16	76
30.13	*76, 77, 78*
30.14	79
30.16	80
30.34	77
32.1ff.	*78*
38.24–26	77

Leviticus
5.15	27
16.10	85
16.21f.	85
19.9f.	93
23.22	93
25.6–7	85
25.10	93
25.25	93
27.1ff.	77
27.3	77
27.25	77

Numbers
3.47	77
3.50	77
7.13–86	77
18.6	77
19.1–10	85
32.22	85

Deuteronomy
14.28f.	93
15.2	93
15.7ff.	93
23.19f.	93
24.6	93
24.10ff.	93
24.19–22	93
32.21	133

Ruth
2.2ff.	75

I Kings
8.62ff.	75

II Kings
11.21–12.14	76
17.24	79

I Chronicles
16.2	75

II Chronicles
24.4–14	76
30.24	75
31.3	75
35.7	75

Nehemiah
10.32f.	75, 75, 76, 91

Job
22.6ff.	93
29.12f.	93
29.15	93

Job
31.16ff.	93

Psalms
126.2	142
126.4f.	142

Proverbs
3.4	85, 89

Isaiah
5.8ff.	93
10.1ff.	93
12.3	142
12.6	142
28.16	133
29.10	133
49.1ff.	133
51.3	142
55.4f.	137
55.10f.	137
55.10	137
61.7	142
61.10	142
65.1	133
65.2	133
65.18	142

Jeremiah
1.5	133
5.26ff.	93

Ezekiel
13.2ff.	47
45.13	75
45.17	75
45.21ff.	75
46.4ff.	75

Index of Biblical References

Daniel		Hosea		Amos	
11.31	25	1.10	133	2.6ff.	93
		2.23	133	9.11	37
		10.12	137		

NEW TESTAMENT

Matthew		Mark		Luke	
5.3	101	6.7–11	24	22.1	75
5.42	101	6.35ff.	101	22.24ff.	107
5.44	121	7.14ff.	27, 37, 55	22.29f.	121
6.2	101	8.4ff.	101		
6.33	109	10.17–30	24	John	
8.20	101	10.21	101	2.14f.	75, 78
10.4	64, 66	10.23ff.	101	3.36	71
10.5f.	113	10.28ff.	101	13.4ff.	107
10.23	113	10.42ff.	107	13.29	101
11.5	101	11.1ff.	101	18.25–27	66
12.6	87	11.15ff.	132		
12.28	109	11.15	75, 78	Acts	
13.22	47	12.13ff.	101	1.3	64, 66
16.19	121	12.41–44	24	1.17	107
17.24–27	75, 86f.	12.41	101	1.25	107
17.24	77, 80	13.14	25	2.1ff.	88
17.25	87	13.22	47, 47	2.42ff.	106
17.26	87	14.12ff.	101	2.42–47	23
17.27	77, 101	14.70–72	66	2.42	102, 107, 151
19.24	109	15.26	101	2.44ff.	90, 102
19.28f.	121	15.40	101	2.46	86
20.26ff.	107			3.1ff.	86
21.12	75, 78	Luke		3.6	23
21.31	109	4.18ff.	101	4.1ff.	24, 66
21.43	109	6.15	64, 66	4.32ff.	23
24.7	25	6.24	101	4.32–5.11	23
24.15	25	6.26	47	4.32	102
25.34ff.	101	6.28	121	4.34	102
25.42ff.	106	8.3	101, 106	4.36ff.	32
25.44f.	107	9.48	107	4.36	112
26.60	47	10.4ff.	101	5.1ff.	102
		10.30ff.	95	5.4	23
Mark		10.40	106	5.17ff.	24, 66
1.13	101	11.28	25	6.1ff.	23, 24, 2.
1.17ff.	101	12.37	106		90, 94, 10
2.23ff.	101	16.19ff.	101		107, 151
3.18	64, 66	17.8	106	6.7	57
4.19	24, 101	19.2ff.	101	6.8ff.	107
6.7ff.	101	19.45f.	75	6.12ff.	24

Index of Biblical References

Acts		Acts		Acts	
6.13f.	112	11.29	32, 107	15.11	36
6.13	47	11.30	26, 29, 30,	15.12	37
7.2ff.	112		52, 97, 107	15.13–21	36
7.54ff.	24	12	53	15.14	27, 37, 57
8.1	25	12.1ff.	24	15.16f.	36
8.4ff.	27, 107	12.3ff.	66	15.17	37
8.14	27, 28, 28, 112	12.12	30	15.20f.	36
8.26ff.	27, 107	12.25	26, 29, 30, 31, 52, 52, 53, 107	15.20	21, 37
9	51			15.21	36
9.1f.	24	12.30	31	15.22	21, 22, 34, 38
9.2	24	13	53, 57	15.23ff.	38
9.26ff.	30	13.2	143	15.23	34, 37, 38, 69
10.1ff.	27, 27	13.4	143	15.24	32, 34
10.2	27	13.5b	30	15.25	37
10.22	27	13.6	47	15.27	22
10.28	27	13.9	143	15.28f.	36
10.44ff.	112	13.13b	30	15.29	21, 37
10.45	65	14	53, 57	15.30–40	67
11	52, 57	14.2	71	15.32f.	21
11.1ff.	36, 37, 112	14.4	96	15.32	22
11.1	27, 28, 37	14.14	96	15.33	30, 38
11.2	65, 66	14.23	19	15.34	30
11.3	27	14.27	35	15.36ff.	54
11.5ff.	27	15	34, 40, 51, 51, 52, 54, 55, 56, 57, 58, 60, 72	15.37ff.	30
11.18	27			15.40	21, 22, 30, 38, 60
11.19ff.	112			15.41	38, 69
11.19	25	15.1ff.	32, 148	16.1ff.	68
11.20ff.	26, 36	15.1–3	54	16.1–3	50
11.20	27	15.1–29	51, 53	16.4	34, 38
11.22	25, 28, 32, 35, 66	15.1	32, 33, 57, 70	16.6f.	143
		15.2a	34	16.8	69
11.23ff.	32	15.2b	34	16.12	69
11.23	28	15.2	32, 34, 35, 42, 52	16.16	68
11.25ff.	113			18	60, 61
11.25f.	26, 28	15.3	34, 35	18.11	38
11.25	57	15.4ff.	34	18.12ff.	38
11.27ff.	25, 104, 148	15.4	34, 35, 52	18.22	21, 22, 42, 60, 60, 61
11.27–30	51, 52, 53, 53	15.5	33, 33, 35, 57		
		15.6ff.	37	18.23– 21.16	13
11.28a	26	15.6–29	36		
11.28b	26	15.6	34, 53, 55	19.10	88
11.28	29, 143	15.7ff.	27, 37	19.21ff.	143
11.29f.	26	15.7–11	36	19.21	14f., 68, 88, 143, 148
11.29–30	26	15.9f.	36		

170

Index of Biblical References

Acts			Acts		Romans	
20.1ff.	148		24.17	70, 148, *150*,	4.10f.	65
20.1–	68			150	4.12	65
21.16			24.21	143	4.16	116
20.2	22		24.22	150, 151	5.2	135
20.3	69, 143		24.26	70, 150	5.5	103
20.4	15, 22,	68,	25.2f.	66	5.8	103
	148, 149		25.2	150	5.15ff.	135
20.5	69		25.7	150	5.16ff.	135
20.6bff.	69		25.8	*150*	6.3ff.	117
20.6	68, 69, 88		25.10	150	6.4ff.	123
20.16	87, 92		25.11f.	150	6.14f.	116, 135
20.17–38	69		25.18f.	151	6.21f.	129
20.22	66		26.6f.	143	7.4ff.	116
20.23	143		26.17f.	143	8.2	116
20.24	108, 143		26.20ff.	143	8.12	120
20.33ff.	147		26.24	151	8.15ff.	103
21	56, 72		26.28f.	156	8.17	123
21.1	68		26.28	151	8.18	121
21.4	69, 143		26.29	143	8.28ff.	103
21.6	69		26.31f.	151	8.31f.	103
21.7	69		27.24	156	8.33	116
21.10ff.	143		28.20	143	8.35	103, 104
21.10f.	25		28.23ff.	143	8.38f.	103
21.11	66		28.30f.	156	9–11	134
21.12	143				9.1ff.	134, 140
21.16	69, 112		Romans		9.1	41
21.17ff.	13		1.5	71, 136	9.6ff.	114, 116
21.17b	34		1.7	116	9.7f.	116
21.18	34		1.10ff.	*14f.*	9.11	140
21.19	108		1.11	122	9.25f.	133
21.20	15, 66, 71		1.12	140	9.26	138
21.20–24	26		1.13	70, 129	9.31	135
21.25	*21*, 37		1.14	120	9.33	133
21.28	21, 66		1.18ff.	110	10.1ff.	134
21.33f.	150		2.8	71	10.1	140
22.21f.	150		2.25	65	10.4	116
22.30ff.	150		2.29	65	10.12	135
23.6ff.	143		3.1	65, 65	10.19	133, 140
23.12ff.	66		3.20ff.	116	10.20	133
23.11	156		3.21ff.	135	10.21	71, 133
23.28f.	151		3.24ff.	135	11.1	133
24.1ff.	150		3.28	116	11.5f.	135
24.5ff.	66		3.30	65, 117	11.5	116
24.5	24		4.4	120, 135	11.6	135
24.14	24		4.9	65, 65	11.7	120

Index of Biblical References

Romans		Romans		I Corinthians	
11.8	133	15.25ff.	90, 104, 134	7.1	15
11.10	120	15.25f.	13, 138	7.3	120
11.11ff.	133, 140	15.25	108, 134	7.17ff.	45, 51, 116
11.13ff.	134	15.26f.	17, *106*, 123	7.17	19
11.13	108	15.26	68, 68, *69*, 93, 100, 105, 111, *124*, 138	7.19	65, 93, 117
11.17ff.	116			7.25 –	15
11.20	65			7.36	120
11.23f.	134	15.27	92, 93, 97, 105, 106, 110, 119, 124, 136	8	*21*, 21
11.25f.	134			8.1ff.	103
11.29	133			8.1	15
11.30f.	14, 71	15.28	128, 129, 141	8.3	103
12.3	136	15.29	122, 142	8.4	117
12.4ff.	104	15.30	103	8.6	117
12.5	103, 117	15.31a	*71*	8.13	103
12.6	135	15.31b	*67*	8.18	21
12.7ff.	117	15.31	16, 108, 119, 122, 125, 134, 137, 142	9.1f.	*44*
12.7	108			9.2	129
12.8	104			9.3ff.	18
12.9f.	103	15.32	140, 142	9.4ff.	97
12.13	14, 59, *69*, 103, 104, 105, 106, 124	16.1	108	9.4	104
		16.3	116	9.7	129
		16.4	19	9.10f.	120
12.14	121	16.7	96	9.10	120
13.7	120	16.16	19, 88	9.11ff.	24, 106
13.8ff.	103	16.21	68	9.14	120
13.8f.	120	16.23	19, 68, 88	9.19ff.	45
13.8	103, 120			9.20f.	*63*
14.1–4	22	I Corinthians		9.20	87
14.14	22	1.2	116, 117	9.23	106, 123
14.23	22	1.4f.	135	10	*21*, 21
15.1	120	1.4	136	10.16ff.	105, 123
15.3	120	1.9	105, 116, 123	10.16f.	117
15.6	103	1.13	117	10.16	106
15.7ff.	120	1.14	68	10.17	117, 123
15.8	65, 108	2.12	135	10.18	116
15.14ff.	134	3.5	108	11.16	19, 117
15.15	136	3.8	117	11.18f.	117
15.16	134	3.10	136	11.22	107
15.19	134	3.11	117	12.1ff.	135
15.20	70	3.16f.	116	12.1	15
15.22ff.	134	4.11	104	12.4ff.	117
15.23	134	4.12	121	12.5	108
15.24ff.	68, 119	4.17	19	12.12f.	103, 117
15.24f.	*14f.*	6.15	117	12.13	114, 117
15.24	70, 140	6.17	117	12.27ff.	117

172

Index of Biblical References

I Corinthians	
12.27	103, 117
13.1ff.	103, 117
13.3	103
14.5	117
14.33f.	19
15.7	96
15.10	136, 139, 141
15.15	47
16.1ff.	90, 91, 104, 125
16.1	19, *68*
16.1–4	*15f., 17*
16.2	88, 89, 90, 92, 93, 102
16.3	19, *69*, 109, 110, 135
16.4	22, 92
16.15	59, 104, 108
16.19	19
17.1	15
17.25	15

II Corinthians	
1.1–8.24	17
1.1	116
1.3	103
1.5ff.	106
1.5	123
1.7	123
1.9	68
1.12	105, 135
1.22	129
2.1ff.	18
2.3f.	17
2.9	17
2.12	69
2.13	18
2.14–7.4	17
3.6	108
3.8	108
4.1	108
5.14f.	117
5.18	108
6.1	135

II Corinthians	
6.3f.	108
6.10	104
6.14	123
6.14–7.1	17
6.16	116
7.3	123
7.6ff.	18
7.8	17
7.12	17
7.13ff.	18
7.15	18
8.1ff.	*68*, 92, 104, 127
8.1	*18*, 18, *19*, 109, 110, 125, 135
8.2ff.	93
8.2f.	102
8.2	*18*, 18, 104, 126
8.3ff.	*18*
8.3	18
8.4f.	92
8.4	70, 105, *106*, 108, 109, 110, 123, 124, 125, 134, 135, 138, 139
8.5	*18*, 126
8.6f.	92
8.6	*18*, 18, 109, 110, 127, 135
8.7ff.	92
8.7f.	128
8.7	109, 110, 135
8.7a	*18*
8.7b	*18*
8.9	18, 97, 109, 110, 120, 126, 135
8.10ff.	92, 93
8.10	*18*, 18, 126
8.11ff.	95
8.11f.	126, 127
8.12ff.	92

II Corinthians	
8.13ff.	16, *17*, 18, *19*, 102
8.13	110
8.14f.	92
8.14	93, 97, *110*, 120, 121
8.16f.	*18*, 127
8.17	18
8.17a	18
8.17b	18
8.18f.	*18*
8.18	*19*, 19
8.19	*19, 21, 22*, 108, 109, 110, 135
8.20f.	16, *19*, 20, 89
8.20	18
8.22f.	*18*
8.23f.	127
8.23	*18, 19, 21, 22*, 96, 97, 124
8.24	*19, 21*, 92, 12'
8.40	*21*
9.1ff.	104
9.1	17, 108, 110, 134, 138
9.2ff.	*22*, 92
9.2	*18*, *68*, 93, 126, 127
9.3f.	*19*
9.3	127
9.4	16, *22*, 68
9.5ff.	*17*, 92
9.5f.	121, 122, 13f
9.5	*18*, 93, 127
9.6ff.	88, 92, 95
9.6f.	127
9.6–10	59, *70*
9.6	121, 146
9.7ff.	127
9.7	93
8.8ff.	95, 102, 10! 122
9.8	109, 110, 12(135
9.10f.	120

173

Index of Biblical References

II Corinthians		Galatians		Galatians	
9.10	137, 146	1.1	*41*	2.7	44, 114
9.11ff.	122, 137	1.2	19	2.8	*44*
9.11	104, 105	1.6ff.	117	2.9ff.	106, 114, 124, 125
9.12f.	109	1.6–12	*41*		
9.12	93, 108, 110, 134, 137, 138	1.6	131	2.9	*43, 43, 44, 44, 45*, 114, 124, 141
9.13ff.	128	1.15f.	*43, 44,* 132, 136		
9.13	70, 104, *105*, *106*, 108, 122, 123, 124, 134	1.15–17a	*41*	2.10	22, *46, 59, 60*, 61, *90, 91, 93*, 100, 103, 104, 111, 138
		1.15	133		
		1.16	42, 114		
9.14	105, 109, 110, 122, 135, 136	1.17f.	112		
		1.18f.	30, 102	2.11ff.	21, 22, 36, *40*, 42, *115*, 141, 147
9.15	109, 110	1.18–19	*41*		
10.1–		1.18–24	51		
13.10	17	1.18	*52, 58*	2.11–14	*52, 54, 56, 62, 63*
10.13	18, 68	1.21	*57*, 69		
11.3	65, 105	1.22f.	112	2.11	64
11.4	117	1.22	19, *41*	2.12	47, *63*, 131
11.7ff.	18	2	34, *40, 41*, 51, *52, 57*, 60	2.13	34, *63*, 64, 67
11.8f.	104			2.14	118
11.8	19, 108	2.1ff.	26, *40, 57*, 102, 106, 141, 148	2.16	37
11.9	97			2.17	108
11.13	47, 96			2.19	63
11.17ff.	18	2.1f.	*21*	2.20ff.	37
11.22ff.	71	2.1–10	*32, 41, 51*, 51, *52, 53, 56*	2.20	103
11.23	108			2.48	47
11.26	47, *48*	2.1–14	53	3.1ff.	131
11.27	104	2.1	42, 51, 52, *58*	3.5	22, 44
11.28	19	2.2	42, *43, 43*, 54	3.6ff.	*49*
11.31	103	2.3ff.	42, *43*, *43*, 131	3.7ff.	116
12.9	136			3.7	114, 116
12.11	120	2.3–5	*46*, 46	3.10	131
12.13ff.	18, 97	2.3	35, *49*	3.20	117
12.13	19	2.4	*46*, 46, 48, 49, *57*, 64	3.26ff.	114
12.14	18, 120			3.26	103
12.17f.	20	2.4f.	46	3.27	117
12.18	18	2.5f.	50	3.28f.	131
12.20	65, 117	2.5	49	3.28	93, 117
13.1	18	2.6ff.	22	3.29	116
13.13	105, 123	2.6f.	44	4.4ff.	103
13.11–		2.6	22, *45*, *54*, 55, 139	4.8ff.	*49*
14.9	17			4.11	*71*
		2.7ff.	136	4.12	131
Galatians		2.7f.	44, *45*, 141	4.21	131
1	*41*	2.7–9	*65*	4.25f.	138

Index of Biblical References

Galatians		Philippians		I Thessalonians	
4.28	116	1.16ff.	156	1.6f.	18, 104
4.29	71	1.20f.	156	2.6	97
4.31	131	1.22	129	2.9	97
5.1–6	49	1.29f.	156	2.14ff.	71
5.2ff.	43	2.1	105, 123	2.14	18, 19, 104
5.3	35, 120	2.2	69	3.12	103
5.4	135	2.4ff.	120	4.9ff.	103
5.6–11	65	2.17	156	4.9f.	126
5.6	45, 51, 93, 103, 117	2.25	97, 104, 124		
		2.30	59	II Thessalonians	
5.11	50	3.2ff.	71	1.4	18
5.13f.	103	3.3	65, 116	1.8f.	154
5.13	116	3.5	65, 65	2.6f.	133
5.22	103, 129	3.7ff.	132	2.15	155
6.6ff.	97	3.10	105, 123	3.6	155
6.6	105, 106, 120, 124	3.8ff.	156	3.8f.	97
		3.18f.	71	3.10ff.	24, 153
6.7–10	59	4.11f.	104	3.13	152
6.9	104	4.14f.	106, 124	3.1ff.	155
6.12f.	71	4.14	123		
6.13–16	49	4.15ff.	69, 104	I Timothy	
6.15	45, 51, 65	4.15	19, 105	1.3ff.	155
6.16	114, 116	4.17	129	1.3f.	154
		6.3	48	1.6f.	154
Ephesians		Colossians		2.4f.	155
2.11ff.	155	1.4ff.	154	2.5ff.	155
2.11	65	1.17ff.	154, 155	2.7	41
3.4ff.	154	1.24ff.	154	3.3	153
4.1ff.	154	1.25ff.	155	3.8	153
4.11ff.	154	2.2f.	154	4.2	47
4.28	152	2.11ff.	155	4.3f.	37
5.6	71	2.11	65	4.7	154
5.15	153	2.16	154	4.16	155
5.23ff.	154	2.19	154	5.3ff.	151
6.5	105	2.20ff.	154	5.3	152
6.21	68	3.5	153	5.8	153
		3.9ff.	154	5.9	151
Philippians		3.11	65, 155	5.10ff.	151
1.1	104, 116	3.14f.	154	5.11	151
1.5	59, 69, 105, 106, 123, 124	3.22	105	5.16	151, 152
		4.10	30	5.17f.	97
1.7	106, 123, 124, 156	4.11	65		
				II Timothy	
1.11	129	I Thessalonians		1.13f.	155
1.12ff.	156	1.4	116	2.16ff.	155

175

Index of Biblical References

II Timothy	
2.23ff.	155
3.2	153
3.14ff.	155
4.2	155
4.12	68
4.20	68

Titus	
1.5	19
1.7	153
1.9	19, 155
1.10	65, 154
1.11	153
1.14ff.	154
1.14f.	37
2.1	155
2.7f.	155
2.15	155
3.3ff.	155
3.8	152
3.9	154
3.14	152

Philemon	
1	124, 156
5	116
6	123
16	103
17	124
18	120
23	156
29	30

Hebrews	
5.1ff.	86
6.7	146

Hebrews	
6.10	108, 146, 152
6.11	146
7.11ff.	86
7.27	86
8.1f.	86
9.12ff.	86
10.5ff.	86
13.5	153
13.9	37
13.10ff.	151
13.16	152

I Peter	
2.9f.	154
3.8	154
3.9	121
4.9	152
5.1ff.	155

II Peter	
2.1	47, 48
2.3	153
2.14f.	153
3.15f.	155

James	
1.1	155
1.5	105
1.27	151, 152
2.2ff.	152
2.6f.	153
2.15	152
2.21ff.	154
3.1ff.	155

James	
4.2ff.	153
5.1ff.	153

I John	
3.17f.	152
4.1	47

II John	
9ff.	155

III John	
5ff.	152

Revelation	
2.2	47
2.6	155
2.9	154
2.14	37
2.15	155
2.20	37
3.9	154
3.17	153
15.4	154
16.13	47
17.1ff.	25
18.8	25
19.20	47
20.10	47
21.3	154
21.8	47
21.24	154
21.26	154
22.2	154
22.18f.	155

www.ingramcontent.com/pod-product-compliance
Lightning Source LLC
Chambersburg PA
CBHW051933160426
43198CB00012B/2137